T0339746

Executing Windows Command Line Investigations

"This book opens a world of Windows command line functionality that investigators never knew existed. Through the use of real world examples and logical application scenarios, the authors have created a must have tool for every forensic examiners kit." – Anthony Martino, Director, Northeast Cybersecurity and Forensics Center

Executing Windows Command Line Investigations

While Ensuring Evidentiary Integrity

Chet Hosmer

Joshua Bartolomie

Rosanne Pelli

ELSEVIER

AMSTERDAM • BOSTON • HEIDELBERG • LONDON
NEW YORK • OXFORD • PARIS • SAN DIEGO
SAN FRANCISCO • SINGAPORE • SYDNEY • TOKYO

Syngress is an Imprint of Elsevier

SYNGRESS

Syngress is an imprint of Elsevier
50 Hampshire Street, 5th Floor, Cambridge, MA 02139, USA

Library of Congress Cataloging-in-Publication Data
A catalog record for this book is available from the Library of Congress

British Library Cataloguing-in-Publication Data
A catalogue record for this book is available from the British Library

ISBN: 978-0-12-809268-2

For information on all Syngress publications
visit our website at https://www.elsevier.com/

www.elsevier.com • www.bookaid.org

Publisher: Todd Green
Acquisition Editor: Chris Katsaropoulos
Editorial Project Manager: Anna Valutkevich
Production Project Manager: Mohana Natarajan
Cover Designer: Mark Rogers

Typeset by Spi Global, India

Dedication

Chet Hosmer
To my Mom, for sharing your love of reading with me.

Joshua Bartolomie
To my beautiful wife Dawn and two amazing daughters Kaylee and Alyson. Thank you for always supporting, and putting up with, me and for inspiring me to always strive to be the best person I can be. To my parents Marjorie and Joseph, who taught me to never limit myself and to not take life too seriously and enjoy it as much as possible, because no one ever gets out of it alive.

Rosanne Pelli
To my husband Frank and my children Frankie and Sophia, thank you for my amazing life! To my parents who always taught me to "go big or stay at home" and to Fred Demma, thank you for giving me my first opportunity in this field and challenging me every day!

Finally, I would like to dedicate this book to the men and women who have worked countless hours in developing cutting-edge cyber technologies, investigating cyber incidents, and protecting our critical infrastructure. Thank you!

Contents

Biography

Chet Hosmer is the founder of Python Forensics, Inc., a non-profit organization focused on the collaborative development of open-source investigative technologies using the Python programming language. Chet serves as a visiting professor at Utica College in the Cybersecurity Graduate Program where his research and teaching focus on advanced steganography/data hiding methods and related defenses. He is also an
Adjunct Faculty Member at Champlain College in the Master of Science in Digital Forensic Science Program where he is researching and working with graduate students to advance the application Python to solve hard problems facing digital investigators.

Chet makes numerous appearances each year to discuss emerging cyber threats including appearances in National Public Radio's Kojo Nnamdi show, ABC's Primetime Thursday, NHK Japan, and ABC News Australia. He is also a frequent contributor to technical and news stories relating to cyber security and forensics and has been interviewed and quoted by IEEE, The New York Times, The Washington Post, Government Computer News, Salon.com, DFI News, and Wired Magazine.

He is the author of three recent Elsevier/Syngress Books: *Python Passive Network Mapping*: **ISBN-13:** 978-0128027219, *Python Forensics*: **ISBN-13:** 978-0124186767, and *Data Hiding* which is co/authored with Mike Raggo: **ISBN-13:** 978-1597497435. Chet delivers keynote and plenary talks on various cyber security related topics around the world, each year.

Joshua Bartolomie (CISSP, CRISC, DFCP, CEECS, CFCE) has 20 years of technical and management experience within the information technology and cyber security domains. Joshua has contributed to and established programs that range from teaching digital forensics to designing, implementing, and evolving cutting edge Security Operations Centers, Incident Response Teams, and Cyber Security Architecture Organizations. Joshua is an active participant in multiple information sharing and collaborative consortiums and has presented at numerous cyber security forums, conferences, and venues.

In his current role, Joshua is responsible for translating corporate business strategies, environmental conditions, infrastructure requirements, and industry best practices into strategic cyber security designs and architectural roadmaps. Joshua holds a Master's Degree in Information Assurance from Norwich University and a Bachelor's of Science in Digital and Computer Forensics from Champlain College.

Rosanne Pelli, is a certified Project Management Professional through the Project Management Institute and CompTIA Security+ professional with Harris Corporation. She has over 10 years of experience in the coordination, programmatic oversight, and management of US government contracts as well as Harris' Secure-U Training Program. During her years of experience, Rosanne has assisted in the management and coordination of various government contracts that focused on the identification and analysis of emerging cyber threats; evaluation and transition of cyber security technologies for tactical use by the cyber security community; technical assistance to federal, state, and local law enforcement communities; development and maintenance of a virtual cyber security training portal; and the development, coordination, and execution of various national and international cyber security training initiatives.

Foreword

Over the course of my 18-year career in computer security, I have never before seen as big a gaping hole in our industry, begging for skilled computer security talent, as we have now. The lack of talent and the failure of technology to optimally equip the skilled resources we employ, have led organizations to suffer material breaches and spend millions of dollars to respond to and recover from those breaches.

The threat landscape continues to grow in sophistication and breadth of scope. Numerous high-profile breaches involving well-known corporations and government entities have been spotlighted by the media. Most of these breaches being compromised through the targeting of employees or unpatched computer systems. While this is still true, the explosion of the Internet of Things and embedded devices has considerably broadened the threat landscape, often doubling or tripling the possible targets and attack vectors available to the threat actor today. In addition to the explosive growth of targets and attack vectors, there is also substantial growth in the number of threat actors themselves. The relative ease of operating a nefarious cyber business is alarming. Malicious code is readily available and is bought and sold on a market. The use of online payments, such as Bitcoin, make it seemingly impossible to trace back.

In today's world, it is generally not a matter of if but when an attacker breaches your environment. After all, we have to protect against everything while the attacker only has to find one thing. As such, the focus of cyber security has shifted from prevention to detection and response. A skilled incident responder or forensics expert can make the difference between having a full-scale breach on your hands and stopping a compromise early in the attacker lifecycle by proactively hunting and analyzing attacks in flight. Incident response and forensics is considerably more than being able to operate expensive tools and administer systems. It is about understanding all aspects of the attacker, their techniques, the lifecycle of a compromise, and the ability to investigate and uncover evidence or indication of compromise every step of that life cycle and do so while maintaining full integrity of the data and the investigation.

Incident Response and forensics are about the depth-of-knowledge and the attention to detail. A highly skilled responder is worth his or her weight in gold and can make the difference between your company being highly successful or finding itself on the cover of the Wall Street Journal, immortalized as yet another victim of a high-profile data breach.

Josh, I would like to personally thank you for passing your immense talent and experience in the area of forensics and incident response forward into a community and world that desperately need it. There are more jobs available today than skilled resources available to fill them; meaning that there are too many organizations ill equipped, under prepared, vulnerable, and unprotected. I look forward to seeing our industry continue to invest and make advancements in the people, process, and technology needed to defend and protect our corporations and our government. I also look forward to seeing this book help educate and train the next generation of cyber security warriors.

James Carder
CISO & VP, LogRhythm Labs

Preface

Tim Patterson and Seattle Computer Products, headquartered in Seattle, WA, USA, made the first release of 86-DOS which was designed to run on an Intel 8086 Computer Kit in Aug. of 1980. Microsoft, headquartered in Redmond, WA, USA, purchased 86-DOS from Seattle Computer Products and hired Tim Patterson later that year. In Aug. of 1981 IBM, headquartered in Armonk, NY, USA, released PC-DOS 1.0, which was developed and owned by Microsoft. IBM insisted that Microsoft retain title and ownership of the product to avoid possible legal issues regarding software infringement. In hindsight many have questioned this decision by IBM which eventually resulted in the evolution of Microsoft as one of the largest software companies in the world.

Within a year after the release of PC-DOS 1.0, Microsoft licensed their version of MS-DOS to hundreds of companies as a general purpose operating system that could run on a wide variety of Intel 8086 based computers. This gave rise to a whole new generation of IBM compatible computers over the next decade. Even early 16-bit versions of Microsoft Windows ran as a Graphical User Interface on top of MS-DOS.

Microsoft still provides an MS-DOS *like* interface today, delivered as the software application *cmd.exe*. This application provides a more direct communication between user entered commands and the underlying operating system. Many consider this a nongraphical command shell where you can run built-in commands or third-party character based applications.

Many investigators and examiners today rely on this "more direct interface" with the operating system to interrogate Microsoft Windows based systems in either live or postmortem scenarios.

This book explores three critical areas. First, to assess the viability of using this command based interface when investigating or examining live systems. Second, to examine the criticality and volatility of evidence integrity. Third, to explore and demonstrate the use of PIRCS (Proactive Incident Response Command Shell) to enhance live investigations. The PIRCS technology provides a Windows Command Line (CLI) *style* interface combined with a secure evidence repository. PIRCS provides a framework for maintaining evidence integrity, validating evidence collection methods, preserving the investigative process, and providing nonrepudiation of actions taken by investigators when interacting with the command line.

The book is applicable to a wide audience and includes a copy of the PIRCS technology to enable experimentation and undergraduate and graduate studies, along with incident response and live investigation applications. The authors of the book and the developers of the technology encourage your comments and suggestions to help advance command line based investigation technologies.

Acknowledgments

Chet Hosmer

Dr. Gary Kessler, the technical editor for this book. Gary's knowledge, guidance, and insight always enhance every chapter.

Chris Katsaropoulos, Anna Valutkevich, and the whole team at Elsevier for your enthusiasm for this topic, and for all the guidance, patience, and support along the way.

To Janet for your encouragement and insightful suggestions on how to make the material accessible by everyone. I want to thank Rosanne and Josh for their collaboration on this book. Their insight, attention to detail and deep subject matter knowledge added significant value to all aspects of the book.

Joshua Bartolomie

To Chet Hosmer and Rosanne Pelli, for all of their hard work and continued drive to ensure this book saw the light of the day and was the best it could be.

To James Carder, thank you for your contribution to this book and for the many years of support, collaboration, and friendship.

Lastly I would like to thank all of the practitioners that continually work to advance the digital forensics and incident response field and who share their knowledge, tools, and methodologies. We would not be where we are today without all of your insights and expertise.

Rosanne Pelli

The Proactive Incident Response Command Shell (PIRCS) technology was based on research sponsored by the Department of Homeland Security (DHS) Science and Technology Directorate, Cyber Security Division (DHS S&T/CSD), BAA 11–02 and Air Force Research Laboratory Information Directorate via contract number FA8750-12-C-0271.[1]

I am extremely grateful to the many practitioners who took the time out of their busy work schedule to discuss their requirements and provide feedback to the PIRCS technology. Also, a special thanks to all the folks within Harris Corporation who supported this project.

To Joshua Bartolomie whose expertise and innovative spirit led to the PIRCS concept and to Chet Hosmer, my sincere gratitude for your patience, support, and guidance, without you this book would not be a reality. Thank you!

---

[1]The views and conclusions contained herein are those of the authors and should not be interpreted as necessarily representing the official policies or endorsements, either expressed or implied, of DHS, Air Force Research Laboratory, or the US Government.

Harris Corporation

Harris Corporation, headquartered in Melbourne, FL, USA, is a leading technology innovator, solving its customers' toughest mission-critical challenges by providing them solutions that connect, inform, and protect. Harris supports customers in more than 125 countries, has approximately $8 billion in annual revenue, and 22,000 employees worldwide. The company is organized into four business segments: Communication Systems, Space and Intelligence Systems, Electronic Systems, and Critical Networks. For more information on Harris Corporation, visit www.harris.com.

The impact of Windows Command Line investigations

triage: Word Origin
1727 from the French triage "a picking out, sorting" From Old French
approximately 14 Century, trier "to pick or cull". During World War I, triage
was the adopted term for sorting the wounded into groups according to the
severity of their injuries.

CHAPTER OUTLINE

INTRODUCTION

As cybercrime activities continue to expand at an alarming rate, our response to these events must keep pace. Reports similar to the following can be found over and over again:

> *According to TrendMicro's 2014 Security Roundup, "2014 was the year of mega breaches, hard-to-patch vulnerabilities, and thriving cybercriminal underground economies. It encapsulated threats of grand proportions, the consequences of which set companies back billions in losses and consumers an unknown figure in lost or stolen personally identifiable information (PII).*
>
> *It was in 2014 when the world witnessed the largest reported hack that led to a staggering loss of around 100 terabytes of data and up to $100 M damages for Sony Pictures Entertainment Inc. (SPE). "Unprecedented in nature" and "an unparalleled and well planned crime" were but a few phrases that described*

Executing Windows Command Line Investigations. http://dx.doi.org/10.1016/B978-0-12-809268-2.00001-8

the Sony Pictures breach in an internal memo released to its employees. This reminds IT professionals of the crucial role that a layered, customized defense plays inside very large networks."

CYBERCRIME METHODS AND VULNERABILITIES

In addition to the increase in cybercrime activities, specific classes of cyber criminals are changing the landscape for both forensic investigation and incident response. Just a few key examples of some current terms:

Cyber Terrorism
    Any use of Information and Communication Technology to attack civilian systems in order to intimidate, coerce, or destroy government or societies as a way to advance political, religious, economic, or ideological goals.
                                                                            Dr. Gary Kessler, 2016.

Hacktivism: The act of breaking into organizational infrastructures for a politically, socially, or terrorist motivated purpose is now becoming a popular method of shaping political debates. This has changed slightly over the past several years as "anonymous" has become less active mainly due to internal divisions. Sony Pictures was the most visible target in recent years, and collecting specific evidence and performing triage in the face of these attacks is still debated today. When such attacks occur it is possible to react such that valuable evidence is lost or compromised. Through the use of triage best practices along with the skillful use of technology, investigators can collect valuable evidence while preserving the integrity of such evidence. In addition, the immediate collection of host and network activity may help to mitigate an attack and quarantine systems and networks from further damage.

Extortion and ransomware: Various forms of cyber extortion and new ransomware scams have emerged. In one of the most publicized cases, the computers of Miss Teen USA, Cassidy Wolf, along with several other young women in southern California were hacked by Jared James Abrahams. He then took control of the victim's webcam and secretly photographed them, demanding nude photographs from the victims. He pled guilty and is serving 18 months in Federal Prison. This has defined the new term, "sextortion."

Businesses and organizations are not exempt from this activity and are being targeted by extortionists as well. The most common approach is to breach an organization network and steal sensitive and personal identifiable information (PII). The extortionist then demands a ransom payment in exchange for not releasing or selling the "exfiltrated" data. In many cases they demand bitcoins and other virtual currencies as payment, allowing the entire transaction to occur in the cyber world. In both of these examples rapid response and triage of evidence from the victim's computers and networks is vital. Another form of ransomware, of course, is like Cryptolocker, that locks files unless you pay for a key … from "companies" that have a help desk and actually give you the key if you pay the ransom. Worse is that many organizations—including at least one police department (Tewksbury, Massachusetts)—have paid the ransom in order to get their files back!!

Cyberbullying, harassment, and stalking: There are both Federal and State Laws that now provide penalties for those engaged in such actions: The Federal stalking statute, 18 USC Section 2261A, was amended to include the use of an "interactive computer service" to "engage in a course of conduct that causes substantial emotional distress to that person or places that person in reasonable fear of the death of, or serious bodily injury to," the victim or a member of the victim's family. The statute requires that the defendant physically travel across state lines, making it inapplicable to many cyberstalking cases. To counter this, almost all States now include laws against cyberstalking, cyberharassment, and cyberbullying. Some states have created new laws, while others have modified harassment or stalking statutes to include cyber. In any case, the timely collection of evidence from victims or potential victim's computers is critical in order to prevent harm and to prosecute those perpetrating the harassment, bullying, or stalking.

Crimes against children: The Internet Crimes Against Children (ICAC) Task Force was created to help Federal, State, and Local law enforcement agencies enhance their investigative responses to offenders who use the Internet, online communication systems, or computer technology to sexually exploit children. Since the perpetrators of such activities have become more sophisticated and elusive, our ability to collect and examine evidence from potential victims, computers, and recent network activity is vital in identifying and tracking those involved. In many cases this needs to be accomplished using triage methods and cannot wait for the backlog processing of computer evidence. In addition, since the parents and guardians typically own the computer systems in use by the minor victims, with their permission first responders can legally access electronic evidence in order to begin triage operations.

Sophisticated botnets: Botnets remain one of the hacker's most relied upon weapons. This malicious software is at the forefront of spamming, distributed denial of service attacks and coordinated hacking activities. One of the most recent additions is "ZeroAccess," said to be controlling over 2 million unsuspecting computers world-wide. The bot "Storm" is estimated to control as many as 50 million computers and operates on a peer-to-peer basis removing the need for a centralized bot herder, making it more difficult to shutdown. In many cases bots (or more specifically their zombie counterparts), exist only in memory and when systems are shutdown traces of the zombie are very difficult to detect. Thus examination of the running state of computer systems using forensic triage of memory and active processes is a vital step in identifying and defeating these threats.

NOVEL VULNERABILITIES

The latest vulnerabilities add yet, another dimension to incident response requirements and forensic triage, not seen before. These require specials tools, technologies, and methods that in many cases require command line level operation and setup. A few examples include:

Heartbleed: is a vulnerability in the OpenSSL software library (notably not a protocol flaw but caused by a coding error) that when exploited can provide hacker access to the memory of data servers. It has been estimated that over a million websites could have been affected and many more applications utilizing OpenSSL. Information contained in the exploited memory could include sensitive data including usernames, passwords, sensitive documents, and a cadre of PII. This vulnerability under certain conditions may reveal the server's private key causing the necessary revocation of server based certificates. Fig. 1.1 depicts the number of revoked certificates in the days following the announcement of the Heartbleed bug.

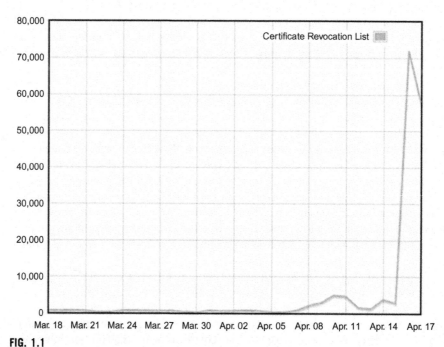

FIG. 1.1

Heartbleed bug catalyst for massive certificate revocations.

POODLE attack vulnerability: POODLE is a design vulnerability found in the way SSL 3.0 handles block cipher mode padding. The POODLE attack allows an attacker to exploit the vulnerability to decrypt and extract information from inside an encrypted transaction. The direct impact is the potential for an attacker to steal a server's digital keys used in encrypted communications and the protection of proprietary internal documents.

Windows XP (zero-day-forever, now that XP is end of life): It is estimated that as many as 31% of home and enterprise computers are still running the Windows XP operating system today. As of Apr. 8, 2014, support and updates for Windows XP has ended leaving these systems vulnerable to exploitation. In addition, leaked versions of the Windows 2000 operating system source code (much of which is shared with Windows XP) gives hackers an avenue to identify and then exploit vulnerabilities in the most tightly held source code base.

In addition, zero-day vulnerabilities continue to impact Microsoft Windows platforms. Fig. 1.2 depicts the timeline of 2014 events as reported by TrendMicro.

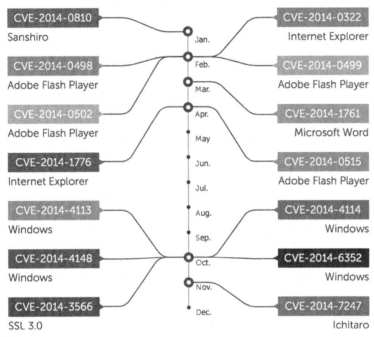

Timeline of major zero-day vulnerabilities in 2014

FIG. 1.2

2014 zero-day vulnerability timeline.

Zero-Day Vulnerabilities "any vulnerability that is exploited prior to anyone (other than the attacker) knowing about the vulnerability."

Common vulnerabilities and exposures (CVE) is a dictionary or catalog of known security threats.

CYBER CRIMINALS USE THE WINDOWS COMMAND LINE

Microsoft Windows based systems continue to dominate the landscape and it is no secret that cyber criminals leverage the Windows Command Line (Fig. 1.3) when infiltrating these devices. As we have identified, both cybercrime methods and vulnerabilities exist within a broad range of Microsoft Windows based environments. These vulnerabilities and the related exploits are often accomplished by leveraging existing capabilities of the underlying operating system and, quite often, accessing those capabilities via the command line.

FIG. 1.3

Why cyber criminals love the command line.

There are several key reasons why this is true:

- Cyber criminals have figured out that leveraging built-in Microsoft tools that assist IT personnel to work efficiently, also support their objectives. This approach also blends perpetrators actions with that of IT personnel. This makes it harder to detect as most system admins and security staff may overlook typical admin activity as an indication of a potential compromise.
- Adding, modifying, or deleting files is much easier to detect and defeat by intrusion prevention systems than simply exploiting and leveraging built-in operating system capabilities.
- Making changes to RAM and associated running processes to deploy and execute malware is far more difficult to detect and respond to.
- Writing Microsoft PowerShell scripts to effect changes across the entire enterprise is an efficient way of wreaking havoc across an organization. In addition, PowerShell offers local, remote, and persistent operational modes giving criminals a wide range of options once they have gained unauthorized access. Even more troubling, based on the specific version of PowerShell that is installed along with the configuration options selected, the amount and depth of information available during and after script execution can be quite scarce. Finally, most remnants of PowerShell script execution are lost after shutdown. This once again points to the value of skillful collection of evidence prior to pulling-the-plug on potentially impacted systems.

- The TCP/IP kernel offers a large array of tools with which to test network connections—for network quality or for network probes.
- Finally, it is quite easy to include a Windows Command Line on a thumb drive with other command line investigative tools. This method has far less impact on a target system than installing and then launching graphical user interface tools or a suite of tools.

TURNING THE TABLES

Performing rapid response to such breaches, threats, and vulnerabilities require investigators to employ triage-based forensic approaches more often today in order to act in a timelier manner and to preserve potential volatile evidence. In order to do this effectively without unknowingly or inadvertently damaging potential evidence requires strict adherence to defined processes and in some cases utilization of specialized tools. We can of course turn the tables and use many of these same capabilities to enhance forensic triage methods in order to collect, examine, and analyze digital evidence.

Forensic triage and incident response using the Windows Command Line are being done today, however a limited number of investigators know how to execute these operations properly. In addition to leveraging these capabilities, we must also be able to "prove" our steps, secure the collected evidence, and document our actions such that if and when the need arises, we can deliver compelling evidence in the courtroom, to legal counsel, or to human resources. Proof is always needed, supporting the facts in the case against the suspects, while at the same time protecting the victims and others that may be involved.

ORGANIZATION OF THE BOOK

We have arranged the book to be accessible to a broad audience of cybercrime investigators, incident response teams, and academic interests. To that end we will provide extensive examples and will delve deeper into topics, lessons learned, and best practices that may in the past have been glossed over in other texts.

Chapter 2 will dive into the importance of the integrity of digital evidence. Within triage and incident response environments additional considerations, methods, and measures need to be considered to ensure that:

1. Any evidence collected and examined should not impede future prosecutions.
2. Actionable evidence collected must be carefully considered and processed to ensure that whatever immediate actions taken are based on verifiable facts.

Chapter 3 will step into the Windows Command Line and first examine built-in Windows OS capabilities that directly aid the investigative process and how to use and interpret the results of those commands. These commands will cover a broad range of capabilities that can deliver information pertaining to user activity, network configuration, running process, and of course the file system contents. In addition, we will present a set of third party command line applications that can delve even deeper into the state of the system. These will include tools to acquire memory, extract registry information, identify dynamic link libraries, and advanced searching and indexing methods. Detailed step-by-step examples will be provided for all of the built in and third party commands utilized.

Chapter 4 introduces the proactive incident response command shell (PIRCS) that provides investigators with a secure environment to execute Windows Commands while preserving evidence and during the investigative process (Fig. 1.4). Specifically, we will address the use of PIRCS, the evidentiary chain of custody capabilities, and real-time activity logging. As with previous chapters a comprehensive look into the use of PIRCS through simple example scenarios will be provided.

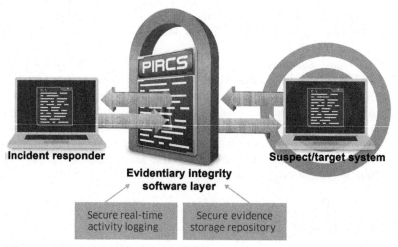

FIG. 1.4

Proactive Incident Response Command Shell (PIRCS).

Chapter 5 provides a set of Use Cases (example scenarios) to further demonstrate the value of the Windows Command Line for both incident response and forensic triage. These Use Cases will leverage the PIRCS environment to provide a step-by-step examination for each Use Case.

Chapter 6 provides a look ahead to the future of the Windows Command Line uses and also examines command line environments available within other operating systems.

Appendices A and B provide reference information for both third party command line tools and technologies along with a detailed guide in the form of a Windows Command Line reference.

CHAPTER 1 REVIEW

In this chapter we examined the impact of current cybercrime activities and novel vulnerabilities along with a discussion of how the Windows Command Line is leveraged by criminals. In addition, we discussed how we plan to turn the tables and utilize the Windows Command Line for both incident response and forensic triage. Finally, we defined the content of Chapters 2–6 along with Appendices A and B.

CHAPTER 1 SUMMARY QUESTIONS

1. Define additional ways insiders could utilize the Windows Command Line to wreak havoc within an organization. Be specific and provide examples.
2. Research and define methods employed by hackers to modify existing running processes (memory modification only). After performing these modifications how can these subtle changes be discovered?
3. What other reasons do attackers leverage the Windows Command Line for criminal purposes?
4. Considering the following simple scenario:
   a. You arrive at active crime scene where a major crime has just occurred.
   b. Immediate action to track down the suspects is vital.
   c. It is determined that evidence on a running Windows computer may contain vital information regarding the crime and associated suspects.
   d. You have the proper authorization to access the Windows computer via the Windows Command Line only which is up and available.
   e. What would be the first command you would type and why?

ADDITIONAL RESOURCES

TrendMicro. (2014). *TrendLabs™ 2014 annual security roundup.* http://blog.trendmicro.com/trendlabs-security-intelligence/2014-annual-security-roundup-magnified-losses-amplified-need-for-cyber-attack-preparedness/. Accessed February 2016.

US-CERT Heartbleed. Alert (TA14-098A) OpenSSL 'Heartbleed' vulnerability (CVE-2014-0160). (n.d.). https://www.us-cert.gov/ncas/alerts/TA14-098A. Accessed February 2016.

US-CERT POODLE. Alert (TA14-290A) SSL 3.0 protocol vulnerability and POODLE attack. (n.d.). https://www.us-cert.gov/ncas/alerts/TA14-290A. Accessed February 2016.

Importance of digital evidence integrity

2

> *Integrity: Word Origin*
> *1400, from the Latin "integritatem" meaning soundness, purity,*
> *wholeness, in perfect condition. "Integrity is doing the right thing, even when*
> *no one is watching"*
> **C.S. Lewis**

CHAPTER OUTLINE

INTRODUCTION

As we begin to consider the collection of evidence using the Windows Command Line, it is important to consider the importance of the resulting integrity of the evidence in question. This chapter will focus on the methods and techniques used to protect digital evidence, be it live or postmortem. In addition, the level of documentation provided when performing live investigations will be crucial in demonstrating the efficacy of the procedures employed by the investigator.

THE IMPORTANCE OF DIGITAL EVIDENCE INTEGRITY

One of the most recognized cases related to the admissibility of scientific evidence is Daubert v. Merrell, Dow Pharmaceuticals Inc., 509 U.S. 579, 595 (1993). In 1999, Kumho Tire Co. v. Carmichael 526 U.S. 137 established that Daubert also applies to technical and scientific evidence. The decision in Daubert defined four specific standards for judges to determine whether scientific evidence should be admissible in court. This four-pronged applies to any scientific procedure, including digital evidence acquisition, examination, and analysis.

Executing Windows Command Line Investigations. http://dx.doi.org/10.1016/B978-0-12-809268-2.00002-X

Daubert states that the following specific factors must be considered about any scientific process used to prepare evidence:

- Whether the theory/method is generally accepted in the relevant scientific community
- Whether the theory/method has been subjected to peer review and publication
- Whether the theory/method has been tested or can be tested
- Whether the potential or error rate is known

Examining these specific factors as they relate to the integrity of digital evidence is critically important. As you can probably already surmise, the Daubert factors likely impact on the admissibility of digital evidence in court. The impacts and considerations are different depending upon the circumstances. For example, comparison of methods and procedures used for bit-by-bit forensic disk imaging differs from the acquisition of evidence from a running system. Both of these methods and their associated procedures differ from the passive capturing of network traffic or that of active interrogation and mapping of network devices.

We must provide a clear baseline understanding regarding the integrity of digital evidence before we dive into using the Windows Command Line or any other method of digital evidence collection. This foundation provides the basis of understanding of the methods, procedures, and technologies that can assist in this process. In addition, we must consider the chain-of-custody related to the digital evidence much like that of evidence collected at a physical crime scene (see Fig. 2.1).

When considering the protection and chain-of-custody of digital evidence several key factors must be considered:

Authentication: The authenticity of the digital evidence is multifaceted.

- Who prepared the digital evidence?
- When did the collection of evidence occur?
- Who witnessed the collection?
- What tools, technology, methods, and procedures were used to acquire the evidence?

Integrity: Once the digital evidence has been collected how will we protect the evidence from accidental or intentional alteration? Some key considerations include:

- How will the evidence be stored? (ie, Disk, Server, and Cloud, etc.)
- What digital integrity mechanism(s) will be employed?
- Who will have access to the digital evidence?
- What access controls will be employed?
- What auditing methods are tightly coupled with the digital evidence?

Nonrepudiation: Life-cycle record keeping from the collection through the disposition of digital evidence provides clear chain-of-custody records. In addition, these records also provide the ability to ensure that no one accessing the digital evidence can deny any and all actions taken by them.

As you can see once again, depending upon the type of digital evidence we are considering—bit-by-bit imaging, live acquisition/triage, or network

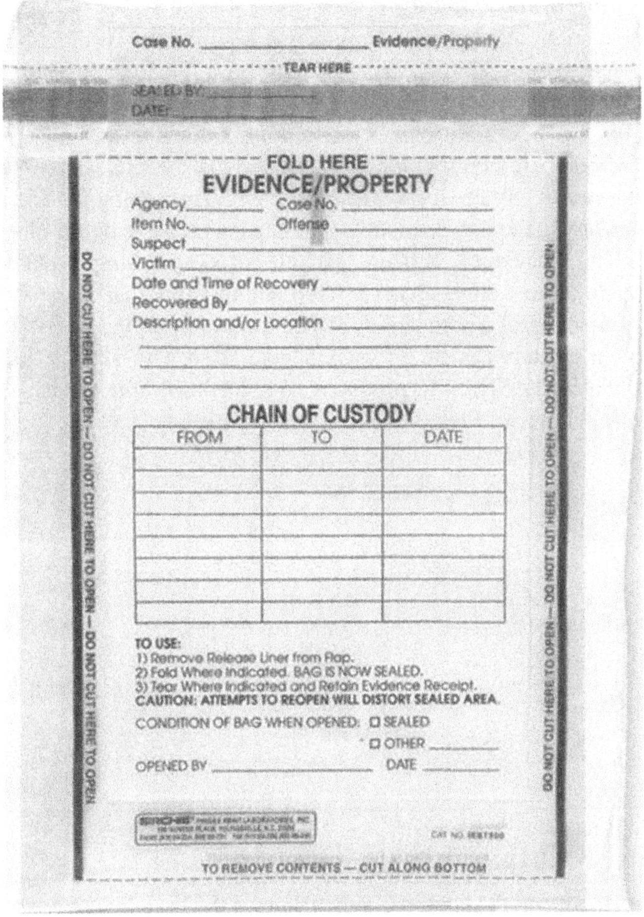

FIG. 2.1

Physical evidence bag.

investigations—the methods employed to protect the integrity of the evidence require careful consideration. To dive a bit deeper we will examine three specific methods that are in use today to protect the integrity of digital evidence. These specific integrity mechanisms include one-way cryptographic hashing, digital signatures, and trusted time stamping.

DIGITAL INTEGRITY MECHANISMS

In order to delve into these mechanisms we provide the fundamentals of each method. In addition, we will map these methods back to the Daubert factors for consideration.

One-way cryptographic hashing

One of the most common methods of protecting the integrity of digital evidence is through the application of one-way cryptographic hash functions (hashing for short). It is vital that those entering the field of digital investigation deeply understand hashing, the benefits that hashing provides, and the limitations of hashing.

Hashing methods are cryptographic algorithms that generate a message digest, commonly referred to as "the hash." In most cases the hashing algorithm is open source allowing anyone to independently generate the message digest of a given file, disk image, memory capture, network packets, or even a simple password. The resulting hash (in almost all cases) is a fixed length value that is most commonly represented as a string of hexadecimal digits; for example, the Message Digest 5 (MD5) algorithm produces a 128 bit hash, Secure Hash Algorithm 1 (SHA-1) produces a 160 bit hash, and SHA-512 produces a 512 bit hash value. Applying the MD5 algorithm to the pangram, "the quick brown fox jumped over a lazy dog" generates the following results (Fig. 2.2).

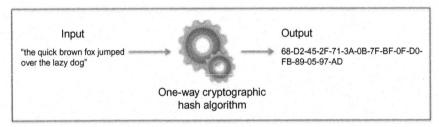

Input		Output
"the quick brown fox jumped over the lazy dog"	→ One-way cryptographic hash algorithm →	68-D2-45-2F-71-3A-0B-7F-BF-0F-D0-FB-89-05-97-AD

FIG. 2.2

MD5 hash of a pangram.

Hashing methods, more specifically the result of the hashing operation produces three important characteristics.

1. Possessing the hash value provides no clues as to the content or length of the original message or file that it is associated with. In other words, hashing algorithms are designed to make it infeasible to derive the original message or file if you only possess the hash itself. (Note: Hash lookups such as *rainbow tables* used for password cracking does not violate this governing principle. In this special case the original password was not *derived* from the hash but rather generated independently and then the results are compared later in order to discover or lookup the password.)
2. It is computationally infeasible to change the contents of the message or file without changing the associated hash. (Note: Under special controlled circumstances the MD5 and even the SHA-1 algorithm has been hacked in this manner, however performing this operation outside of these special circumstances is still considered infeasible.)

3. It is infeasible to find two messages or files that differ in content, but produce the same hash ... this is considered collision resistance.

Based on these characteristics, how do the general hashing algorithms stack up against the Daubert tests for determining the admissibility of digital evidence?

Daubert Factor	Hashing for Digital Evidence Integrity
The theory/method is generally accepted in the relevant scientific community	The mathematics and computer science community, with the following caveat, has generally accepted the method of hashing digital evidence for integrity preservation. Caveat: The hash generated for the acquired evidence in question must be secured. The hashing algorithm itself contains no special controls; allowing anyone to generate or regenerate the hash value after changing the evidence in question. Thus it is important that the hash be protected once generated. Furthermore, the hash value should be generated during the evidence acquisition process and included with the chain-of-custody documentation
The theory/method has been subjected to peer review and publication	The general area of hashing has been peer reviewed in scientific publications. In addition, several of the hashing algorithms (SHA-1-SHA-512) have been developed by the National Institute of Standards and Technology (NIST) and scrutinized by researchers around the globe
The theory/method has been tested or can be tested	The general theory has been tested and practiced for more than 20 years. In addition, numerous independent software implementations of each hashing algorithm have been developed that produce the same results
Whether the potential or known rate of error is acceptable	There have been notable attacks on the MD5 and SHA-1 algorithms. But these attempts have had limited impact on the integrity of evidence. However, the procedures and methods that surround the generation and protection of the generated hash values still remains an open issue today

So what does this mean for establishing and protecting the integrity of digital evidence? Can hashing be used? The simple answer is yes. However, this requires careful handling of both, the original evidence and the resulting hash values. Let's examine three specific cases where digital hashing is applied today and examine the value that they deliver to investigations.

- Hashing static evidence
- Hashing volatile or live evidence
- Searching for specific evidence

Hashing static evidence

Static evidence, such as confiscated disk drives, USB devices, SD-cards, photographs acquired from cameras, phones or mobile devices, document files, and virtual machine images and the like can all be hashed and logged as evidence. The hash values for each piece of evidence can also be logged and stored separately for future use. Once the original evidence has been sealed away, copies can be produced and provided to examiners (prosecution and defense) and then examined for both inculpatory and exculpatory value. At any time during this examination or analysis process the evidence can be rehashed and then compared with the stored original hash values to ensure that the evidence has not changed. The process of examining, analyzing, and reverifying can continue without ever affecting the original evidence. During the examination process, reports and the outcome of the analysis process can produce secondary results. These results, once generated can then in turn be stored, hashed, and shared with the parties involved. For example, if the original evidence included a set of JPEG images that were extracted from an iPhone, and the examination process extracted metadata from the images (camera model and serial number, geo location tags and timestamp data), the resulting evidence can also be hashed and stored as part of the case.

Hashing volatile or live evidence

When acquiring, probing, or triaging live running systems, evidence collected during that process will likely change during the course of acquisition. For example, when extracting random access memory (RAM) from a system, all that can be accomplished is taking a snapshot, which is the equivalent of taking a photograph of a crime scene. The moment after the snapshot is taken, the environment will change. You can place as much crime scene tape around a physical crime scene as you want, but change will occur a nano-second after the shot is taken. The same is true for system memory.

Unlike taking a photograph of a physical crime scene after the fact, the act of imaging memory itself will change the contents of memory, since the technologies that take the memory snapshot must be loaded and executed by the processor in the very memory you are taking a snapshot of. However, all of this can be accounted for and isolated. Most importantly you want to hash and log the evidence collected (in this case the memory image) as soon as the snapshot is completed. You can then verify later that the snapshot that was taken at the scene has not been altered. You can imagine that questions will be raised such as: who took the snapshot, when was the snapshot taken, what tools were used to take the snapshot or even what impact does the snapshot process have on the rest of the memory that was acquired? More specifically, did the process delete, modify, or add information in memory? The answer is a resounding yes ... but we know the changes that were made.

Will performing operations like this or other live acquisitions on the system make changes to data stored on the media? The answer again is yes. To give you the simplest example, if you walk up to a running system and simply move the mouse; at that point, changes are written to memory, the registry, and the disk. The question is then why would we consider doing this? Well, consider what evidence and potential evidence is lost or destroyed forever if we simply pull the plug. Modern systems today come standard with 8–64 GB of memory, servers can have as much as 2 TB as of this writing, and this will quickly increase. Since this memory is volatile, the moment we pull the plug it is essentially gone. We may be able to extract some information from the swap file, but not all. In addition, reconstructing the network connections that were in place, the files that were open, and the users actively logged in and other stateful information that may be valuable is likely lost.

Malware that is memory resident along with the associated connections and behaviors are also likely lost or at the least very difficult to reconstruct. Consider the situation where a suspect, minutes earlier inserted a USB memory device and transferred data from the system, network server, or the cloud to the device. That information could have significant bearing on the case.

Finally, in cases where speed is important, it is common practice that imaging drives and performing postmortem investigations on the imaged data is typically measured in days, weeks, months, or years ... or we are still waiting! On the other hand, using the Windows Command Line, other simple command line tools, or PowerShell make it possible to capture vital information relevant to the investigation in minutes, preserving and protecting the integrity of that information along with the exact commands that the investigator took, and then shutting down the system, imaging the media, and beginning the postmortem process.

Searching for specific evidence

Hashing can be used to generate a signature of malware, sensitive documents, or contraband such as child pornography that has been seized during an investigation. Since the size of each hash is small in comparison to the items that were hashed, the hashes can be searched using a search key. For example, each file on a system could easily be hashed and then compared to a list of items that are in the search list. This search will only find exact matches; even a single bit difference will cause a mismatch. Consider the example where you have a hash list of all the operating system files that should be present and unaltered on a system. You could then perform a search to find any unexpected or unauthorized changes that could indicate a breach of the condition of the evidence.

Hash types and origins

Many different or competing hash types exist today that should be considered. The following table provides an overview of the most popular hashing types along with some valuable facts regarding each.

Hash Type	Dateline—Creator	Size in Bits	Notes
MD5	1991, by Ron Rivest replacing the earlier MD4 algorithm	128	In 2004, Xiaoyun Wang and Hongbo Yu from Shandong University, Jinan 250100, China, devised a differential attack against MD5 demonstrating that under certain laboratory conditions they could decrease the collision resistance of the algorithm
SHA-1	1993, NIST. The algorithm is loosely based on the work of Rivest and the MD5 algorithm	160	In Oct. 2015, the freestart collision attack utilized a 64 GPU cluster to perform the attack on SHA-1. It was able to demonstrate collisions in as little as 10 days. The NIST stated that: "SHA-1 shall not be used for digital signature generation after Dec. 31, 2013"
RIPEMD-128 and RIPEMD-160	1996, RIPEMD (RACE Integrity Primitives Evaluation Message Digest) is a family of cryptographic hash functions developed in Leuven, Belgium	128–160	Since the RIPEMD algorithms are loosely based on the MD4 algorithm developed by Rivest, it is estimated that some of the same attack methods used against MD5 could be applied to RIPEMD. However, since the RIPEMD is used less often than either MD5 or NIST/SHA algorithms, it has been of less focus of attackers
SHA-2	2002, NIST. Which includes: SHA-224, SHA-256, SHA-384, SHA-512, SHA-512/224, and SHA-512/256	224–512	SHA-2 includes significant changes from its predecessor, SHA-1 expecting to improve collision resistance. However, in 2015 Florian Mendel, Tomislav Nad, and Martin Schlaffer from Graz University of Technology, Austria have proposed new improved methods that can potentially cause collisions of these advanced methods

Continued

Hash Type	Dateline—Creator	Size in Bits	Notes
SHA-3	In 2014, NIST published the draft FIPS 202 SHA-3 Standard: entitled "Permutation-Based Hash and Extendable-Output Functions." FIPS 202 was approved on Aug. 5, 2015. Which includes: SHA3-224, SHA3-256, and SHA3-512	224–512	The new method deviates from the previous SHA-1 and SHA-2 methods of hashing. As a matter of fact, the development of the new standard and method was the outgrowth of a competition that NIST established to develop the new standard. On Oct. 2, 2012, the Keccak algorithm was selected as the winner of the competition. Main contributors to the algorithm included: Guido Bertoni, Joan Daemen

There is one question that may occur to the reader at this point. If MD5 and SHA-1, and even the SHA-2 family of hashes, have come under collision-based attacks and scrutiny, why is it that most of the forensic community is still using MD5 or SHA-1? The simple answer is that most of the toolmakers in the forensic community do not feel that the attacks on MD5 or SHA are credible threats to the integrity of digital evidence. This thinking should be reevaluated and not only should the community move quickly to SHA-2 and more specifically SHA2-512, other considerations for the protection of hash values need to be reevaluated, along with the standardization of the protection and chain-of-custody of the generated hash values. When you bring this issue to both the toolmakers and law enforcement, the first reaction tends to be that somehow their trust or code is being questioned. On the surface this is an understandable reaction as the defense always challenges both the experts themselves and the handling; the efficacy of the tools; the chain-of-custody; and processing of digital evidence. However, this is not in anyway an attack on their process, procedures, or even the tools, rather it is a way to strengthen or even eliminate the challenges that may come forth. On the digital evidence side, there are ways to protect the integrity of digital evidence such that testimony by those who performed the acquisition and applied the integrity mechanisms can be validated independently and require little or no testimony. This is important because in many cases those that actually performed the acquisition, applied the integrity mechanisms, and walked the chain-of-custody, might not be available to testify or the time frame between acquisition to court can be months or years. In addition, as we continue to move from static evidence acquisition to live acquisition, the waters continue to become muddier. Therefore, we need to consider best-practices that could improve or enhance the integrity of digital evidence. The next sections of this text look at this directly.

Digital signatures

The application and use of digital signatures is widespread in business, finance, healthcare, and legal arenas. However, the application of digital signatures for preserving the integrity of digital evidence is limited. Digital signatures provide the ability to bind a private key (in most cases assigned to an individual) to sign or encrypt a hash value generated for a specific piece of digital evidence. For example this could be a file, a disk image, a memory capture, or possibly packets captured during the recording of a network activity. The advantage of a digital signature is that the source of a digital file can be attributed to an individual by utilizing the public key of that individual to verify the signature. The contents of the signature (the hash) can then be used to validate authenticity that the associated evidence has not changed since the signing. See Figs. 2.3 and 2.4.

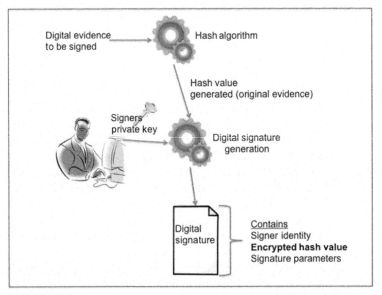

FIG. 2.3

Digital signature creation process.

The process is quite straightforward. The process of hashing the evidence whether it be static or volatile, is the same; however once the hash is generated the individual performing the operation would sign (using their issued private key) the hash. This generates a digital signature binding the identity of the individual with the signing of the evidence. The benefit of this method of course is that a third party can validate the original evidence by simply obtaining a copy of the original evidence and the digital signature associated with it.

One of the minor issues with this process however, is evident when the private key associated with the signing is compromised; the digital certificate must be revoked, invalidating the digital signature. If this occurs, the original evidence would have to be hashed and re-signed to generate a new signature using the new private key. One other limitation is that the time associated with the signing is not bound to

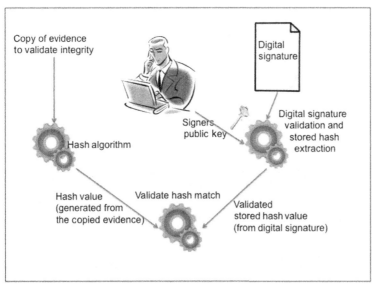

FIG. 2.4

Digital signature validation process.

the digital signature. Therefore, we can now prove the signature is valid, we can associate the signature with the signer, and the hash matches the original evidence ... but we cannot determine the exact time the signing occurred.

Signature types and origins

A few competing Digital Signature Algorithms (DSAs) exist today that should be considered. The following table provides an overview of the most popular types along with some valuable facts regarding each.

Signature Algorithm	Timeline and Creator	Notes
Rivest, Shamir, Adleman (RSA)	1977 by Ron Rivest, Adi Shamir and Leonard Adleman	The concept of digital signatures dates back to the beginning of public-key cryptography (PKC). In 1976, Whitfield Diffie and Martin Hellman devised the concept of PKC which included methods for key exchange and digital signatures. The general model that Diffie and Hellman created was further developed by Rivest, Shamir, and Adleman in 1977 and is the most proven and most popular algorithm in use today.

Continued

Signature Algorithm	Timeline and Creator	Notes
Digital Signature Algorithm	1991 by the NIST, a core element of the Digital Signature Standard	David W. Kravitz is credited with the invention of the algorithm. The standard was patented in 1991, however, NIST has made the patent available worldwide royalty free.
Elliptic Curve Digital Signature Algorithm (ECDSA)	1999, accepted in an ANSI standard. The algorithm was recognized as a standard by the ISO in 1998 and also recognized and accepted by NIST in 2000	Neal Koblitz and Victor Miller invented the algorithm in 1985. The fundamental security basis for the elliptic curve cryptosystems is the computational intractability of the elliptic curve discrete logarithm problem. It is generally viewed as stronger and more secure than RSA and DSA and has characteristics that make it utilize less power, making it ideally suited for low power mobile devices.

Based on these characteristics, how do DSAs stack up against the Daubert factors for protecting the integrity of digital evidence?

Daubert Factor	Digital Signatures for Evidence Integrity
The theory/method is generally accepted in the scientific community	The scientific, business, industry, finance, payment systems, and market transactions all accept and more importantly rely on digital signatures for integrity preservation. Caveat: The implementation and management of the related public key and certificate of such infrastructures is paramount.
The theory/method has been subjected to peer review and publication	The subject of digital signatures has been peer reviewed in computer science and cryptographic publications.
The theory/method has been tested or can be tested	The general theory has been tested and practiced for nearly 40 years.
Whether the potential or known rate of error is acceptable	There have been notable impacts on private keying material and the widespread revocation of keys and certificates. The most notable was the 2014 Heartbleed incident that required the revocation and reissuing of over 100,000 certificates.

Trusted time stamping

To understand what trusted time stamping is we must first understand a little about time itself and what is necessary if we are to utilize time as a digital evidence integrity mechanism. From ancient societies to the present day, time has been interpreted in many ways. Time is essentially an agreement that allows society to function in an orderly fashion—where all parties are easily able to understand the representation. Some examples of time measurement include (Fig. 2.5):

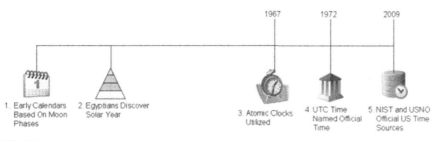

FIG. 2.5

A brief history of time keeping.

- The first calendars known to man were based upon the moon because everyone could easily agree on this as a universal measure of time.
- Moving forward, the Egyptians were the first to understand the solar year and they were able to develop a calendar based on the rotation of the earth around the sun.
- In 1967, an international agreement defined the unit of time as the second, measured by the decay of Cesium using precision instruments known as atomic clocks.
- In 1972, the Treaty of the Meter (established in 1875) was expanded to include the current time reference known as Coordinated Universal Time (UTC), which replaced Greenwich Mean Time (GMT) as the world's official time.
- Today, more than fifty national laboratories operate over three hundred atomic clocks in order to provide a consistent and accurate UTC. In the United States, we have two official sources of time: the NIST in Bolder, Colorado, for commercial time, and the United States Naval Observatory (USNO) in Washington, DC, for military time.

The process of digitally signing evidence that includes a trusted source of time, utilizes the same types of public key infrastructure processes used by digital signatures. Trusted third parties then combine time gathered from official time sources with digital signatures to produce a trusted timestamp. Utilizing such a capability to timestamp digital evidence (mainly message digests or hashes) can then prove the existence of a hash at a specific moment in time. The diagram in Fig. 2.6 depicts how a timestamp could be applied, then used.

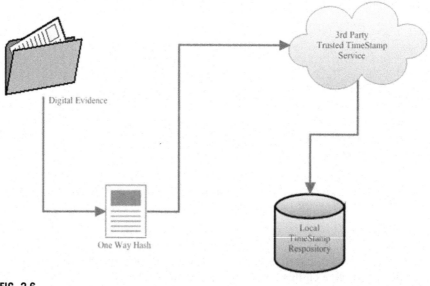

Digital Evidence

One Way Hash

3rd Party Trusted TimeStamp Service

Local TimeStamp Respository

FIG. 2.6

Applying trusted timestamps to digital evidence.

Timestamp generation is accomplished by providing a one-way cryptographic hash to a trusted time stamping service. (Note: Only the hash, not the evidence is provided.) The service then generates a digital signature with an embedded secure source of time.

The next step is to validate the timestamp and the associated evidence. For time stamp validation, the process requires two steps as depicted in Fig. 2.7.

The one-way hash is generated for the evidence and is then compared with the original value generated during the collection; this is effectively what is done today to validate evidence hash values. The second step is to validate whether the timestamp contains the same hash value, and that the integrity of the time stamp is also valid. Validating the third party digital signature of the timestamp does this.

This approach is able to simultaneously secure the timestamp and provide the evidentiary trail of the time source within the timestamp. Once you have created a timestamp that is resistant to manipulation and provides an authenticated audit trail, you can electronically "bind" these secured date/time stamps to digital

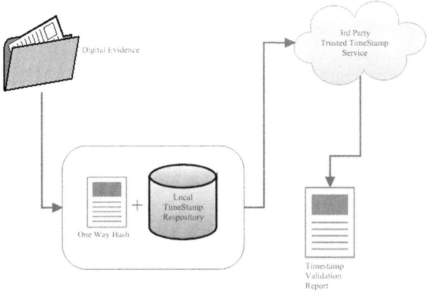

FIG. 2.7

Validating trusted timestamps.

evidence. A qualified third party—either the original service or another trusted third party service—can then verify this data independently.

Despite the broad accessibility of accurate time (watches, computer clocks, and time servers, etc.), the incorporation of trusted time within a system requires a secure, auditable digital date/time stamp.

Once again, based on these characteristics, how do trusted timestamps stack up against the Daubert requirements for establishing the integrity of digital evidence?

Daubert Factor	Trusted Time Stamping for Evidence Integrity
The theory/method is generally accepted in the scientific community	The scientific, business, industry, finance, payment systems, and market transactions utilize trusted timestamps to prove the "when" of these transactions.
The theory/method has been subjected to peer review and publication	The processes described in Internet Engineering Task Force (IETF) Request for Comments (RFC) 3161 provides proof that a specific time-stamped item of information (a datum) existed before a particular time.
The theory/method has been tested or can be tested	The general theory has been tested and practiced for over 15 years. However, the practice has had little exposure within digital forensics.

Continued

Daubert Factor	Trusted Time Stamping for Evidence Integrity
Whether the potential or known rate of error is acceptable	There have not been any errors or vulnerabilities with trusted timestamps beyond those associated with digital signatures themselves

SUMMARY

The investigation methods, procedures, and urgency that we face today require us to rethink the basics regarding integrity protection of digital evidence. We are required to respond more quickly, collect evidence and vital information at the scene of the crime, while the crime could very likely be continuing to unfold. Obviously we need a better way. Whether we are collecting evidence from traditional computers and servers, mobile phones or tablets, the cloud, automobiles, or live network traffic; our need to gather actionable intelligence while securing the integrity of the evidence and our process of collection is vital. Oftentimes, the evidence itself is not contested, but what can causes evidence to be thrown out or discounted is the methods, documentation, or lack thereof, when collecting the evidence in question.

CHAPTER 2 REVIEW

In this chapter we took a practical look at the importance of integrity as it relates to digital evidence. We examined the differences between static and live evidence to examine how these integrity methods and procedures should apply. We also examined the legal standing regarding the admissibility of evidence using the Daubert case results and factors. We examined those factors against integrity methods and processes in place today. We also took a cursory look at different hashing and digital signature standards currently in use, along with some attacks that could potentially impact them today and in the future.

CHAPTER 2 SUMMARY QUESTIONS

1. Define and provide examples of static digital evidence.
2. Define and provide examples of volatile digital evidence.
3. What are the specific risks associated with using one-way cryptographic hashes to protect the integrity of evidence?
4. What processes and procedures would you define to improve the integrity of evidence protected by digital hashes?
5. If you were to choose today ... which hashing algorithm would you choose to protect the integrity of digital evidence and why?

6. What difficulties do you see when applying digital signatures to forensic evidence?
7. What other methods (such as biometrics), would you consider applying to the integrity of digital evidence?
8. If Trusted Time Stamping were applied to digital evidence, what positive impacts would it have on static evidence and on volatile evidence?
9. What difficulties do you see in adoption of Trusted Time Stamping when applied to digital evidence?

ADDITIONAL RESOURCES

Daubert v. Merrell Dow Pharmaceuticals Inc., 509 U.S. 579, 595. (1993). https://www.law.cornell.edu/supct/html/92-102.ZO.html.

Garrie, D. B., & Morrissy, J. D. (2014). *Forensic evidence in the courtroom: understanding content and quality*. http://scholarlycommons.law.northwestern.edu/cgi/viewcontent.cgi?article=1218&context=njtip. Accessed February 2016.

Hosmer, C. (2002). Proving the integrity of digital evidence with time. *International Journal of Digital Evidence*, *1*(1). https://www.utica.edu/academic/institutes/ecii/publications/articles/9C4EBC25-B4A3-6584-C38C511467A6B862.pdf.

Hosmer, C. (2006). Digital evidence bag. *Communications of the ACM—Next-Generation Cyber Forensics*, *49*(2), 69–70.

Hosmer, C. (2009). Evolution of the one-way cryptographic hash, part I and part II. *Forensic Magazine*. http://www.forensicmag.com/articles/2009/07/evolution-one-way-cryptographic-hash-part-1.

IETF. Internet X.509 Public Key Infrastructure Time-Stamp Protocol (TSP) RFC 3161. (n.d.). https://www.ietf.org/rfc/rfc3161.txt. Accessed February 2016.

Johnson, D., Menezes, A., Vanstone, S., & Certicom Research, Canada. *The Elliptic Curve Digital Signature Algorithm (ECDSA)*. (n.d.). http://cs.ucsb.edu/~koc/ccs130h/notes/ecdsa-cert.pdf. Accessed February 2016.

NIST. (2015). *Secure Hash Standard FIPS 180-4*. http://csrc.nist.gov/publications/fips/fips180-4/fips-180-4.pdf. Accessed February 2016.

O'Donnell, A. *Rainbow tables your password's worst nightmare*. (n.d.). http://netsecurity.about.com/od/hackertools/a/Rainbow-Tables.htm. Accessed February 2016.

SWGIT. (2008). Best practices for maintaining the integrity of digital images and digital video. *Forensic Science Communication*, *10*(2). https://www.fbi.gov/about-us/lab/forensic-science-communications/fsc/april2008/index.htm/standards/2008_04_standards01.htm.

Wang, X., & Yu, H. (2005). How to break MD5 and other hash functions. In *Advances in Cryptology—EUROCRYPT 2005*. http://diyhpl.us/~bryan/papers2/security/advances-in-cryptology/Advances%20in%20Cryptology%20-%20EUROCRYPT%202005,%2024%20conf.(LNCS3494,%20Springer,%202005)(ISBN%203540259104)(588s).pdf#page=31.

Windows Command Line Interface

3

Hacker: Word Origin
Early 13th century – originally a surname for someone who makes tools for
chopping. In the 1960's used at the Massachusetts Institute of Technology
(MIT) to define someone who works like a hack when writing and
experimenting with software or one who enjoys computer programming for the
art of it. In modern times it has become associated with someone who gains
unauthorized access to computers or someone who develops software to
break into computers and networks.

CHAPTER OUTLINE

INTRODUCTION

Responding to incidents that involve Microsoft Windows machines can present the investigator with several forensic options. The incident encountered (ie, data breach, malware activity, insider attacks, leakage of sensitive information, human resource violations, victim abduction or abuse, or even capital crimes) will in most cases drive or dictate the investigative steps. In many cases shutting down or replacing the impacted system with a ready backup is infeasible or not prudent. For example:

- An adequate backup is not available for the system(s) in question.
- The system is actively processing vital data such as while maintaining a critical infrastructure control system.
- The system is responsible for processing customer data where shutting down a system would cause significant financial hardship.
- Shutting down the system would cause the loss of important volatile evidence.

Executing Windows Command Line Investigations. http://dx.doi.org/10.1016/B978-0-12-809268-2.00003-1

Homeland Security Presidential Policy Directive 21 (PPD-21) defines 16 critical infrastructure sectors that are vital to the United States. Sectors include: Chemical; Commercial Facilities; Communications; Critical Manufacturing; Dams; Defense Industrial Base; Emergency Services; Energy; Financial Services; Food and Agriculture; Government Facilities; Healthcare and Public Health; Information Technology; Nuclear Reactors, Materials, and Waste; Transportation Systems; and Water and Wastewater Systems.

In order to properly collect evidence and relevant information from these systems, a live investigative response is required. The process of collecting this evidence is important. Generally speaking, you would collect the most volatile evidence first, especially evidence that would be impacted most by these live collection methods. For example, if you plan to acquire memory, you would perform this operation before executing a search of the file system, as these actions would dramatically change the contents of memory.

WHAT IS THE WINDOWS COMMAND LINE INTERFACE?

Before diving into specific examples of using the Windows Command Line Interface (CLI) to collect live volatile data, let's first define what the Windows CLI is. The Windows CLI is most commonly referred to as the Command Prompt, but officially it is referred to by Microsoft as the "Windows Command Processor." The Windows Command Processor is a Windows application that is available on most versions of Microsoft Windows where the application provides the ability to enter specific commands.

The Windows Command Processor is sometimes referred to as the DOS prompt, the DOS Box, or MS-DOS. This Windows Command Processor emulates many DOS commands and provides even greater capability, but is a standalone Windows Application. It should be noted that early version of the Windows Operating System (OS) actually ran on top of DOS.

These commands can be used to probe the system, perform administrative functions, execute specialized scripts that automate operations, troubleshoot or isolate problems, or perform live investigations if an incident occurs.

So how does the Windows Command Processor work? This seems like a reasonable question, however the answer depends on what version of Windows you are using, as each version has a slightly different method of invoking the application. Figs. 3.1 and 3.2 depict launching the Command Prompt in Windows 7 and Windows 8, respectively.

Alternatively on Windows 8 and Windows 10, you can press the Windows Key +X as shown in Fig. 3.3.

This brings up the Windows Tools Menu where you can select a number of built-in Windows commands and configuration options including Command Prompt and Command Prompt (Admin) (Fig. 3.4).

FIG. 3.1

Windows 7 command prompt execution.

FIG. 3.2

Windows 8.1 command prompt execution using the start button.

FIG. 3.3

Windows tools menu shortcut.

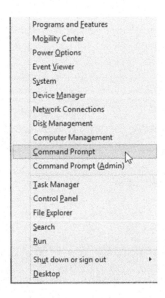

FIG. 3.4

Launching the windows tools menu via the keyboard.

One simple trick that can be used is to right click on the Command Prompt application (Fig. 3.5) and add the Application to the Windows Task Bar (Fig. 3.6). With this, you can single click on the Windows Task Bar Icon to open the Command Prompt.

Now that the Command Prompt is on the Task Bar, you can right click to bring up the menu that either allows you to execute the Command Prompt or Unpin the Command Prompt Application from the Task Bar. If you then right click on the Command Prompt selection you can choose Open, Run as Administrator, Unpin from Task Bar, or bring up the Command Prompt Properties menu. By selecting *Run as Administrator* you can invoke the Command Prompt with Admin privilege (see Fig. 3.7).

It is important to note that for this to work on the machine you are investigating, the current user must have Admin rights. If so, the User Account Control dialog box will be displayed (Fig. 3.8). By selecting OK, the Command Prompt will open with Administrative Privilege.

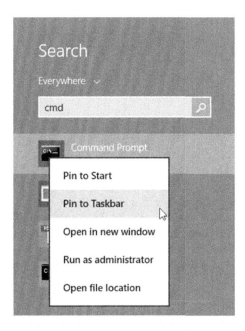

FIG. 3.5

Adding the command prompt to the Windows taskbar.

FIG. 3.6

Windows taskbar after adding the command prompt.

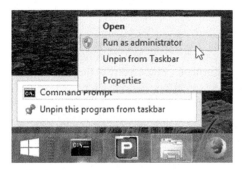

FIG. 3.7

Elevate the command prompt to administrator privilege.

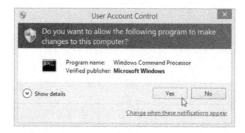

FIG. 3.8

User account control dialog box.

Notice the differences depicted in Figs. 3.9 and 3.10. In Fig. 3.9, the Title Bar is "Command Prompt" and the starting path is "C:\Users\Chester" which is the active users home directory in this example. Whereas in Fig. 3.10, we successfully elevated the privilege of the command prompt, and the Title Bar now indicates "Administrator: Command Prompt" and the starting path is "C:\Windows\system32," the home directory of Windows.

FIG. 3.9

Command prompt launched in user mode.

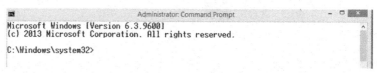

FIG. 3.10

Command prompt launched in administrator mode.

Once the command prompt is up and running, you can customize the default settings to suit your specific needs. Since many of the commands and command results can be tedious and lengthy, creating an environment where commands can be more visible can be helpful (ie, increased screen real estate, larger fonts, more contrast, and additional history). Specific configuration and preferences depend on the user. Figs. 3.11 through 3.15 provide examples for configuring the Command Prompt.

In Fig. 3.11, Right click on the Command Prompt Title Bar revealing a menu that includes a *Properties* selection. This brings up the Command Prompt Properties Dialog Box, from here there are several submenus that allow you to configure your properties.

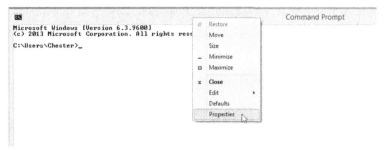

FIG. 3.11

Right click and select properties.

Fig. 3.12 depicts the *Options* Tab and an example of preferred settings for Buffer Size, Number of Buffers, Cursor Size, etc. The important selections here are Buffer Size and Number of Buffers. *Buffer Size* specifies the number of commands that are retained in the command buffer history. The buffer provides a historical record of the commands you have executed. When running a Command Prompt, you can then utilize the Up and Down arrow keys to navigate through the previously entered commands. The default value is 50 commands, but it can be made as large as 999. The next important option is the, "*Number of Buffers*" and is the one that is most confusing. *Number of Buffers* specifies the number of concurrent instances of the Command Prompt where each could retain their own historical buffer. For example, if you change the value to 10, you will be able to have up to 10 Command Prompt instances opened, each with its own historical buffer.

FIG. 3.12

Command prompt dialog box *options* selection.

Moving to the right and selecting the *Font* Tab allows you to configure your font size with a display at the bottom depicting how your selection will appear (Fig. 3.13).

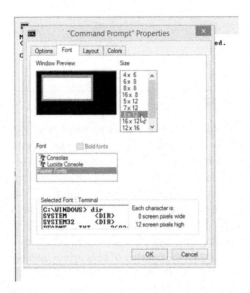

FIG. 3.13

Command prompt *font* selection.

Again moving to the right and selecting the *Layout* Tab (Fig. 3.14) you can configure the size of the Command Prompt window. The Screen *Buffer Size* allows you to configure how many characters are displayed on each line in the Command Prompt window. *Window Position* determines where the Command Prompt window is displayed in relationship to the left and top edges of your desktop or you may elect to choose *Let System Position Window* option.

Finally, moving to the far right, the *Colors* Tab allows you to select the specific colors associated with the *Screen* and *Popup* Text (Fig. 3.15). Each allows you to specify both the foreground and background colors. The Colors Tab depicts a sample rendering of your settings as well.

Please note that launching a newly configured Command Prompt that deviates from the standard black and white colors provides an output that is not preferred by publishers and printers as this would require significant use of ink and could possibly bleed through pages (see Fig. 3.16). Thus you will see screenshots throughout this book that use the Command Prompt with a Black Text on a White Background.

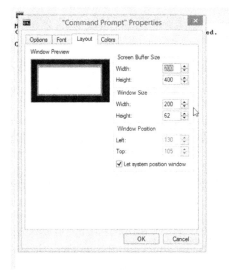

FIG. 3.14

Command prompt *layout* selection.

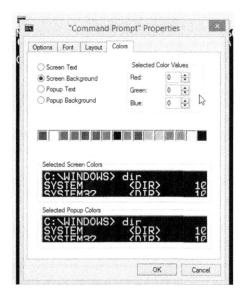

FIG. 3.15

Command prompt *colors* selection.

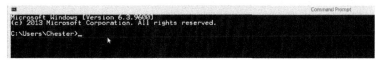

FIG. 3.16

Sample white on black command line window.

BREAKING DOWN WINDOWS COMMANDS BY INVESTIGATION PROCESSES

The Internet is filled with Windows Command Line references and HowTo's for virtually every command available. However, finding recommendations for command sequence considerations, the investigative rationale, potential time implications, or the potential impact on the data being accessed is limited at best. In this section we will group the Windows CLI Investigation Process by sequence. Depending on your investigation, this sequence may change based upon the immediate demands and timeframes that you may have. In addition, for this chapter we will focus only on built-in Windows Commands. Third-party command line applications with be covered later in the book, but for this chapter our assumption is that you are limited to the Windows Command Prompt with built-in commands. In Chapter 4, we will layout the use of the Proactive Incident Response Command Shell (PIRCS) that we will utilize to securely perform Windows CLI investigations. In Chapter 5, we will outline several specific case studies, sometimes referred to as "use cases," when performing investigations based on a specific need.

Windows CLI—starting a live investigation

Now that the Command Prompt is open and in front of you, lets revisit the question below that we originally posed back in Chapter 1.

Considering the following simple scenario:

a. You arrive at an active crime scene where a major crime has just occurred.
b. Immediate action to track down the suspect(s) is vital.
c. It has been determined that evidence on a running Windows computer may contain vital information regarding the crime and associated suspect(s).
d. You have the proper authorization to access the Windows computer via the Windows Command Line only, which is currently up and available.
e. What would be the first command you would type and why?

Note, we will discuss in detail how to record and secure all of your actions when we bring PIRCS into the equation in Chapters 4 and 5.

For all inline command line examples, we will be using a fixed spaced italicized font. The bold portion represents what is typed, while the unbolded text is what the application outputs.

For example, typing the command *cd* as shown here, will simply report back the current path.

```
C:\Users\Chester>cd
C:\Users\Chester>
```

There are several good options here, but let's start out simple. One of the first commands that you should learn about is *echo*. Echo is a command that is available on most CLIs—not only on Windows, it is also available on Unix, Linux, MacOS X,

OS/2, and many other popular OSs. Let's take a look at the basic structure of the command prompt itself. The default prompt looks like this, with the greater than sign indicating that the Command Prompt is ready for a command to be entered.

```
C:\Users\Chester>
```

As you can see, the default prompt provides the full path of information regarding the current directory followed by the 'greater than' sign ">." It is important to note that users can change their prompt and even eliminate the path data from the prompt itself. You just type commands following the 'greater than' sign to invoke actions.

Let's take a look at some of the first commands that you are likely to execute. *Echo* as the name implies allows you to output a string of characters to the display by simply typing *echo* followed by the string you wish to be displayed.

For example:

```
C:\Users\Chester>echo Investigator Name: Joe Friday
Investigator Name: Joe Friday

C:\Users\Chester>echo Location: 123 Main St, New York, New York 10044
Location: 123 Main St, New York, New York 10044

C:\Users\Chester>echo Case: Potential Child Victim
Case: Potential Child Victim
```

These simple echo commands provide a method for investigators to make notations much like you would in a log book. Thus the first three echo commands that were executed provide the investigator's name, the location of the investigation, and the reason for the investigation.

We can include more content to these echo messages by accessing some common Windows Environment Variables as follows:

Windows Environment Variables are used to define specific values that can be used by running processes. For example environment variables can define the path or directory where temporary files are stored. They can also specify directories such as the Home directory for a specific user. They can also be used to hold information about the system such as the OS version, the path for specific commands or applications, and they can hold dynamic values such as the current Date and Time.

Note: When using this method, you must include the Environment Variable between opening and closing percent signs as shown here. If the user has modified the prompt to camouflage the current directory information you can always determine this by using the CD command or you can embed the CD command in an echo like this:

```
C:\Users\Chester>echo %CD%
C:\Users\Chester
```

To obtain the name assigned to the computer you are investigating you can utilize the COMPUTERNAME environment variable.

```
C:\Users\Chester>echo Computer Name %COMPUTERNAME%
Computer Name PYTHONLAPTOP
```

Another important piece of system data that is useful to generate is date and time, this can be generated from the command line as well using an echo command. The forensic value and importance of Windows System time depends on many factors:

- Is the time accurate?
- What is the Time Zone at the current geographic location?
- What Time Zone is the computer set to?
- What is the current Universal Coordinated Time (UTC) in relationship to the computer itself?

```
C:\Users\Chester>echo Investigator Observed Time: Mon 12/21/2015
  11:54 AM Eastern Time
Investigator Observed Time: Mon 12/21/2015 11:54 AM Eastern Time

C:\Users\Chester>echo %date%
Mon 12/21/2015

C:\Users\Chester>echo %time%
11:52:41.65
```

The Computer Time Zone is not readily available as an environment variable. However, by using the *systeminfo* command we can extract just the time zone from the plethora of information that is delivered by *systeminfo*. We will cover the *systeminfo* command in the next sequence in greater detail, but like other commands, *systeminfo* simply outputs lines of text that contain details about the system we are investigating. Instead of dumping all that data to the screen, we have piped the output of the *systeminfo* command into yet another command named *find*. The find command uses the text output from the system command along with the matching string information, in this case "Time Zone" to identify matches. The vertical character|(pronounced "pipe") redirects the output of the *systeminfo* command into the *find* command. The resulting command outputs the current Time Zone assigned to the system.

```
C:\Users\Chester>systeminfo| find "Time Zone"
Time Zone: (UTC-05:00) Eastern Time (US & Canada)
```

You may be wondering how you know the proper syntax to use for specific commands like *systeminfo*, *find*, and *echo*. Virtually all the standard Windows CLI commands include a help option that provides this information. Most third-party commands also include this information, but this will depend upon the implementation of the program itself as to whether it supports help and what method is used to access the help information. To access help for the standard Windows CLI commands, type the command followed by the command line switch / ?. This will print the help information for the command that is specified to the screen. For those new to the Command Line, interpreting the cryptic help output requires a bit of patience and practice.

```
C:\Users\Chester> find / ?

Searches for a text string in a file or files.
FIND [/V] [/C] [/N] [/I] [/OFF[LINE]] "string" [[drive:][path]
 filename[ ...]]

/V Displays all lines NOT containing the specified string.
/C Displays only the count of lines containing the string.
/N Displays line numbers with the displayed lines.
/I Ignores the case of characters when searching.
/OFF[LINE] Do not skip files with offline attribute set.

"string" Specifies the text string to find.

[drive:][path]filenamSpecifies a file or files to search.

If a path is not specified, FIND searches the text typed at the prompt or
piped from another command.
```

The *find* command is actually quite easy to understand and thus is a good one to start with. The command only has a few switches that change the command's behavior. In our case, we didn't require any switches as the standard behavior is what we wanted. First, we could use the /I switch so that the case of the words "Time Zone" could be less strict. Second, if we wanted to know what the output line number from *systeminfo* that produced the Time Zone, we could add the /N switch. For example:

```
C:\Users\Chester> systeminfo | find "time zone" / I / N
[24]Time Zone: (UTC-05:00) Eastern Time (US & Canada)
```

As you can see we first changed the "Time Zone" to "time zone" and using the /N option allowed us to find the string "Time Zone" in the output from *systeminfo*. Also, you may have noticed the [24] at the beginning of the output line. This indicates that the *find* command located the "Time Zone" string on the 24th line of the *systeminfo* output.

Some additional environment variables that are useful to echo and retained as part of the investigation include the OS, the Home Drive for this computer and the Home Path of the current user. The HOMEDRIVE variable is the drive letter on the computer that is connected to the current user's home directory. The drive letter to use is defined in the user's account properties within the domain. The HOMEPATH variable provides the full path to the current user's home directory. The USER-NAME variable provides the logon ID of the currently logged in user. The TMP and TEMP variables provide the full path to the user's temporary files directories.

```
C:\Users\Chester>echo OS: %OS%
OS: Windows_NT

C:\Users\Chester>echo Home Drive: %HOMEDRIVE%
Home Drive: C:

C:\Users\Chester>echo Home Path: %HOMEPATH%
Home Path: \Users\Chester

C:\Users\Chester>echo User Name: %USERNAME%
User Name: Chester

C:\Users\Chester>echo %TEMP%
C:\Users\Chester\AppData\Local\Temp

C:\Users\Chester>echo %TMP%
C:\Users\Chester\AppData\Local\Temp
```

There is a quick way of simply displaying all the current Windows Environment variables by typing the command *set*.

```
C:\Users\Chester>set

ALLUSERSPROFILE=C:\ProgramData
APPDATA=C:\Users\Chester\AppData\Roaming
asl.log=Destination=file
CommonProgramFiles=C:\Program Files\Common Files
CommonProgramFiles(x86)=C:\Program Files (x86)\Common Files
CommonProgramW6432=C:\Program Files\Common Files
COMPUTERNAME=PYTHONLAPTOP
ComSpec=C:\Windows\system32\cmd.exe
FP_NO_HOST_CHECK=NO
HOMEDRIVE=C:
HOMEPATH=\Users\Chester
LOCALAPPDATA=C:\Users\Chester\AppData\Local
LOGONSERVER=\\MicrosoftAccount
NUMBER_OF_PROCESSORS=4
OS=Windows_NT
Path=C:\Python27\;C:\Python27\Scripts; ... [truncated]
PATHEXT=.COM;.EXE;.BAT;.CMD;.VBS;.VBE;.JS;.JSE;.WSF;.WSH;
PROCESSOR_ARCHITECTURE=AMD64
```

```
PROCESSOR_IDENTIFIER=Intel64 Family 6 Model 69 Stepping 1,
 GenuineIntel
PROCESSOR_LEVEL=6
PROCESSOR_REVISION=4501
ProgramData=C:\ProgramData
ProgramFiles=C:\Program Files
ProgramFiles(x86)=C:\Program Files (x86)
ProgramW6432=C:\Program Files
PROMPT=$P$G
PSModulePath=C:\Windows\system32\WindowsPowerShell\v1.0\Modules\
PUBLIC=C:\Users\Public
PythonPath=c:\Python27
SESSIONNAME=Console
SystemDrive=C:
SystemRoot=C:\Windows
TEMP=C:\Users\Chester\AppData\Local\Temp
TMP=C:\Users\Chester\AppData\Local\Temp
USERDOMAIN=PYTHONLAPTOP
USERDOMAIN_ROAMINGPROFILE=PYTHONLAPTOP
USERNAME=Chester
USERPROFILE=C:\Users\Chester
windir=C:\Windows
```

Now that we have established some of the basics regarding the computer we are investigating, we can move on to collecting and examining more information regarding the system. Before we do however, it is good practice to stage the investigation periodically and generate new time and date results as we complete each section.

```
C:\Users\Chester>echo %time%
14:17:06.16

C:\Users\Chester>echo %date%
Mon 12/21/2015
```

You may be thinking at this point, "Wait a minute; if it is good practice to print this information to the screen and review it, what about a more permanent record of the operations that I am performing, not simply having the information scroll off into oblivion?" You are correct, of course, as you recall we set our history buffer to 999 lines. As you will see in Chapters 4 and 5 we will be employing PIRCS to store and secure the results of these commands. However, what are the options without PIRCS or some other integrated logging method? Without installing other software or making special network connections, your options are limited, cumbersome, or some would say untenable. The problem stems from the single handed nature of the Windows Command Line, where the only possible outputs of commands are "standard out" or "standard error." You can redirect the output of a command to a file, of course, using the "greater than" symbol (>) or use "double greater than" symbols (>>) to write and append data to an existing file. The simplest way of doing this is to insert a new clean evidence drive into a USB port (Fig. 3.17).

FIG. 3.17

Insert new clean evidence drive.

(Note: This action will, of course, leave trace evidence in the Windows Registry, Memory, and Hard Drive.) Once the drive has been inserted we can formulate a new command that redirects the output of a command to the evidence drive as shown here. (Note: The drive letter will likely vary from computer to computer based on many factors.)

```
C:\Users\Chester>echo Time: %time% Date: %date% >> d:\log.txt
```

This command would append the output of the time and date value to the log.txt file on the USB drive (assuming that the USB drive is denoted D:). However, the problem with this approach is actually twofold:

(1) Only the output of the command is redirected to the output file or appended (not the command itself). You then end up with data in the file without the context associated with the command that was entered.
(2) The output is only written or appended to the file and it is not written to the screen. So as an investigator, you would have to continue to examine the contents of the file to see the results of each command.

One alternative is to invoke the Microsoft PowerShell that has many additional capabilities that include creating a transcript of all activity. You can invoke the PowerShell from within the Command Prompt as follows.

```
C:\Users\Chester>powershell
Windows PowerShell
```

```
Copyright (C) 2014 Microsoft Corporation. All rights reserved.

PS C:\Users\Chester>
```

Once in the PowerShell, you can invoke the transcription service that will then log all of your operations. You invoke the transcription service as follows. (Note this assumes that you have inserted a removable drive D: that will store your evidence.)

```
PS C:\Users\Chester> set-location D:\
PS D:\> start-transcript d:\evidence.log -append -noclobber
Transcript started, output file is d:\evidence.log
PS D:\>
```

At this point you can execute PowerShell commands. These commands and their corresponding results will be written to the evidence.log file. To demonstrate, I used the date and time zone example and the results contained in the evidence file are shown here.

```
**********************
Windows PowerShell transcript end
End time: 20151221160627
**********************
**********************
Windows PowerShell transcript start
Start time: 20151221161115
Username: PYTHONLAPTOP\Chester
RunAs User: PYTHONLAPTOP\Chester
Machine: PYTHONLAPTOP (Microsoft Windows NT 6.3.9600.0)
Host Application: powershell
Process ID: 4408
**********************
Transcript started, output file is d:\evidence.log

PS D:\> date
Monday, December 21, 2015 4:13:17 PM

PS D:\> systeminfo | find "time zone" / I
Time Zone: (UTC-05:00) Eastern Time (US & Canada)

(It should be noted that the systeminfo command will fully execute and
 will add trace evidence in memory of the actions taken.)
```

Another option is to periodically copy and paste the information from Command Prompt to a file. Once again, assuming that you have inserted an evidence storage device like a USB device we can perform the following:

(1) Use the command prompt to execute the desired commands.

(2) Right click anywhere inside the Command Prompt window and select "Mark" as shown in Fig. 3.18.

(3) Next select the starting point and select the text you wish to copy as shown in Fig. 3.19.

(4) When you have the text selected, press the "Enter" key and the selected text will be placed in the paste buffer. (Note: Many people are accustomed to using the Ctrl-C combination when copying selected text. This does NOT work in the Command Prompt application.)

(5) Now execute the following command.

$$C:\backslash Users\backslash Chester> start\ notepad.exe$$

The *start* command as the name suggests allows you to start the specified application directly from the Command Line. Since notepad.exe is built in to most standard Windows installations you can launch notepad directly from the command line. (Note: This does assume that the Windows installation and paths are setup properly and this method will again add trace evidence in memory.) If the command is successful, simply right click inside the notepad window and paste the contents from the Command Line copy that you just performed as shown in Fig. 3.20.

(6) Finally, save the notepad file to your evidence drive as shown in Fig. 3.21.

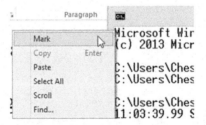

FIG. 3.18

Select the mark option within the command prompt window.

Now that we have established a few alternatives (all have pro's and con's associated with them) we will focus the remainder of the chapter on commands and command execution and leave the logging and secure storage of the command line results to our coverage of PIRCS in Chapters 4 and 5.

Windows CLI—collecting vital system information

Now we have some basic understanding of the Windows Command Line and have performed some perfunctory commands to set the stage for our investigation. We have established who the investigator is, the location of the computer, the current time, date, time zone settings of the computer in question, the Computer Name,

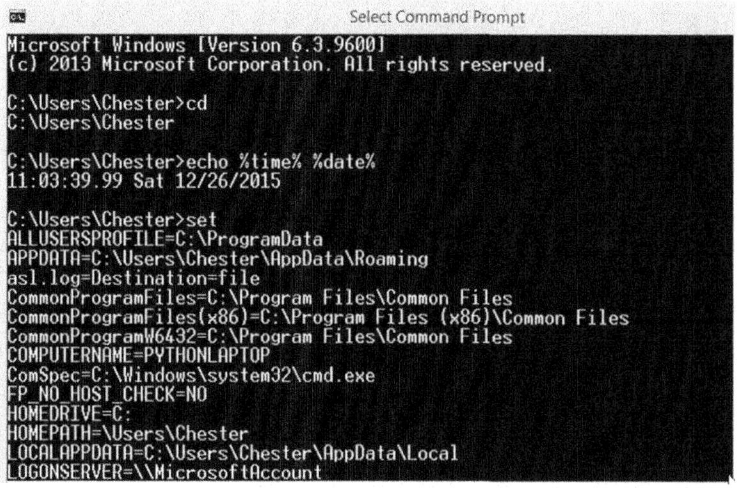

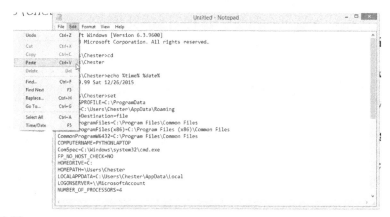

FIG. 3.19

Select the desired text to copy.

FIG. 3.20

Paste the copied text into the notepad document.

FIG. 3.21

Save the notepad document to the evidence drive.

the User Name of the currently logged in User, the User Home Drive, Home Path, and the current user's Temporary Directories.

Now let's take a deeper dive into system and devices. One of the key questions is what commands can we execute? By utilizing the built-in *Help* command we can obtain a list of commands that are readily available for the current system. This is the result you can expect from a standard Windows 8.1 installation.

```
C:\Users\Chester>help
For more information on a specific command, type HELP command-name

ASSOC       Displays or modifies file extension associations.
ATTRIB      Displays or changes file attributes.
BREAK       Sets or clears extended CTRL+C checking.
BCDEDIT     Sets properties in boot database to control boot loading.
CACLS       Displays or modifies access control lists (ACLs) of files.
CALL        Calls one batch program from another.
CD          Displays the name of or changes the current directory.
CHCP        Displays or sets the active code page number.
CHDIR       Displays the name of or changes the current directory.
CHKDSK      Checks a disk and displays a status report.
CHKNTFS     Displays or modifies the checking of disk at boot time.
CLS         Clears the screen.
CMD         Starts a new instance of the Windows command interpreter.
COLOR       Sets the default console foreground and background colors.
COMP        Compares the contents of two files or sets of files.
COMPACT     Displays or alters the compression of files on NTFS
              partitions.
CONVERT     Converts FAT volumes to NTFS. You cannot convert the current
              drive.
COPY        Copies one or more files to another location.
DATE        Displays or sets the date.
DEL         Deletes one or more files.
DIR         Displays a list of files and subdirectories in a directory.
DISKCOMP    Compares the contents of two floppy disks.
DISKCOPY    Copies the contents of one floppy disk to another.
DISKPART    Displays or configures Disk Partition properties.
DOSKEY      Edits command lines, recalls Windows commands, and creates
              macros.
DRIVERQUERY Displays current device driver status and properties.
ECHO        Displays messages, or turns command echoing on or off.
ENDLOCAL    Ends localization of environment changes in a batch file.
ERASE       Deletes one or more files.
EXIT        Quits the CMD.EXE program (command interpreter).
FC          Compares two files or sets of files, and displays the differ
              ences between them.
```

FIND	Searches for a text string in a file or files.
FINDSTR	Searches for strings in files.
FOR	Runs a specified command for each file in a set of files.
FORMAT	Formats a disk for use with Windows.
FSUTIL	Displays or configures the file system properties.
FTYPE	Displays or modifies file types used in file extension associations.
GOTO	Directs the Windows command interpreter to a labeled line in a batch program.
GPRESULT	Displays Group Policy information for machine or user.
GRAFTABL	Enables Windows to display an extended character set in graphics mode.
HELP	Provides Help information for Windows commands.
ICACLS	Display, modify, backup, or restore ACLs for files and directories.
IF	Performs conditional processing in batch programs.
LABEL	Creates, changes, or deletes the volume label of a disk.
MD	Creates a directory.
MKDIR	Creates a directory.
MKLINK	Creates Symbolic Links and Hard Links
MODE	Configures a system device.
MORE	Displays output one screen at a time.
MOVE	Moves one or more files from one directory to another directory.
OPENFILES	Displays files opened by remote users for a file share.
PATH	Displays or sets a search path for executable files.
PAUSE	Suspends processing of a batch file and displays a message.
POPD	Restores the previous value of the current directory saved by PUSHD.
PRINT	Prints a text file.
PROMPT	Changes the Windows command prompt.
PUSHD	Saves the current directory then changes it.
RD	Removes a directory.
RECOVER	Recovers readable information from a bad or defective disk.
REM	Records comments (remarks) in batch files or CONFIG.SYS.
REN	Renames a file or files.
RENAME	Renames a file or files.
REPLACE	Replaces files.
RMDIR	Removes a directory.
ROBOCOPY	Advanced utility to copy files and directory trees
SET	Displays, sets, or removes Windows environment variables.
SETLOCAL	Begins localization of environment changes in a batch file.
SC	Displays or configures services (background processes).
SCHTASKS	Schedules commands and programs to run on a computer.
SHIFT	Shifts the position of replaceable parameters in batch files.

```
SHUTDOWN     Allows proper local or remote shutdown of machine.
SORT         Sorts input.
START        Starts a separate window to run a specified program or
               command.
SUBST        Associates a path with a drive letter.
SYSTEMINFO   Displays machine specific properties and configuration.
TASKLIST     Displays all currently running tasks including services.
TASKKILL     Kill or stop a running process or application.
TIME         Displays or sets the system time.
TITLE        Sets the window title for a CMD.EXE session.
TREE         Graphically displays the directory structure of a drive or
               path.
TYPE         Displays the contents of a text file.
VER          Displays the Windows version.
VERIFY       Tells Windows whether to verify that your files are written
               correctly to a disk.
VOL          Displays a disk volume label and serial number.
XCOPY        Copies files and directory trees.
WMIC         Displays WMI information inside interactive command shell.
```

For more information on tools see the command-line reference in the online help.

Capture important system information

Collecting system information can reveal important details regarding the current system and the general running state of the computer under investigation. Let's take a look at some commands that will help in discovering this basic information. We earlier used the *systeminfo* command to extract the system time zone information in order to establish a complete time reference for the computer we are investigating. As you can see executing *systeminfo* enables us to capture the fundamental baseline of the computer under investigation using a single command.

```
C:\Users\Chester> systeminfo
```

```
Host Name:                PYTHONLAPTOP
OS Name:                  Microsoft Windows 8.1
OS Version:               6.3.9600 N/A Build 9600
OS Manufacturer:          Microsoft Corporation
OS Configuration:         Standalone Workstation
OS Build Type:            Multiprocessor Free
Registered Owner:         cdh@python-forensics.org
Registered Organization:  Python Forensics, Inc.
Product ID:               00258-61471-70681-AAOEM
Original Install Date:    7/26/2014, 10:58:26 PM
System Boot Time:         12/18/2015, 8:18:35 AM
```

```
System Manufacturer:         Dell Inc.
System Model:                Inspiron 5447
System Type:                 x64-based PC
Processor(s):                1 Processor(s) Installed.
                             [01]: Intel64 Family 6 Model 69 Stepping 1
                              GenuineIntel ~1700 Mhz
BIOS Version:                Dell Inc. A04, 5/9/2014
Windows Directory:           C:\Windows
System Directory:            C:\Windows\system32
Boot Device:                 \Device\HarddiskVolume1
System Locale:               en-us;English (United States)
Input Locale:                en-us;English (United States)
Time Zone:                   (UTC-05:00) Eastern Time (US & Canada)
Total Physical Memory:       8,073 MB
Available Physical Memory:   5,004 MB
Virtual Memory: Max Size:    10,361 MB
Virtual Memory: Available:   6,747 MB
Virtual Memory: In Use:      3,614 MB
Page File Location(s):       C:\pagefile.sys
Domain:                      WORKGROUP
Logon Server:                \\MicrosoftAccount
Hotfix(s):                   219 Hotfix(s) Installed.

                             [01]:  KB2899189_Microsoft-Windows-Camera-
                             Codec-Package
                             [02]: KB2894852
... truncated for brevity
                             [218]: KB3112336
                             [219]: KB3119147

Network Card(s):             5 NIC(s) Installed.
                             [01]: Intel(R) Dual Band Wireless-AC 3160
                                    Connection Name: Wi-Fi
                                    Status: Media disconnected
                             [02]: Realtek PCIe FE Family Controller
                                    Connection Name: Ethernet
                                    DHCP Enabled:    Yes
                                    DHCP Server:     192.168.0.1
                                    IP address(es)
                                    [01]: 192.168.0.122
                                    [02]: fe80::1a5:f691:5963:fde
                                    [03]: 2606:a000:eae0:5800:
                                           1a5:f691:5963:fde
                             [03]: Bluetooth Device (Personal Area Network)
```

Network Connection

Connection Name: Bluetooth

Status: Media disconnected
[04]: VMware Virtual Ethernet Adapter for
      VMnet1
Connection Name: VMware Network
      Adapter VMnet1
DHCP Enabled: No
IP address(es)
[01]: 192.168.163.1
[02]: fe80::dd94:ea3c:3ceb:e7dd
[05]: VMware Virtual Ethernet Adapter for
      VMnet8
Connection Name: VMware Network
      Adapter VMnet8
DHCP Enabled: No
IP address(es)
[01]: 192.168.21.1
[02]: fe80::525:3f59:c937:d5e3

Hyper-V Requirements:

VM Monitor Mode Extensions: Yes
Virtualization Enabled: Yes
Second Level Address Translation: Yes
Data Execution Prevention : Yes

Basic disk information

The next question to address is what are the logical disk drives attached to the system? This will provide us a bit more information regarding how the system is configured, along with the identification of disks where evidence may be stored. In order to accomplish this at the command line we are going to invoke the *wmic* command. WMIC is an abbreviation for Windows Management Instrumentation Command and when used properly and carefully, can provide investigators with beneficial information. The *wmic logicaldisk* command provides quite a bit of useful information regarding the status and operation of the logical disks currently available on the system. The following simplest command will return the caption (basically drive letter of the logical disks available). As you can see there are two logical disks available C: and D:.

```
C:\Users\Chester> wmic logicaldisk get caption
Caption
C:
D:
```

We can obtain a bit more information by specifying the specific data about the logical disks we are interested in by adding to the information we "get" from the *logicaldisk* specifier. For example:

```
C:\Users\Chester> wmic logicaldisk get caption, filesystem, size, free
 space, description

Caption  Description      FileSystem  FreeSpace      Size
C:       Local Fixed Disk  NTFS       832790732800   987900145664
D:       Removable Disk    FAT32      3991699456     4001546240
```

This command execution reveals that the C: drive is a local fixed disk with a size of approximately 920 GB (Gigabytes) with approximately 775 GB of free space, formatted with the New Technology File System (NTFS) filesystem. The D: drive is a Removable Disk (the evidence drive that was previously inserted) with a size of approximately 3.7 and 3.71 GB of free space, formatted with a FAT32 filesystem. Note, the values listed for Size and FreeSpace by the wmic logical disk command are in bytes. In order to calculate GB you need to convert the bytes into the equivalent GB's. The basics are as follows:

```
1 Kilobyte = 1,024 bytes
1 Megabyte = 1,048,576 bytes or 1,024 kilobytes
1 GB       = 1,073,741,824 bytes or 1,024 megabytes
1 TB       = 1,099,511,627,776 bytes or 1,024 gigabytes
```

Logical Disk: In contrast to a Physical Disk which refers to the actual hardware itself, logical disks are actually volumes that are part of, or contained on, a Physical Disk. Therefore, you may have multiple logical disks contained on a single Physical Disk. The configuration of Physical Disks has changed in recent years with the advent of solid state drives (SSDs) that have no spinning platters or read/write heads.

NTFS: Refers to New Technology File System. NTFS is a proprietary File System from Microsoft. The File System has improvements over its predecessor—the FAT file system—in performance, file system size, maximum file size, reliability, and security. The maximum size of NTFSs is dependent on the underlying hardware, however based on the hardware today, most peg the upper limit to 2 TB (terabytes).

Digging a bit deeper into the configuration of the available disks requires the use of the diskpart command. Using diskpart to examine storage devices has a couple of drawbacks or special considerations. First, diskpart requires administration rights which can be elevated automatically if the current user has administrative privilege. Secondly, using diskpart can potentially damage your disk and make information unrecoverable. Thus, we are only going to walk through some safe and simple commands within diskpart that are used to extract or list information. In order to use diskpart, you should start the Command Prompt as Administrator. Then simply type diskpart as shown in Fig. 3.22. Notice that the title bar now reflects "Administrator: Command Prompt—diskpart."

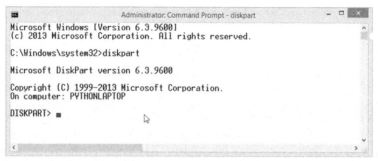

FIG. 3.22

Launching the administrator prompt and *diskpart*.

The simplest way to extract some meaningful information from *diskpart* is to use the following *list* commands (*list disk, list volume, and list vdisk*)

```
DISKPART> list disk

  Disk ###  Status          Size     Free     Dyn  Gpt
  --------  -------------   -------  -------   ---  ---
  Disk 0    Online           931 GB     0 B         *
  Disk 1    Online          3822 MB     0 B
```

The *list disk* command provides a list of disks and information about them, including their size, amount of available free space, and whether the disk is a basic or dynamic disk. Note Disk 0 and Disk 1 are the physically attached disks—not logical.

Now let's obtain the information regarding the volumes contained on each disk.

```
DISKPART> list volume
```

Volume ###	Ltr	Label	Fs	Type	Size	Status	Info
Volume 0	C	OS	NTFS	Partition	920 GB	Healthy	Boot
Volume 1		ESP	FAT32	Partition	500 MB	Healthy	System
Volume 2		WINRETOOLS	NTFS	Partition	750 MB	Healthy	Hidden
Volume 3		PBR Image	NTFS	Partition	10 GB	Healthy	Hidden
Volume 4	D	EVIDENCE	FAT32	Removable	3818 MB	Healthy	

You may notice that the **System** and **Hidden** Volumes were not accounted for when using the *wmic* command. Volume 1 ESP refers to the EFI System Partition which is used by the boot loader to load specific files used by the OS along with any special system utilities. EFI stands for the Unified Extensible Firmware Interface. Volume 2 WINRETOOLS and PRB Image are used for system recovery. The value of this is to utilize the lowest level tools that are built into the OS to discover information regarding all the disk partitions and volumes. It should be noted that sophisticated methods exist that provide surreptitious methods of hiding both, partitions and volumes. These are best exposed during postmortem processing using specialized tools designed to uncover these advanced methods. However, using the built-in tools during live investigations provide a solid investigative baseline.

Next, we will interrogate the system for the existence of any virtual disks. A virtual hard disk works much like a conventional physical hard disk. These disks can be memory resident or exist on an existing physical disk, they can be fixed in size or they can be dynamically modified. Executing the `list vdisk` command will expose any virtual disks. The system currently being investigated did not have any virtual disks as shown below.

```
DISKPART> list vdisk
There are no virtual disks to show.
```

To dive even deeper, you can select a specific disk—in this example disk 0, which is the main hard disk on the laptop. Once selected, you can list the partition information and examine information related to the different types of partitions. This includes the SYSTEM, the Original Equipment Manufacturer partition that contains information—typically drivers from DELL in this example. The reserved partitions, primary partitions, and the recovery partition information are revealed.

```
DISKPART> select disk 0

Disk 0 is now the selected disk.

DISKPART> list partition

  Partition ###  Type              Size     Offset
  -------------  ----------------  -------  -------
  Partition 1    System            500 MB   1024 KB
  Partition 2    OEM                40 MB    501 MB
  Partition 3    Reserved          128 MB   541 MB
  Partition 4    Recovery          750 MB   669 MB
  Partition 5    Primary           920 GB  1419 MB
  Partition 6    Recovery           10 GB   921 GB
```

At this point, the investigative value of the information we have gleaned from the logical and physical disk inquiries may not be readily apparent. However, this information will be useful during an investigation especially in malware related attacks in which low level changes have been made to the system. In addition, this information is vital when establishing the baseline of the system under investigation.

Type *exit* to quit DISKPART.

Basic network information
The next area of immediate consideration is the basic network information, in other words—how is the system under investigation connected to the outside world?

A good place to start is with the *ipconfig* command, which is short for Internet Protocol Configuration. To obtain the full breadth of information available, the *ipconfig /all* command is used as shown below.

As you will see, the information provided by *ipconfig* is voluminous. The command provides basic information such as the Host Name, Internet Protocol Addresses, and the Network Interface physical address (typically to as the MAC address), DNS Suffix (which will typically give you a clue regarding the Internet Service Provider that the system uses). In addition, information about wired, wireless, Bluetooth, and virtual machine network interfaces are provided.

```
C:\Users\Chester> ipconfig /all

Windows IP Configuration

        Host Name . . . . . . . . . . . . . . : PythonLaptop
        Primary Dns Suffix . . . . . . . . . :
        Node Type . . . . . . . . . . . . . . : Hybrid
        IP Routing Enabled. . . . . . . . . . : No
        WINS Proxy Enabled. . . . . . . . . . : No
        DNS Suffix Search List. . . . . . . : sc.rr.com

Ethernet adapter Bluetooth Network Connection:

        Media State . . . . . . . . . . . . . : Media disconnected
        Connection-specific DNS Suffix . :
        Description . . . . . . . . . . . . . : Bluetooth Device (Personal Area
                                                Network)
        Physical Address. . . . . . . . . . . : A0-88-69-5C-EB-D4
        DHCP Enabled. . . . . . . . . . . . . : Yes
        Autoconfiguration Enabled . . . . : Yes

Ethernet adapter Ethernet:

        Connection-specific DNS Suffix . : sc.rr.com
        Description . . . . . . . . . . . . . : Realtek PCIe FE Family Controller
        Physical Address. . . . . . . . . . . : 34-17-EB-56-A5-E7
        DHCP Enabled. . . . . . . . . . . . . : Yes
        Autoconfiguration Enabled . . . . : Yes
        IPv6 Address. . . . . . . . . . . . . : 2606:a000:eae0:5800:1a5:f691:
                                                5963:fde(Preferred)
        Link-local IPv6 Address . . . . . . : fe80::1a5:f691:5963:fde%4
                                                (Preferred)
        IPv4 Address. . . . . . . . . . . . . : 192.168.0.122(Preferred)
        Subnet Mask . . . . . . . . . . . . . : 255.255.255.0
        Lease Obtained. . . . . . . . . . . : Saturday, December 19, 2015
                                                10:47:27 AM
```

```
        Lease Expires . . . . . . . . . . . . .: Sunday, December 27, 2015
                                               10:47:31 PM
        Default Gateway . . . . . . . . . . .: fe80::21d:d3ff:fe88:23c1%4
                                               192.168.0.1
        DHCP Server . . . . . . . . . . . . .: 192.168.0.1
        DHCPv6 IAID . . . . . . . . . . . . .: 154408939
        DHCPv6 Client DUID. . . . . . . . . : 00-01-00-01-1B-29-7F-91-34-17-
                                               EB-56-A5-E7
        DNS Servers . . . . . . . . . . . . .: 209.18.47.61
                                               209.18.47.62
        NetBIOS over Tcpip. . . . . . . . . .: Enabled

Wireless LAN adapter Wi-Fi:

        Media State . . . . . . . . . . . . .: Media disconnected
        Connection-specific DNS Suffix . .: sc.rr.com
        Description . . . . . . . . . . . . . . .: Intel(R) Dual Band Wireless-AC 3160
        Physical Address. . . . . . . . . . .: A0-88-69-5C-EB-D0
        DHCP Enabled. . . . . . . . . . . . .: Yes
        Autoconfiguration Enabled . . . . .: Yes

Ethernet adapter VMware Network Adapter VMnet1:

        Connection-specific DNS Suffix . :
        Description . . . . . . . . . . . . . .: VMware Virtual Ethernet Adapter for
                                               VMnet1
        Physical Address. . . . . . . . . . .: 00-50-56-C0-00-01
        DHCP Enabled. . . . . . . . . . . . .: No
        Autoconfiguration Enabled . . . . .: Yes
        Link-local IPv6 Address . . . . . .: fe80::dd94:ea3c:3ceb:e7dd%6
                                               (Preferred)
        IPv4 Address. . . . . . . . . . . . .: 192.168.163.1(Preferred)
        Subnet Mask . . . . . . . . . . . . .: 255.255.255.0
        Default Gateway . . . . . . . . . . .:
        DHCPv6 IAID . . . . . . . . . . . . .: 419450966
        DHCPv6 Client DUID. . . . . . . . . .: 00-01-00-01-1B-29-7F-91-34-17-
                                               EB-56-A5-E7
        DNS Servers . . . . . . . . . . . . .: fec0:0:0:ffff::1%1
                                               fec0:0:0:ffff::2%1
                                               fec0:0:0:ffff::3%1
        NetBIOS over Tcpip. . . . . . . . . .: Enabled

Ethernet adapter VMware Network Adapter VMnet8:

        Connection-specific DNS Suffix . :
```

```
Description. . . . . . . . . . . . . . : VMware Virtual Ethernet Adapter for
                                        VMnet8
Physical Address. . . . . . . . . . : 00-50-56-C0-00-08
DHCP Enabled. . . . . . . . . . . . : No
Autoconfiguration Enabled . . . . : Yes
Link-local IPv6 Address . . . . . . : fe80::525:3f59:c937:d5e3%7
                                        (Preferred)
IPv4 Address. . . . . . . . . . . . : 192.168.21.1(Preferred)
Subnet Mask . . . . . . . . . . . . : 255.255.255.0
Default Gateway . . . . . . . . . . :
DHCPv6 IAID . . . . . . . . . . . . : 453005398
DHCPv6 Client DUID. . . . . . . . . : 00-01-00-01-1B-29-7F-91-34-17-
                                        EB-56-A5-E7
DNS Servers . . . . . . . . . . . . : fec0:0:0:ffff::1%1
                                        fec0:0:0:ffff::2%1
                                        fec0:0:0:ffff::3%1
NetBIOS over Tcpip. . . . . . . . . : Enabled

Tunnel adapter isatap.{9B4481DE-5DB3-47ED-ABFD-62F7EED11E50}:

Media State . . . . . . . . . . . . : Media disconnected
Connection-specific DNS Suffix . . :
Description . . . . . . . . . . . . : Microsoft ISATAP Adapter
Physical Address. . . . . . . . . . : 00-00-00-00-00-00-00-E0
DHCP Enabled. . . . . . . . . . . . : No
Autoconfiguration Enabled . . . . . : Yes

Tunnel adapter isatap.{BF5D73E5-8683-49AA-B8C5-410490BC55FF}:

Media State . . . . . . . . . . . . : Media disconnected
Connection-specific DNS Suffix . . :
Description . . . . . . . . . . . . : Microsoft ISATAP Adapter #10
Physical Address. . . . . . . . . . : 00-00-00-00-00-00-00-E0
DHCP Enabled. . . . . . . . . . . . : No
Autoconfiguration Enabled . . . . . : Yes

Tunnel adapter isatap.sc.rr.com:

Media State . . . . . . . . . . . . : Media disconnected
Connection-specific DNS Suffix . . : sc.rr.com
Description . . . . . . . . . . . . : Microsoft ISATAP Adapter #11
Physical Address. . . . . . . . . . : 00-00-00-00-00-00-00-E0
DHCP Enabled. . . . . . . . . . . . : No
Autoconfiguration Enabled . . . . . : Yes
```

Another important command option under ipconfig is the *ipconfig/displaydns* command. Executing this command provides details of the domain name services in play for the currently logged in user. More specifically, this command displays the resolver cache of DNS translations for the system. For example, if you access the domain name microsoft.weather.com a domain name server returns the specific IP address for microsoft.weather.com, translating the domain into an addressable IP address. In order to limit these DNS translations, windows will cache them in memory such that each time you access microsoft.weather.com the translation can occur on your local system. If the cache were to become poisoned, in other words a malicious application were to redirect the IP address associated with microsoft.weather.com to an intermediary you would think you were getting your weather data from Microsoft, when in reality you would be entering information at some rogue website that is pretending to be microsoft.weather.com.

Here is a truncated example of the command, as the results can be voluminous based on the user's Internet activity. One of the important fields within each record is Time To Live. This field defines how long (in seconds) before the cache will be refreshed with new information from the Internet. Cache values are typically short (3-5 minutes), if you see a Time to Live that is long for example hours, this should be considered suspicious.

```
C:\Users\Chester> ipconfig /displaydns

service.weather.microsoft.com

- - - - - - - - - - - - - - - - - - - - - - - - - - - - - - - - -

Record Name . . . . . : service.weather.microsoft.com

Record Type . . . . . : 5

Time To Live. . . . . : 193

Data Length . . . . . : 8

Section . . . . . . . : Answer

CNAME Record . . . . : wildcard.weather.microsoft.com.edgekey.net
```

The information presented here again provides investigative value along with a baseline of the system under investigation.

Moving up from the hardware and protocol layers of the network, we can also query other network and security related aspects. For example, you may wish to examine the state of the computer's internal firewall settings. This can determine if the firewall is running or potentially has been tampered with. In order to perform nondestructive act, it is best to use firewall commands that extract the current configuration information. Currently, the best way to access the firewall configuration from the command line is by using the *netsh advfirewall* command. (In the future PowerShell will likely be the preferred approach.) The command *netsh* is a command-line scripting utility that allows you to locally or even remotely display or modify the computer's network configuration.

Typing *netsh help* will provide you with the list of supported *netsh* commands.

```
C:\Users\Chester>netsh help

The following commands are available:

Commands in this context:
?              - Displays a list of commands.
add            - Adds a configuration entry to a list of entries.
advfirewall    - Changes to the 'netsh advfirewall' context.
bridge         - Changes to the 'netsh bridge' context.
delete         - Deletes a configuration entry from a list of entries.
dhcpclient     - Changes to the 'netsh dhcpclient' context.
dnsclient      - Changes to the 'netsh dnsclient' context.
dump           - Displays a configuration script.
exec           - Runs a script file.
firewall       - Changes to the 'netsh firewall' context.
help           - Displays a list of commands.
http           - Changes to the 'netsh http' context.
interface      - Changes to the 'netsh interface' context.
ipsec          - Changes to the 'netsh ipsec' context.
lan            - Changes to the 'netsh lan' context.
mbn            - Changes to the 'netsh mbn' context.
namespace      - Changes to the 'netsh namespace' context.
nap            - Changes to the 'netsh nap' context.
netio          - Changes to the 'netsh netio' context.
p2p            - Changes to the 'netsh p2p' context.
ras            - Changes to the 'netsh ras' context.
rpc            - Changes to the 'netsh rpc' context.
set            - Updates configuration settings.
show           - Displays information.
trace          - Changes to the 'netsh trace' context.
wcn            - Changes to the 'netsh wcn' context.
wfp            - Changes to the 'netsh wfp' context.
winhttp        - Changes to the 'netsh winhttp' context.
winsock        - Changes to the 'netsh winsock' context.
wlan           - Changes to the 'netsh wlan' context.
```

As you can see, there are dozens of commands that allow you to inspect and examine various aspects of the network configuration, and there are many commands to inspect the firewall settings. To list the possible *advfirewall* commands you would do the following.

```
C:\Users\Chester>netsh advfirewall

The following commands are available:

Commands in this context:
?              - Displays a list of commands.
consec         - Changes to the 'netsh advfirewall consec' context.
dump           - Displays a configuration script.
export         - Exports the current policy to a file.
firewall       - Changes to the 'netsh advfirewall firewall' context.
help           - Displays a list of commands.
import         - Imports a policy file into the current policy store.
mainmode       - Changes to the 'netsh advfirewall mainmode' context.
monitor        - Changes to the 'netsh advfirewall monitor' context.
reset          - Resets the policy to the default out-of-box policy.
set            - Sets the per-profile or global settings.
show           - Displays profile or global properties.
```

The least impactful command here is *show*, and can display either the profile or the global properties. To further investigate the specific commands available under the *advfirewall show* context you can execute the following command:

```
C:\Users\Chester>netsh advfirewall show

The following commands are available:

Commands in this context:

show allprofiles      - Displays properties for all profiles.
show currentprofile   - Displays properties for the active
                          profile.
show domainprofile    - Displays properties for the domain
                          properties.
show global           - Displays the global properties.
show privateprofile   - Displays properties for the private
                          profile.
show publicprofile    - Displays properties for the public
                          profile.
show store            - Displays the policy store for the current
                          interactive session.
```

As an example, the following command would be used to expose the configuration of the currently active profile, while other profiles can also be examined driven by the investigation and case scenario.

```
C:\Users\Chester>netsh advfirewall show currentprofile

Public Profile Settings:
- - - - - - - - - - - - - - - - - - - - - - - - - - - - - - - - - - - - - - - - - - - - - - - - -
State                            ON
Firewall Policy                  BlockInbound,AllowOutbound
LocalFirewallRules               N/A (GPO-store only)
LocalConSecRules                 N/A (GPO-store only)
InboundUserNotification          Enable
RemoteManagement                 Disable
UnicastResponseToMulticast       Enable

Logging:
LogAllowedConnections            Disable
LogDroppedConnections            Disable
FileName %systemroot%\system32\LogFiles\Firewall\pfirewall.log
MaxFileSize                      4096
```

Examining the results, we find several key pieces of information.

(1) The Firewall is on.
(2) The Policy is set to block all inbound and outbound traffic.
(3) The path of the firewall.log file if we wish to examine it.
(4) The MaxFileSize of the log.

As you can see there are literally hundreds of command combinations available within *netsh* to examine a variety of network settings and activities. This section has provided the basics for accessing the *netsh* from the command line, how to identify the command, sub-commands and command options, or context.

A final word of caution: It is important that you fully understand each command and have practiced the commands before using them during a live investigation. In addition, be careful to select commands that only view, display, show, or list information, so you limit any modification to the system under investigation.

Windows CLI—collecting volatile evidence

Next we will examine several commands that interrogate and extract volatile information from the system under investigation. Several key areas will be covered here including Memory, Running Processes, Active Network Activities, and Event Logs.

System Memory: There is not a native Windows memory capture capability available for the command or from the GUI for that matter. There are several third-party tools that do a good job with limited system impact. However, to do this correctly, the third-party tool must install a signed kernel level driver to access protected memory. (Note, this statement only covers systems running in protected mode. Windows XP systems for example have less kernel protection and the memory from these systems can be extracted without the installation of a signed driver.) Even with the installation of these special signed kernel drivers, certain areas of system memory are still not accessible, however the areas that are excluded have limited probative value.

A question remains, before we pull the plug, can we access any memory secrets from the system under investigation without installing third-party tools? Yes—the Windows OS uses a memory paging scheme. When the system is running low on physical memory because of the number of applications that are running, or certain applications like web browsers are caching large amounts of information, Windows automatically moves the least used "pages" of memory out to a hidden file named pagefile.sys. To determine where the pagefile.sys file is, along with some information about it, we can utilize a *wmic* command, namely *wmic pagefile*.

```
C:\Users\Chester>wmic pagefile
AllocatedBaseSize    Caption            CurrentUsage   Description
2288                 C:\pagefile.sys    289            C:\pagefile.sys

InstallDate                    Name                PeakUsage
20140610225212.145283-240 C:\pagefile.sys 2241

TempPageFile
FALSE
```

(Note: To make this more readable in book form I have reformatted the output of the command.)

Now that we know where the page file is located, under normal conditions Windows marks the file as a hidden system file. In order to reveal the basic file information we use another command to examine the file system contents—the *dir* command. Since the file is likely to be a hidden system file, we have to use a special version of the *dir* command. As before, if you are not sure of the command or possible command parameters you can always type:

```
C:\>dir /?
Displays a list of files and subdirectories in a directory.

DIR [drive:][path][filename] [/A[[:]attributes]]  [/B]  [/C]  [/D]
                             [/L]  [/N]  [/O[[:]sortorder]] [/P]
                             [/Q]  [/R]  [/S]  [/T[[:]timefield]]
                             [/W]  [/X]  [/4]
                             [drive:][path][filename]
```

Specifies drive, directory,
and/or files to list.

/A   *Displays files with specified attributes.*
          attributes   D   Directories   R   Read-only files
                       H   Hidden files   A   Files ready for archiving
                       S   System files   I   Not content indexed files
                       L   Reparse Points -   Prefix meaning not
/B   *Uses bare format (no heading information or summary).*
/C   *Display the thousand separator in file sizes. This is the*
          default. Use /-C to disable display of separator.
/D   *Same as wide but files are list sorted by column.*
/L   *Uses lowercase.*
/N   *New long list format where filenames are on the far right.*
/O   *List by files in sorted order.*

sortorder N   By name (alphabetic)   S   By size (smallest first)
         E   By extension (alphabetic)   D   By date/time (oldest first)
         G   Group directories first   -   Prefix to reverse order
/P   *Pauses after each screenful of information.*
/Q   *Display the owner of the file.*
/R   *Display alternate data streams of the file.*
/S   *Displays files in specified directory and all subdirectories.*
/T   *Controls which time field displayed or used for sorting*
timefield C   Creation
          A   Last Access
          W   Last Written
/W   *Uses wide list format.*
/X   *This displays the short names generated for non- 8dot3 file*
          names. The format is that of /N with the short name inserted
          before the long name. If no short name is present, blanks are dis-
          played in its place.
/4   *Displays four-digit years*

In this example we want to use the */A:HS-D* option to display only the HIDDEN SYSTEM files and exclude the directories. We know based on the *wmic pagefile -* command previously executed, that the pagefile.sys file should be in the C:\ directory. Thus the command would be:

C:\Users\Chester>dir c:\ /A:HS-D
Volume in drive C is OS
Volume Serial Number is 8621-BAFB

Directory of c:

```
08/22/2013 12:31 AM      427,680 bootmgr
06/18/2013 07:18 AM            1 BOOTNXT
12/18/2015 08:18 AM    6,772,088,832 hiberfil.sys
12/26/2015 10:47 AM    2,399,141,888 pagefile.sys
12/18/2015 08:18 AM      268,435,456 swapfile.sys
              5 File(s) 9,440,093,857 bytes
              0 Dir(s) 831,361,867,776 bytes free
```

As you can see pagefile.sys is listed here as expected and is quite large ~2.4 GB. However, we also find two other memory related files here of interest, namely, hiberfil.sys and swapfile.sys. Since hibernation was enabled on this computer, a great resource of memory analysis is hiberfile.sys when available; this file contains the kernel and all the applications and the application state as of the last hibernation point. Since this is a Windows 8.1 system, there is also a swapfile.sys. The swap file is another type of paging file, this one relates to the Windows 8.x and 10.x metro applications which can also provide investigative clues depending on the user's use of Metro applications.

Metro applications are touch-screen-friendly applications written especially for Microsoft's WinRT programming environment. These applications were originally created for Microsoft Surface tablets and Windows phones, however Windows 8 and Windows 10 environments also support Metro applications using either touch or mouse based interfaces.

Now that we see that memory rich files are available and potentially useful, there is a catch. These files are locked by the system during normal operations and cannot be read by users or even the administrator via the command line. However, we have two options.

(1) We can use third-party tools that can copy these files.
(2) We can simply note that these files are available and should be examined at a later time.

Windows CLI—running processes and services

The applications, associated processes, and system services that are running or in use can provide useful investigative information and of course provide a baseline of the state of the system under investigation. To perform this operation from the command line, we use the `tasklist` command. The `tasklist` command has a number of options that mostly deal with either the formatting of the output or filtering of the results. As with other commands, you can simply type: `tasklist /?` to obtain the list of options.

```
C:\Users\Chester>tasklist /?


TASKLIST [/S system [/U username [/P [password]]]]
         [/M [module] | /SVC | /V] [/FI filter] [/FO format] [/NH]

Description:
    This tool displays a list of currently running processes on
    either a local or remote machine.

Parameter List:
    /S     system          Specifies the remote system to connect to.

    /U     [domain\]user   Specifies the user context under which
                           the command should execute.

    /P     [password]      Specifies the password for the given
                           user context. Prompts for input if omitted.

    /M     [module]        Lists all tasks currently using the given
                           exe/dll name. If the module name is not
                           specified all loaded modules are displayed.

    /SVC                   Displays services hosted in each process.

    /APPS                  Displays Store Apps and their accociated
                           processes.

    /V                     Displays verbose task information.

    /FI    filter          Displays a set of tasks that match a
                           given criteria specified by the filter.

    /FO    format          Specifies the output format.
                           Valid values: "TABLE", "LIST", "CSV".

    /NH                    Specifies that the "Column Header" should
                           not be displayed in the output.
                           Valid only for "TABLE" and "CSV" formats.

    /?                     Displays this help message.

    Filters:
    Filter Name     Valid Operators          Valid Value(s)
    -----------     ---------------          ------------------------
    STATUS          eq, ne                   RUNNING | SUSPENDED
                                             NOT RESPONDING | UNKNOWN
    IMAGENAME       eq, ne                   Image name
    PID             eq, ne, gt, lt, ge, le   PID value
    SESSION         eq, ne, gt, lt, ge, le   Session number
    SESSIONNAME     eq, ne                   Session name
    CPUTIME         eq, ne, gt, lt, ge, le   CPU time in the format
                                             of hh:mm:ss.
                                             hh - hours,
                                             mm - minutes, ss - seconds
    MEMUSAGE        eq, ne, gt, lt, ge, le   Memory usage in KB
    USERNAME        eq, ne                   User name in [domain\]user
                                             format
    SERVICES        eq, ne                   Service name
    WINDOWTITLE     eq, ne                   Window title
    MODULES         eq, ne                   DLL name
```

To keep this simple, first I will execute the command with no options and pipe the output to the *sort* command. This will sort the tasklist alphabetically making it easier to review the results for brevity. Note that we are showing a very short truncated result.

```
C:\Users\Chester>tasklist | sort
```

Image Name	PID	Session Name	Session #	Mem Usage
cmd.exe	7560	Console	2	2,352 K
Dropbox.exe	4012	Console	2	136,948 K
firefox.exe	3920	Console	2	
SkyDrive.exe	664	Console	2	6,128 K
SkypeC2CPNRSvc.exe	1760	Services	0	2,044 K
tasklist.exe	4256	Console	2	5,704 K
vmware-authd.exe	2800	Services	0	3,864 K
winword.exe	3712	Console	2	86,936 K

For the *abbreviated* output we kept a few of the processes of interest. These include cmd.exe (this is the command prompt we are running from). Other notable processes of investigative interest include Dropbox and Skydrive (this is valuable to the investigative process, as files stored in the Dropbox or Skydrive may be difficult to obtain after shutdown). Since Dropbox can be accessed from other computers, the content of the Dropbox file could be modified or deleted elsewhere, although local copies of the file will exist on the local disk. Another process of interest is firefox.exe indicating that the user is currently browsing the Internet. We also notice Skype processes indicating that the user may be communicating via voice or chat messaging or transferring files using Skype. Next, we see a *vmware* process indicating that there may be virtual machines on this system that may contain additional investigative data. Finally, we see that *winword* is running indicating the user which we can deduce, that it is *likely* that the user has a document open for editing. By changing the command, we can obtain additional information. First, you should specify the /Vor verbose option, which will provide greater details regarding each process. Next you could use either format output option /FO to specify the type of output. Two popular output formats are TABLE and CSV (comma separated value). This is valuable if you plan to analyze the running processes and services later using a spreadsheet program like Microsoft Excel. Here is an abbreviated example of the CSV output:

```
C:\Users\Chester>tasklist /v /FO CSV | sort

"Image Name","PID","Session Name","Session#","Mem Usage","Status",
    "User Name","CPU Time","Window Title"

"cmd.exe","7560","Console","2","2,392    K","Running","PYTHONLAPTOP\
    Chester","0:00:00","Command Prompt"

"Dropbox.exe","4012","Console","2","137,844    K","Running","PYTHON-
    LAPTOP\Chester","0:09:06","N/A"

"firefox.exe","3920","Console","2","617,708    K","Running","PYTHON-
    LAPTOP\Chester","6:11:51","Amazon.com: Online Shopping for Elec-
    tronics, Apparel, Computers, Books, DVDs & more - Mozilla Firefox"
```

To better understand the resulting output along with the potential forensic value, let's take a look at each of the output elements in order as shown below (Table 3.1).

Table 3.1 Tasklist Elements

Output Element	Description	Investigative Value
Image name	The name of the running process or the executable filename	Quickly identifies well- known processes
PID	The process identifier. The OS assigns a unique number to each process. It is possible to have multiple processes with the same name, but the PID will be unique	This PID can be used to associate network activity with a specific process
Session name	For local machine investigations, this element will be "Console" or "Services." If this process is running over a network then the name of the network session will be recorded	In most cases will be used to identify if this is a local process or a system service
Session number	The session number associated with the session	The session can be used to associate network activity with a specific session process
Memory usage	At the current instant in time, this will define how much memory is allocated to this process. The value is display in K bytes. Note: 1K=1024 bytes	Can provide clues to investigators regarding unusual memory usage
Status	This will provide the state of the process. For example: RUNNING: The process is running normally. SUSPENDED: The process has stopped running. NOT RESPONDING: Windows is not able to communicate with the process. UNKNOWN: Windows is not able to determine the status of the process.	If a process such as firewall or virus protection has been SUSPENDED it can indicate that a malicious application is in control or at least that the system is less secure
User name	The account that activated the process	Who started the application running, more specifically what user or system account?
CPU time	The amount of CPU time that has been used by this process since it was started. Listed in hours: minutes:seconds	This can help identify recently started applications
Windows title	Windows title bar for the process—if available	In the case of processes like the Firefox web browser, it will display information regarding the most current active website

As you can see the verbose output provides much greater detail and context for the investigator.

Next, there are times when you need to focus your examination on the tasklist. There are many filters available for this purpose. The filter shown here, *tasklist /FI "SESSIONNAME ne CONSOLE"* outputs only processes that have *SESSIONNAME* other that is not equal to *CONSOLE* (the *ne* stands for NOT EQUAL). Thus the output of the command results is a list of *Services* rather than user launched processes.

```
C:\Users\Chester>tasklist /FI "SESSIONNAME ne CONSOLE"

Image Name                   PID Session Name      Session#   Mem Usage
========================= ======== ================ =========== ============
System Idle Process            0 Services               0         4 K
System                         4 Services               0     6,600 K
smss.exe                     348 Services               0       340 K
csrss.exe                    556 Services               0     2,160 K
wininit.exe                  616 Services               0       836 K
services.exe                 700 Services               0     6,764 K
svchost.exe                  796 Services               0    10,732 K
AppleMobileDeviceService.    1668 Services               0     3,124 K
mDNSResponder.exe           1684 Services               0     3,204 K
SkypeC2CAutoUpdateSvc.exe   1732 Services               0     5,160 K
SkypeC2CPNRSvc.exe          1760 Services               0     2,044 K
CodeMeter.exe               2648 Services               0     7,748 K
vmware-authd.exe            2800 Services               0     3,864 K
vmnetdhcp.exe               2824 Services               0     7,916 K
vmware-usbarbitrator64.ex   2840 Services               0     2,324 K
```

Finally, when examining processes, we would also like to map the dynamic link libraries that are loaded by all processes or by a specific process. The following command will do this for Dropbox.exe and Firefox.exe.

```
C:\Users\Chester>tasklist /M /FI "ImageName eq Dropbox.exe"

Image Name                   PID Modules
========================= ======== ============================================
Dropbox.exe                 4012 ntdll.dll, wow64.dll, wow64win.dll,
                                  wow64cpu.dll
```

```
C:\Users\Chester>tasklist /M /FI "ImageName eq Firefox.exe"

Image Name                   PID Modules
========================= ======== ============================================
firefox.exe                 3920 ntdll.dll, wow64.dll, wow64win.dll,
                                  wow64cpu.dll
```

It is important to note that most advanced malicious applications attach themselves to legitimate processes, therefore the examination of memory snapshots are necessary to provide a complete picture of the running processes and associated DLL's. However, tasklist provides a great starting point and baseline for our investigative process.

Windows CLI—active network activities

Now that we can identify the running processes and specific details related to these processes, we need to take a look at how those processes are communicating with the external environment via the network. From the command line we can use the *netstat* command to probe active network information.

To determine the command line operation of *netstat* we query the help command.

```
C:\Users\Chester>netstat /?

Displays protocol statistics and current TCP/IP network connections.

NETSTAT [-a] [-b] [-e] [-f] [-n] [-o] [-p proto] [-r] [-s] [-x] [-t]
   [interval]
```

-a	Displays all connections and listening ports.
-b	Displays the executable involved in creating each connection or listening port. In some cases well-known executables host multiple independent components, and in these cases the sequence of components involved in creating the connection or listening port is displayed. In this case the executable name is in [] at the bottom, on top is the component it called, and so forth until TCP/IP was reached. Note that this option can be time-consuming and will fail unless you have sufficient permissions.
-e	Displays Ethernet statistics. This may be combined with the -s option.
-f	Displays Fully Qualified Domain Names (FQDN) for foreign addresses.
-n	Displays addresses and port numbers in numerical form.
-o	Displays the owning process ID associated with each connection.
-p	proto Shows connections for the protocol specified by proto; proto may be any of: TCP, UDP, TCPv6, or UDPv6. If used with the -s option to display per-protocol statistics, proto may be any of: IP, IPv6, ICMP, ICMPv6, TCP, TCPv6, UDP, or UDPv6.
-r	Displays the routing table.
-s	Displays per-protocol statistics. By default, statistics are shown for IP, IPv6, ICMP, ICMPv6, TCP, TCPv6, UDP, and UDPv6; the -p option may be used to specify a subset of the default.
-t	Displays the current connection offload state.
-x	Displays NetworkDirect connections, listeners, and shared endpoints.
-y	Displays the TCP connection template for all connections. Cannot be combined with the other options.

```
interval   Redisplays selected statistics, pausing interval seconds
           between each display. Press CTRL+C to stop redisplaying sta-
           tistics. If omitted, netstat will print the current configu-
           ration information once.
```

For the first examination of network activity, we generate some general statistics about each network interface by using the `-s` option.

This command provides statistics surrounding general IPv4 and IPv6, ICMPv4 and ICMPv6, and Transmission Control Protocol (TCP)/User Datagram Protocol (UDP) over IPv4/IPv6 activities. Again, this provides a baseline of the recent network activity on this computer (activity since the last reboot).

```
C:\Users\Chester> netstat -s

IPv4 Statistics

Packets Received                     = 1585347
Received Header Errors               = 749
Received Address Errors              = 2102
Datagrams Forwarded                  = 0
Unknown Protocols Received           = 0
Received Packets Discarded           = 994305
Received Packets Delivered           = 1486864
Output Requests                      = 551823
Routing Discards                     = 0
Discarded Output Packets             = 339
Output Packet No Route               = 28
Reassembly Required                  = 0
Reassembly Successful                = 0
Reassembly Failures                  = 0
Datagrams Successfully Fragmented    = 0
Datagrams Failing Fragmentation      = 0
Fragments Created                    = 0

IPv6 Statistics

Packets Received                     = 538634
Received Header Errors               = 0
Received Address Errors              = 10502
Datagrams Forwarded                  = 0
Unknown Protocols Received           = 15
Received Packets Discarded           = 40486
Received Packets Delivered           = 528104
Output Requests                      = 259204
Routing Discards                     = 0
```

```
Discarded Output Packets              = 0
Output Packet No Route                = 19
Reassembly Required                   = 0
Reassembly Successful                 = 0
Reassembly Failures                   = 0
Datagrams Successfully Fragmented     = 0
Datagrams Failing Fragmentation       = 0
Fragments Created                     = 0
```

ICMPv4 Statistics

	Received	Sent
Messages	28	32440
Errors	0	0
Destination Unreachable	23	32406
Time Exceeded	0	0
Parameter Problems	0	0
Source Quenches	0	0
Redirects	0	0
Echo Replies	5	0
Echos	0	34
Timestamps	0	0
Timestamp Replies	0	0
Address Masks	0	0
Address Mask Replies	0	0
Router Solicitations	0	0
Router Advertisements	0	0

ICMPv6 Statistics

	Received	Sent
Messages	360068	77843
Errors	0	0
Destination Unreachable	3	119
Packet Too Big	0	0
Time Exceeded	0	0
Parameter Problems	0	3
Echos	0	66665
Echo Replies	66484	0
MLD Queries	0	0
MLD Reports	22	0
MLD Dones	12	0
Router Solicitations	0	21
Router Advertisements	282346	0

```
Neighbor Solicitations     10893           125
Neighbor Advertisements    308             10910
Redirects                  0               0
Router Renumberings        0               0

TCP Statistics for IPv4

Active Opens                       = 17994
Passive Opens                      = 76
Failed Connection Attempts         = 123
Reset Connections                  = 2141
Current Connections                = 16
Segments Received                  = 937502
Segments Sent                      = 764115
Segments Retransmitted             = 26953

TCP Statistics for IPv6

Active Opens                       = 3870
Passive Opens                      = 4
Failed Connection Attempts         = 30
Reset Connections                  = 247
Current Connections                = 1
Segments Received                  = 162436
Segments Sent                      = 105465
Segments Retransmitted             = 7383

UDP Statistics for IPv4

Datagrams Received         = 198258
No Ports                   = 238979
Receive Errors             = 755328
Datagrams Sent             = 208850

UDP Statistics for IPv6

Datagrams Received         = 6080
No Ports                   = 40330
Receive Errors             = 119
Datagrams Sent             = 71018
```

For the next command, let's start with a simple netstat command that reports on all (-a) connections and listening ports, displays the numerical values (-n) for the port numbers and addresses and displays the process ID or PID of the owning process (-o). Here is the command with truncated results.

```
C:\Users\Chester>netstat -ano

Active Connections

Proto  Local Address          Foreign Address      State         PID
TCP    0.0.0.0:135            0.0.0.0:0            LISTENING     836
TCP    127.0.0.1:843          0.0.0.0:0            LISTENING     4012
TCP    127.0.0.1:5354         0.0.0.0:0            LISTENING     1684
TCP    127.0.0.1:5354         127.0.0.1:49156      ESTABLISHED   1684
TCP    127.0.0.1:5354         127.0.0.1:49157      ESTABLISHED   1684
TCP    127.0.0.1:17600        0.0.0.0:0            LISTENING     4012
TCP    127.0.0.1:27015        0.0.0.0:0            LISTENING     1668
TCP    127.0.0.1:28790        0.0.0.0:0            LISTENING     2556
TCP    127.0.0.1:28900        0.0.0.0:0            LISTENING     2212
TCP    127.0.0.1:49156        127.0.0.1:5354       ESTABLISHED   1668
TCP    127.0.0.1:49157        127.0.0.1:5354       ESTABLISHED   1668
TCP    127.0.0.1:49928        127.0.0.1:49929      ESTABLISHED   4012
TCP    127.0.0.1:49929        127.0.0.1:49928      ESTABLISHED   4012
TCP    127.0.0.1:63256        127.0.0.1:63257      ESTABLISHED   3920
TCP    127.0.0.1:63257        127.0.0.1:63256      ESTABLISHED   3920
TCP    192.168.0.114:139      0.0.0.0:0            LISTENING     4
TCP    192.168.0.114:52233    108.160.172.241:443  CLOSE_WAIT    4012
TCP    192.168.0.114:53466    108.160.172.241:443  CLOSE_WAIT    4012
TCP    192.168.0.114:53507    45.58.70.1:443       CLOSE_WAIT    4012
TCP    192.168.0.114:53702    108.160.172.241:443  ESTABLISHED   4012
TCP    192.168.0.114:53858    108.160.170.34:443   ESTABLISHED   4012
TCP    192.168.0.114:54156    108.160.172.193:443  CLOSE_WAIT    4012
TCP    192.168.0.114:54242    54.209.218.255:443   CLOSE_WAIT    4012
TCP    192.168.0.114:54243    54.192.207.181:443   ESTABLISHED   4012
TCP    192.168.0.114:54244    52.25.78.214:443     ESTABLISHED   3920
TCP    192.168.0.114:54245    54.230.205.208:443   TIME_WAIT     0
TCP    192.168.0.114:54246    54.230.205.208:443   TIME_WAIT     0
TCP    192.168.0.114:54247    23.235.46.239:80     TIME_WAIT     0
TCP    192.168.0.114:54248    54.239.17.7:80       ESTABLISHED   3920
TCP    192.168.0.114:54249    54.192.206.189:80    ESTABLISHED   3920
TCP    192.168.0.114:54250    54.192.206.189:80    ESTABLISHED   3920
TCP    192.168.0.114:54251    54.192.206.189:80    ESTABLISHED   3920
TCP    192.168.0.114:54252    54.192.206.189:80    ESTABLISHED   3920
TCP    192.168.0.114:54253    54.192.206.108:80    ESTABLISHED   3920
TCP    192.168.0.114:54254    54.192.206.108:80    ESTABLISHED   3920
TCP    192.168.0.114:54255    54.192.206.189:80    ESTABLISHED   3920
TCP    192.168.0.114:54256    54.192.206.108:80    ESTABLISHED   3920
TCP    192.168.0.114:54257    54.192.206.108:80    ESTABLISHED   3920
TCP    192.168.0.114:54258    54.192.206.108:80    ESTABLISHED   3920
```

```
TCP    192.168.0.114:54259    54.192.204.254:443    ESTABLISHED    3920
TCP    192.168.0.114:54260    54.192.204.254:443    ESTABLISHED    3920
TCP    192.168.0.114:54261    54.192.206.183:80     ESTABLISHED    3920
TCP    192.168.0.114:54262    54.192.206.183:80     ESTABLISHED    3920
TCP    192.168.0.114:54263    54.192.206.183:80     ESTABLISHED    3920
TCP    192.168.0.114:54264    54.192.206.183:80     ESTABLISHED    3920
TCP    192.168.0.114:54265    54.192.206.183:80     ESTABLISHED    3920
TCP    192.168.0.114:54266    54.192.206.183:80     ESTABLISHED    3920
TCP    192.168.0.114:54267    74.125.138.148:80     ESTABLISHED    3920
TCP    192.168.0.114:54268    54.239.22.50:80       FIN_WAIT_1     3920
TCP    192.168.0.114:54270    54.192.206.165:80     ESTABLISHED    3920
TCP    192.168.0.114:54271    54.192.206.165:80     ESTABLISHED    3920
TCP    192.168.0.114:54272    72.21.194.87:80       ESTABLISHED    3920
TCP    192.168.0.114:54273    72.21.194.87:80       ESTABLISHED    3920
TCP    192.168.0.114:54274    54.239.17.7:80        ESTABLISHED    3920
TCP    192.168.0.114:54275    54.239.17.7:443       ESTABLISHED    3920
TCP    192.168.0.114:54276    54.239.17.7:80        ESTABLISHED    3920
TCP    192.168.0.114:54277    54.239.17.7:80        ESTABLISHED    3920
TCP    192.168.0.114:54278    54.192.206.108:80     ESTABLISHED    3920
TCP    192.168.0.114:54279    54.239.22.50:80       ESTABLISHED    3920
TCP    192.168.0.114:54280    54.239.22.50:80       ESTABLISHED    3920
TCP    192.168.0.114:54281    54.239.22.50:80       ESTABLISHED    3920
TCP    192.168.0.114:54282    54.239.22.50:80       ESTABLISHED    3920
TCP    192.168.0.114:54283    54.239.22.50:80       ESTABLISHED    3920
TCP    192.168.0.114:54284    54.239.22.50:80       ESTABLISHED    3920
TCP    192.168.0.114:54285    54.239.23.147:80      ESTABLISHED    3920
TCP    192.168.0.114:54286    54.239.23.147:80      ESTABLISHED    3920
TCP    192.168.0.114:54287    54.239.22.50:80       SYN_SENT       3920
TCP    192.168.21.1:139       0.0.0.0:0             LISTENING      4
TCP    192.168.163.1:139      0.0.0.0:0             LISTENING      4
TCP    [::]:135               [::]:0                LISTENING      836
TCP    [::]:445               [::]:0                LISTENING      4
TCP    [::]:1947              [::]:0                LISTENING      2000
TCP    [::]:22350             [::]:0                LISTENING      2648
TCP    [::]:26143             [::]:0                LISTENING      4
TCP    [::]:49152             [::]:0                LISTENING      616
UDP    0.0.0.0:3702           *:*                   1868
UDP    0.0.0.0:3702           *:*                   1868
UDP    0.0.0.0:4500           *:*                   952
UDP    0.0.0.0:5355           *:*                   1108
UDP    0.0.0.0:22350          *:*                   2648
UDP    0.0.0.0:50098          *:*                   1868
UDP    0.0.0.0:50882          *:*                   1684
```

UDP	0.0.0.0:52767	*:*	2000
UDP	127.0.0.1:1900	*:*	3376
UDP	127.0.0.1:50880	*:*	1668
UDP	127.0.0.1:50881	*:*	1668
UDP	127.0.0.1:56432	*:*	3376
UDP	192.168.0.114:137	*:*	4
UDP	192.168.0.114:138	*:*	4
UDP	192.168.0.114:1900	*:*	3376
UDP	192.168.0.114:5353	*:*	1684
UDP	192.168.21.1:137	*:*	4
UDP	192.168.21.1:138	*:*	4
UDP	192.168.21.1:1900	*:*	3376
UDP	192.168.21.1:5353	*:*	1684
UDP	192.168.163.1:137	*:*	4
UDP	192.168.163.1:138	*:*	4
UDP	192.168.163.1:1900	*:*	3376
UDP	192.168.163.1:5353	*:*	1684
UDP	[::]:123	*:*	308
UDP	[::]:500	*:*	952
UDP	[::]:1947	*:*	2000
UDP	[::]:3702	*:*	1868
UDP	[::]:3702	*:*	1868
UDP	[::]:4500	*:*	952
UDP	[::]:5355	*:*	1108
UDP	[::]:50099	*:*	1868
UDP	[::]:50883	*:*	1684
UDP	[::1]:1900	*:*	3376
UDP	[::1]:5353	*:*	1684
UDP	[::1]:59308	*:*	3376

Even in truncated form, this is a lot of information to process and investigate. It is certainly reasonable to capture this and store it as the baseline, but how would we go about investigating this. As you can see each line in the output of the netstat -ano - command contains the information given in Table 3.2.

Table 3.2 Netstat Elements

Proto	Proto is short for protocol. For our results they are either TCP or UDP
Local address	The local IP address and port number of the local network interface. *Note this can also be a special IP address on the local computer such as 127.0.0.0 or 0.0.0.0*
Foreign address	The remote IP address and port number of the remote network interface. *Note this can also be a special IP address on the local computer such as 127.0.0.0 or 0.0.0.0*
State	Indicates the current state of any TCP connections
PID	The numeric identifier of the process associated with this connection

Next we would connect the network activity with the specific processes that were generated from the *tasklist* command. Examining the results of the *tasklist* command, we can easily identify a couple of processes that should have active network connections (Firefox.exe and Dropbox.exe). Let's say we wish to only output information related to these two processes and only display the results if the connection state is equal to ESTABLISHED. Examining the *tasklist* output, we can identify the PID for Firefox.exe (3920) and Dropbox.exe (4012). We can accomplish this by connecting the output of the netstat command with the findstr command using a pipe operator (|). The resulting command and output are shown here.

We start by identifying the established network connections associated with Dropbox.exe.

```
C:\Users\Chester>netstat -ano | findstr 4012 | findstr ESTABLISHED
TCP 192.168.0.114:53702 108.160.172.241:443 ESTABLISHED 4012
TCP 192.168.0.114:54306 108.160.169.184:443 ESTABLISHED 4012
TCP 192.168.0.114:54523 54.192.207.181:443 ESTABLISHED 4012
```

Next, we identify the established network connections associated with Firefox. exe (truncated for brevity). We should note that established connections with Firefox are going to change dramatically based on the current activity in the browser. The connections with Dropbox.exe tend to be a bit more stable and the established connections persist. On the contrary, the connections with the web browser Firefox are fleeting.

```
C:\Users\Chester>netstat -ano | findstr 3920 | findstr ESTABLISHED
TCP 192.168.0.114:54577 54.239.26.91:80   ESTABLISHED 3920
TCP 192.168.0.114:54581 54.239.17.7:80    ESTABLISHED 3920
TCP 192.168.0.114:54582 54.239.17.7:80    ESTABLISHED 3920
TCP 192.168.0.114:54584 54.192.206.245:80 ESTABLISHED 3920
TCP 192.168.0.114:54585 54.192.206.245:80 ESTABLISHED 3920
TCP 192.168.0.114:54586 54.192.206.245:80 ESTABLISHED 3920
TCP 192.168.0.114:54587 54.192.206.186:80 ESTABLISHED 3920
TCP 192.168.0.114:54588 54.192.206.186:80 ESTABLISHED 3920
```

One additional area of concern is that of the current routing table. Routing tables are basically a set of rules that govern how IP packets are directed. All devices, including computers, switches, routers, firewalls, and other network appliances contain a routing table. Since routing tables contain specific IP addresses, if the tables were to be maliciously altered (often referred to as poisoning) packets could be directed to intermediary network devices in order to intercept or alter the packets leaving a network based on these poisoned routing rules.

The *netstat* command provides a simple way of capturing the current routing table using the -*r* option. Before turning off or shutting down the system it is prudent to capture the current state of the routing table, as the table is typically not persistent and would be more difficult to reconstruct postmortem.

The routing table shown below was generated by the *netstat* command: The results include an **Interface list** that identifies all current network interfaces, including Bluetooth, Payment Card Industry (PCI) hardwired interfaces, wireless, and VMware virtual interfaces. It also, includes the **IPv4 and IPv6 routing tables** governing the direction of packets based on IP type.

```
C:\Users\Chester>netstat -r
===========================================================================
Interface List
11...a0 88 69 5c eb d4 ......Bluetooth Device (Personal Area Network)
 4...34 17 eb 56 a5 e7 .......Realtek PCIe FE Family Controller
 3...a0 88 69 5c eb d0 .......Intel(R) Dual Band Wireless-AC 3160
 6...00 50 56 c0 00 01 .......VMware Virtual Ethernet Adapter for VMnet1
 7...00 50 56 c0 00 08 .......VMware Virtual Ethernet Adapter for VMnet8
 1...........................Software Loopback Interface 1
10...00 00 00 00 00 00 00 e0 Microsoft ISATAP Adapter
 8...00 00 00 00 00 00 00 e0 Microsoft ISATAP Adapter #10
 9...00 00 00 00 00 00 00 e0 Microsoft ISATAP Adapter #11
===========================================================================
```

```
IPv4 Route Table
===========================================================================
Active Routes:
```

Network Destination	Netmask	Gateway	Interface	Metric
0.0.0.0	0.0.0.0	192.168.0.1	192.168.0.114	20
127.0.0.0	255.0.0.0	On-link	127.0.0.1	306
127.0.0.1	255.255.255.255	On-link	127.0.0.1	306
127.255.255.255	255.255.255.255	On-link	127.0.0.1	306
192.168.0.0	255.255.255.0	On-link	192.168.0.114	276
192.168.0.114	255.255.255.255	On-link	192.168.0.114	276
192.168.0.255	255.255.255.255	On-link	192.168.0.114	276
192.168.21.0	255.255.255.0	On-link	192.168.21.1	276
192.168.21.1	255.255.255.255	On-link	192.168.21.1	276
192.168.21.255	255.255.255.255	On-link	192.168.21.1	276
192.168.163.0	255.255.255.0	On-link	192.168.163.1	276
192.168.163.1	255.255.255.255	On-link	192.168.163.1	276
192.168.163.255	255.255.255.255	On-link	192.168.163.1	276
224.0.0.0	240.0.0.0	On-link	127.0.0.1	306
224.0.0.0	240.0.0.0	On-link	192.168.0.114	276
224.0.0.0	240.0.0.0	On-link	192.168.163.1	276
224.0.0.0	240.0.0.0	On-link	192.168.21.1	276
255.255.255.255	255.255.255.255	On-link	127.0.0.1	306
255.255.255.255	255.255.255.255	On-link	192.168.0.114	276
255.255.255.255	255.255.255.255	On-link	192.168.163.1	276
255.255.255.255	255.255.255.255	On-link	192.168.21.1	276

```
===========================================================================
Persistent Routes:
  None
```

```
IPv6 Route Table
===============================================================================
Active Routes:
 If Metric Network Destination         Gateway
  4    276 ::/0                        fe80::21d:d3ff:fe88:23c1
  1    306 ::1/128                     On-link
  4    276 2606:a000:eac2:9300::/64    On-link
  4    276 2606:a000:eac2:9300:1a5:f691:5963:fde/128
                                       On-link
  4    276 2606:a000:eac2:9300:4c54:9ca:235e:d010/128
                                       On-link
  4    276 2606:a000:eae0:5800::/64    On-link
  4    276 2606:a000:eae0:5800:1a5:f691:5963:fde/128
                                       On-link
  4    276 fe80::/64                   On-link
  6    276 fe80::/64                   On-link
  7    276 fe80::/64                   On-link
  4    276 fe80::1a5:f691:5963:fde/128
                                       On-link
  7    276 fe80::525:3f59:c937:d5e3/128
                                       On-link
  6    276 fe80::dd94:ea3c:3ceb:e7dd/128
                                       On-link
  1    306 ff00::/8                    On-link
  4    276 ff00::/8                    On-link
  6    276 ff00::/8                    On-link
  7    276 ff00::/8                    On-link
===============================================================================
Persistent Routes:
  None
```

Windows CLI—event logs evidence capture

Windows store event logs in several logs named *Application*, *Security*, *System*, and *Setup*. The log types do change for different Windows versions. There is not a direct method of viewing or analyzing the events logs directly from the command line without using third-party utilities like Windows Powershell or a special version specific to Windows utilities that require installation. However, if recent events are vital to the live investigation, the built-in windows event viewer application can be launched from the command line. As you would understand, launching this requires elevated privilege—in other words the current logged in user must have administrator rights. In addition, launching this application will leave additional trace evidence on this target system that would need to be accounted for. Assuming you have the proper credentials you can launch the event viewer as follows:

```
C:\Users\Chester>eventvwr
```

This command (if successful) will launch the Graphical User Interface Event Viewer Application depicted in Fig. 3.23.

We are viewing the recent System Events and have selected the WinLogin event in the center panel indicating when the last Windows login occurred. You can

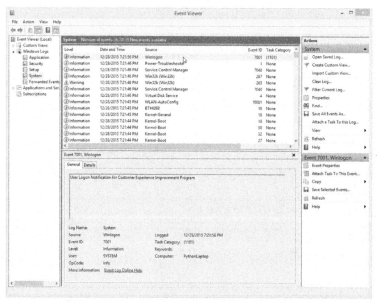

FIG. 3.23

Windows event viewer.

examine the recent events from the System, Security, Application, and Setup logs as they pertain to your investigation.

Next, we can move to the far right top panel and select the Save All Events As selection, as shown in Fig. 3.24.

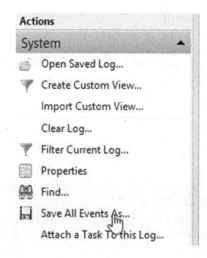

FIG. 3.24

Select save all events as.

This will in-turn bring up the Save As Dialog Box as shown in Fig. 3.25.

FIG. 3.25

Save as settings.

Here we have specified the destination to be our D: drive which has a disk label of *Evidence*. We have specified the filename as Evidence-EventLog with the comma-separated-value or .csv type. This will cause all the Windows events to be written to our Evidence Drive as shown in Fig. 3.26.

FIG. 3.26

Evidence-EventLog.csv saved to the D: drive.

Finally, we open the newly created Evidence-EventLog.csv file with Microsoft Excel and view the evidence record in spreadsheet format as shown in Fig. 3.27.

	A	B	C	D	E	F
1	Level	Date and Time	Source	Event ID	Task Category	
2	Information	12/28/2015 19:26	Microsoft	20001		-7005 Driver Management concluded the process to install driver wpdfs.inf_amd64_0e7:
3	Information	12/28/2015 19:26	Microsoft	24577	Driver Post-Install Configuration	Media player and imaging program compatibility layers were successfully register
4	Information	12/28/2015 19:26	Microsoft	24579	Driver Post-Install Configuration	Autoplay registration was skipped for device %1.
5	Information	12/28/2015 19:26	Microsoft	24576	Driver Installation	Drivers were successfully installed for device WPD Device.
6	Information	12/28/2015 19:26	Microsoft	20003		-7005 Driver Management has concluded the process to add Service WUDFWpdFs for De
7	Information	12/28/2015 19:26	Microsoft	10100	Installation or update of device drivers.	The driver package installation has succeeded.
8	Information	12/28/2015 19:26	Microsoft	10002	Installation or update of device drivers.	The UMDF service WpdFs (CLSID {112D6495-AC4C-46F8-B663-6A4266C53313}) was (
9	Information	12/28/2015 19:26	Microsoft	10000	Installation or update of device drivers.	A driver package which uses user-mode driver framework version 2.0.0 is being in
10	Information	12/28/2015 19:21	Microsoft	15	None	Hive \??\C:\Users\Chester\AppData\Local\Microsoft\Windows\UsrClass.dat was i
11	Information	12/28/2015 19:21	Microsoft	16	None	The access history in hive \??\C:\Users\Chester\ntuser.dat was cleared updating :
12	Information	12/28/2015 19:21	Microsoft	7001		-1101 User Logon Notification for Customer Experience Improvement Program

FIG. 3.27

Evidence-EventLog.csv saved to the D: drive.

This process will preserve the Windows event logs for future examination. This information may become important in the future to determine who logged into the system at what date and time, when authorized changes to the system were made, what Windows updates were applied and when, and when new software or hardware was installed, etc. Examining this log in a live setting can provide pertinent information regarding the most recent activity or activities performed during a specific time period.

Windows CLI—collecting static evidence and quick searching

Now that we have provided a glimpse at collecting volatile information using the Windows CLI, let's move to more static information that can be captured during live investigations or could be left to postmortem activities. In some investigative situations, examining the filesystem in a live triage situation is important. To establish a baseline of a filesystem (directories and files) you can use the *tree* command.

```
C:\Users\Chester> tree /?
Graphically displays the folder structure of a drive or path.
TREE [drive:][path] [/F] [/A]

/F Display the names of the files in each folder.
/A Use ASCII instead of extended characters.
```

As you can see, this is a very simple command that only requires the drive and path that you wish to generate a graphic tree structure of the filesystem. The /F option provides the individual file names contained in each directory. In order to make this useful, (especially today with systems containing over 100,000 files), we pipe the output of the command to the command *more*. This allows us to examine the output of the command in a page-by-page controlled environment.

Note this is truncated output.

```
C:\Users\Chester>tree c:\Users /F | more
Folder PATH listing for volume OS
Volume serial number is 8621-BAFB
C:\USERS
├───Chester
│   │   .rekallrc
│   │   dir
│   │   powershell
│   │   Saved
│   │
│   ├───.ipython
│   │   └───profile_default
│   │       │   history.sqlite
│   │       │
│   │       ├───db
│   │       ├───log
│   │       ├───pid
│   │       ├───security
│   │       ├───startup
│   │       │       README
│   │       │
│   │       └───static
│   │           └───custom
│   │                   custom.css
│   │                   custom.js
│   │
│   ├───Contacts
│   ├───Desktop
│   │   │   CH-03 Draft - Backup.docx
│   │   │   DEFCON FINAL 2015.pptx
│   │   │   Evidence.log
│   │   │   file.txt
│   │   │   GMU Briefing - Final.pptx
│   │   │   log.txt
│   │   │   pyIndex.py
│   │   │   spoofer.py
│   │   │
│   │   ├───DEF-CON
│   │   │   │   dumbSearch.py
│   │   │   │   haystack
│   │   │   │   haystack.log
│   │   │   │   haystack.py
│   │   │   │   haystacker.py
│   │   │   │   oui.txt
│   │   │   │   pygoogle.py
│   │   │   │   pygoogle.pyc
```

As you can see this provides a text based graphical like file listing to provide a quick and basic filesystem dump. You can also redirect the output of the command to a file as shown here:

```
C:\Users\Chester> tree c:\Users /F > D:\FileSystemTree.txt
```

It is important to note that the *tree* command does NOT display Hidden or System files.

To provide a more complete filesystem record using built-in commands we can resort to the *dir* or directory command. The command, as shown below, will perform a full search of the filesystem as reported by Windows. The */A* switch will display all file types including Hidden and System. The */s* will traverse all subdirectories and the */p* option will display the results one page at a time.

```
C:\Users\Chester>dir c:\ /A /s /p
Volume in drive C is OS
Volume Serial Number is 8621-BAFB

Directory of c:\

10/16/2014 08:33 AM  <DIR>              $Recycle.Bin
09/01/2015 08:24 AM  <DIR>              $Windows.~BT
06/10/2014 10:35 PM  <DIR>              Apps
08/22/2013 12:31 AM          427,680    bootmgr
06/18/2013 07:18 AM                1    BOOTNXT
08/19/2014 01:53 PM  <DIR>              CodeReplacement
08/19/2014 01:50 PM  <DIR>              DB
12/05/2013 05:16 PM              114    DBAR_Ver.txt
04/29/2015 07:17 AM  <DIR>              DELL
06/10/2014 11:00 PM           27,289    dell.sdr
08/22/2013 09:45 AM  <JUNCTION>         Documents and Settings [C:\Users]
08/04/2014 12:33 PM  <DIR>              DQ
06/10/2014 10:11 PM  <DIR>              Drivers
12/18/2015 08:18 AM    6,772,088,832    hiberfil.sys
05/18/2015 12:50 PM  <DIR>              IMAGES
06/10/2014 10:33 PM  <DIR>              Intel
07/26/2014 10:08 PM  <DIR>              MSOCache
05/16/2015 02:20 PM  <DIR>              NLP
12/26/2015 10:47 AM    2,399,141,888    pagefile.sys
08/22/2013 10:22 AM  <DIR>              PerfLogs
12/03/2014 09:05 AM  <DIR>              PORTS
11/12/2015 10:41 AM  <DIR>              Program Files
12/26/2015 12:01 PM  <DIR>              Program Files (x86)
12/18/2015 08:20 AM  <DIR>              ProgramData
05/16/2015 01:51 PM  <DIR>              Python27
01/09/2015 03:43 PM  <DIR>              RGB TEST
08/19/2014 01:50 PM  <DIR>              Samples
08/20/2014 08:46 AM  <DIR>              SeperateDBTables
12/18/2015 08:18 AM      268,435,456    swapfile.sys
06/11/2014 12:25 AM  <DIR>              System Recovery
```

```
12/23/2015 03:44 AM  <DIR>              System Volume Information
06/10/2014 10:39 PM  <DIR>              Temp
09/15/2015 05:48 PM  <DIR>              TEST
05/18/2015 12:47 PM  <DIR>              TESTIMG
09/15/2015 05:48 PM  <DIR>              TESTOLD
05/20/2015 09:54 AM  <DIR>              TST
07/26/2014 09:58 PM  <DIR>              Users
10/28/2015 02:26 PM  <DIR>              Windows
07/28/2014 08:05 PM          15,560     WirelessDiagLog.csv
       8 File(s)     9,440,136,820 bytes
```

We can, of course, redirect this output as well to a file on the evidence drive to take this inventory snapshot of files contained on any connected drive.

```
C:\Users\Chester>dir c:\ /A /s > D:\c-drivefilesystem.txt
```

We can also use the *dir* command to only provide the output of specific filenames as well. For example, if we wish to take a quick look of files that have .jpg extensions:

```
C:\Users\Chester>cd c:\
c:\>dir /s *.jpg | more
Volume in drive C is OS
Volume Serial Number is 8621-BAFB

Directory of c:\$Recycle.Bin\S-1-5-21-843926835-1922831853-10881780
   43-1001

08/24/2015    12:45 PM         544   $IOKH6SR.jpg
04/24/2015    05:30 PM         544   $I37E2T7.jpg
12/19/2015    11:48 AM         544   $I6SWGRU.jpg
04/24/2015    05:26 PM         544   $I7VMH6L.jpg
04/30/2015    09:00 AM         544   $ICZGOL6.jpg
12/19/2015    02:38 PM         544   $IGM8R2O.jpg
08/29/2015    07:09 AM         544   $IKLC9L6.jpg
08/24/2015    12:44 PM     115,216   $ROKH6SR.jpg
04/24/2015    05:29 PM     120,368   $R37E2T7.jpg
12/17/2015    04:43 PM      23,745   $R6SWGRU.jpg
04/24/2015    05:24 PM     113,138   $R7VMH6L.jpg
04/30/2015    08:59 AM     114,258   $RCZGOL6.jpg
12/17/2015    04:50 PM      73,301   $RGM8R2O.jpg
08/29/2015    07:08 AM     115,216   $RKLC9L6.jpg
       14 File(s)     679,050 bytes

Directory of c:\$Recycle.Bin\S-1-5-21-843926835-1922831853-10881780
   43-1001\$R69IV7D\08242014
```

```
02/09/2012 12:57 PM        32,019 stego.jpg
      1 File(s)     32,019 bytes

Directory      of      c:\$Recycle.Bin\S-1-5-21-843926835-1922831853-
   1088178043-1001\$RE6HLEN

02/09/2012 12:57 PM        32,019 stego.jpg
      1 File(s)     32,019 bytes

Directory      of      c:\$Recycle.Bin\S-1-5-21-843926835-1922831853-
   1088178043-1001\$RQP4IO6

09/19/2013 08:39 PM        91,329 file.jpg
      1 File(s)     91,329 bytes

Directory of c:\IMAGES

11/18/2015  02:41 PM        624,744 Biking.jpg
11/18/2015  02:41 PM      1,224,201 Castle.JPG
11/18/2015  02:41 PM        446,759 Cat.jpg
11/18/2015  02:41 PM        600,630 Deutchland.JPG
11/18/2015  02:41 PM        304,930 Disney.jpg
11/18/2015  02:41 PM         96,831 dscn0011.jpg
11/18/2015  02:41 PM         98,012 kinderscout.jpg
- - More - -
```

As you notice, this command picks up all the files even those included in the Windows hidden *recyclebin* directory. You can then direct the output of this command to a file as shown here.

```
C:\Users\Chester> cd c:\
c:\>dir /s *.jpg > D:\JPEGFileList.txt
```

Obviously, you can then choose any file extension you would like to inventory their locations in the same manner *.mp3, *.gif, *.mp4, etc.

Finally, if you wish to generate a list of filenames with the full path and exclude the date, time, and size information, you can utilize the */b* option as shown here.

```
C:\Users\Chester> cd c:\
c:\>dir /s /b *.jpg > D:\JPEGSimpleFileList.txt
c:\>dir /s /b *.jpg | more
c:\$Recycle.Bin\S-1-5-21-843926835-1922831853-1088178043-1001\
   $I0KH6SR.jpg
c:\$Recycle.Bin\S-1-5-21-843926835-1922831853-1088178043-1001\
   $I37E2T7.jpg
```

```
c:\$Recycle.Bin\S-1-5-21-843926835-1922831853-1088178043-1001\
 $I6SWGRU.jpg
c:\$Recycle.Bin\S-1-5-21-843926835-1922831853-1088178043-1001\
 $I7VMH6L.jpg
c:\$Recycle.Bin\S-1-5-21-843926835-1922831853-1088178043-1001\
 $ICZGOL6.jpg
c:\$Recycle.Bin\S-1-5-21-843926835-1922831853-1088178043-1001\
 $IGM8R2O.jpg
c:\$Recycle.Bin\S-1-5-21-843926835-1922831853-1088178043-1001\
 $IKLC9L6.jpg
c:\$Recycle.Bin\S-1-5-21-843926835-1922831853-1088178043-1001\
 $ROKH6SR.jpg
c:\$Recycle.Bin\S-1-5-21-843926835-1922831853-1088178043-1001\
 $R37E2T7.jpg
c:\$Recycle.Bin\S-1-5-21-843926835-1922831853-1088178043-1001\
 $R6SWGRU.jpg
c:\$Recycle.Bin\S-1-5-21-843926835-1922831853-1088178043-1001\
 $R7VMH6L.jpg
c:\$Recycle.Bin\S-1-5-21-843926835-1922831853-1088178043-1001\
 $RCZGOL6.jpg
c:\$Recycle.Bin\S-1-5-21-843926835-1922831853-1088178043-1001\
 $RGM8R2O.jpg
c:\$Recycle.Bin\S-1-5-21-843926835-1922831853-1088178043-1001\
 $RKLC9L6.jpg
c:\$Recycle.Bin\S-1-5-21-843926835-1922831853-1088178043-1001\
 $R69IV7D\08242014\stego.jpg
c:\$Recycle.Bin\S-1-5-21-843926835-1922831853-1088178043-1001\
 $RE6HLEN\stego.jpg
c:\$Recycle.Bin\S-1-5-21-843926835-1922831853-1088178043-1001\
 $RQP4IO6\file.jpg
c:\IMAGES\Biking.jpg
c:\IMAGES\Castle.JPG
c:\IMAGES\Cat.jpg
c:\IMAGES\Deutchland.JPG
c:\IMAGES\Disney.jpg
c:\IMAGES\dscn0011.jpg
c:\IMAGES\kinderscout.jpg
c:\IMAGES\Munich.JPG
c:\IMAGES\Rome.jpg
c:\IMAGES\Turtle.jpg
c:\IMAGES\zzz.jpg
c:\Program Files\Common Files\microsoft shared\Stationery\Bears.jpg
c:\Program Files\Common Files\microsoft shared\Stationery\Blue_
 Gradient.jpg
c:\Program Files\Common Files\microsoft shared\Stationery\Garden.jpg
```

```
c:\Program Files\Common Files\microsoft shared\Stationery\Green
   Bubbles.jpg
c:\Program Files\Common Files\microsoft shared\Stationery\Hand
   Prints.jpg
c:\Program Files\Common Files\microsoft shared\Stationery\Monet.jpg
c:\Program Files\Common Files\microsoft shared\Stationery\Notebook.
   jpg
c:\Program Files\Common Files\microsoft shared\Stationery\Orange
   Circles.jpg
c:\Program Files\Common Files\microsoft shared\Stationery\Peacock.
   jpg
c:\Program Files\Common Files\microsoft shared\Stationery\Pine_
   Lumber.jpg
c:\Program Files\Common Files\microsoft shared\Stationery\Pretty_
   Peacock.jpg
c:\Program Files\Common Files\microsoft shared\Stationery\Psychedelic.
   jpg
c:\Program Files\Common Files\microsoft shared\Stationery\Roses.jpg
c:\Program Files\Common Files\microsoft shared\Stationery\Sand_
   Paper.jpg
c:\Program Files\Common Files\microsoft shared\Stationery\ShadesOf
   Blue.jpg
c:\Program Files\Common Files\microsoft shared\Stationery\Small_
   News.jpg
c:\Program Files\Common Files\microsoft shared\Stationery\SoftBlue.
   jpg
c:\Program Files\Common Files\microsoft shared\Stationery\Stars.jpg
- -More - -
```

An important note of caution here has to be made. The methods of collecting file paths based on file extensions alone can produce both false positive and false negative results if the extensions have been altered accidentally or maliciously. Other more detailed examinations of the contents of the files, not just the names of the files, must be done during a thorough postmortem investigation. However, this quick look can reveal files of interest that may aid in the immediate live investigation.

Alternate data streams

With the introduction of the NTFS also came the addition of ADS, or the Alternate Data Stream capability. ADS is basically the ability to store data using a "stream name" hidden behind a simple file. In order to access the hidden stream you need to know the name of the secret or hidden stream along with the file the stream is attached to. Or, I like to define it as a "front."

What is a data stream? Data stream objects are one continuous uninterrupted string of bytes. This means there exist a defined start and a defined end for the stream, but nothing else is specified. Thus, this long string of data bytes can be used for any purpose, and the internal structure can and usually is defined based on the type of data contained within the stream. For example objects like mp3, mp4, jpeg, etc. can be considered streams that have a specified begin and end, but contain a well-defined internal structure.

The best way to describe how ADS works is by demonstration: I created a directory to hold the new ADS, *ads_demo*. Next, I launched the notepad application from the command line to create the simple file novel.txt. Fig. 3.28 depicts the innocuous file content that was created.

FIG. 3.28

Notepad creation of an innocuous text file.

```
c:\Users\Chester\ads_demo> start notepad novel.txt
```

Once completed, the file is then saved as normal, and the "front" file has now been successfully created. Next, I use the *dir* command to list the updated contents of the *ads_demo* directory. As expected, the file novel.txt is now listed as part of the *ads_demo* directory.

```
c:\Users\Chester\ads_demo> dir
Volume in drive C is OS
Volume Serial Number is 8621-BAFB

Directory of c:\Users\Chester\ads_demo

01/04/2016   11:38 AM    <DIR>          .
01/04/2016   11:38 AM    <DIR>          ..
01/04/2016   11:43 AM                75 novel.txt
             1 File(s)              75 bytes
             2 Dir(s) 810,505,195,520 bytes free
```

At this point I use the *type* command to type out the contents of the file novel.txt. Again, as expected, we see the contents of the novel.txt file that was just created.

```
c:\Users\Chester\ads_demo>type novel.txt

The Great American Novel.

Chapter 1

It was a cool summer evening ....
```

Next we can create the secret ADS and attach it to the novel.txt file. Again we use the notepad application to create the hidden or secret text. Notice the title bar shown in Fig. 3.29 now displays novel.txt:secret indicating we have opened the ADS and not the simple file. We now type in our secret message as shown in Fig. 3.29.

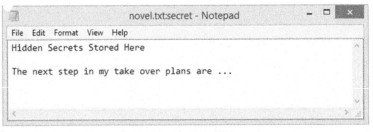

FIG. 3.29

Notepad creation of the ADS secret text.

```
c:\Users\Chester\ads_demo>notepad novel.txt:secret.txt
```

Once we have saved the contents of our ADS (our hidden content in this example), we list the directory once again using the simple *dir* command. You notice that nothing has changed—the same novel.txt file is listed with the same size, date, and timestamp.

```
c:\Users\Chester\ads_demo>dir
Volume in drive C is OS
Volume Serial Number is 8621-BAFB

Directory of c:\Users\Chester\ads_demo

01/04/2016  11:38 AM    <DIR>          .
01/04/2016  11:38 AM    <DIR>          ..
01/04/2016  11:43 AM                75 novel.txt
               1 File(s)             75 bytes
               2 Dir(s) 810,505,195,520 bytes free
```

However, if we list the directory using the *dir /R* command, the directory listing reveals any ADSs. As we can see, the stream secret.txt with a size of 73 bytes is hidden behind the novel.txt file.

```
c:\Users\Chester\ads_demo>dir /R
Volume in drive C is OS
Volume Serial Number is 8621-BAFB

Directory of c:\Users\Chester\ads_demo

01/04/2016  11:38 AM    <DIR>          .
01/04/2016  11:38 AM    <DIR>          ..
01/04/2016  11:43 AM                75 novel.txt
                                    73 novel.txt:secret.txt:$DATA
               1 File(s)            75 bytes
               2 Dir(s)  810,505,191,424 bytes free
```

In order to reveal the contents of the secret.txt file for this example, we redirect the secret text stream into the *more* command as shown here.

```
c:\Users\Chester\ads_demo>more < novel.txt:secret.txt

Hidden Secrets Stored Here

The next step in my take over plans are ...
```

It is important to note that ADS can be used to do more than hide simple text data. They can also be used to store malicious code that can be launched under the cover of well-known innocuous applications. Thus, as command line investigators, you should always be aware of the possibilities of the presence of ADS and use the *dir /R* command to uncover them.

Windows CLI—ending a live investigation

When ending a live investigation, the investigator as with the beginning, *echo* their comments and pertinent system information. For example:

```
C:\Users\Chester>echo Investigator Name: Joe Friday
Investigator Name: Joe Friday

C:\Users\Chester>echo Location: 123 Main St, New York, New York 10044
Location: 123 Main St, New York, New York 10044

C:\Users\Chester>echo Case: Potential Child Victim
Case: Potential Child Victim
```

```
C:\Users\Chester>echo Investigator Observed Time: Mon 12/28/2015
  9:22 PM Eastern Time
Investigator Observed Time: Mon 12/28/2015 9:22 AM Eastern Time

c:\Users\Chester>echo %date%
Mon 12/28/2015

c:\Users\Chester>echo %time%
21:20:51.10

c:\Users\Chester>systeminfo | find "time zone" /I /N
[24]Time Zone:(UTC-05:00) Eastern Time (US & Canada)
```

CHAPTER 3 REVIEW

The Windows Command Line provides investigators with numerous options when performing live investigations. These commands, if selected carefully, can gather on-scene clues about the system under investigation with minimal impact on the integrity of the hard-drive evidence. We have only scratched the surface of the commands that are available and defined a logical process for collecting system information, volatile information, identifying files containing system memory, collecting, and correlating running processes with current network activity. We have also touched on the methods for mapping the file system and performing rudimentary searches for specific file types.

CHAPTER 3 SUMMARY QUESTIONS

1. What additional information would you as an investigator *echo* when starting a Windows CLI Investigation?
2. What additional information would you as an investigator *echo* when ending a Windows CLI Investigation?
3. What additional information would you consider vital when examining the results of the *systeminfo* command?
4. Examine the possible *wmic* commands available. Identify at least three additional commands that you would consider vital during a Windows CLI Investigation.
   Experiment with these commands and then:
   a. Provide examples of the command execution.
   b. Specify the information that these commands would deliver to the investigation.
   c. Assess the impact that these commands would have on the system under investigation.
5. What additional information would you consider vital when examining the results of the *ipconfig* command?

6. Examine the possible `netsh` commands available. Identify at least three additional commands that you would consider vital during a Windows CLI Investigation.

  Experiment with these commands and then:
  a. Provide examples of the command execution.
  b. Specify the information that these commands would deliver to the investigation.
  c. Assess the impact that these commands would have on the system under investigation.

7. Research and then experiment with third-party command line tools that could copy locked system files such as: pagefil.sys, hiberfil.sys, and swapfil.sys. In addition, research and examine third-party tools that could then extract important evidence from these memory rich files.

8. What additional information would you consider vital when examining the results of the `tasklist` command?

9. Examine the possible `netstat` commands available. Identify at least three additional commands that you would consider vital during a Windows CLI Investigation.

  Experiment with these commands and then:
  a. Provide examples of the command execution.
  b. Specify the information that these commands would deliver to the investigation.
  c. Assess the impact that these commands would have on the system under investigation.

10. What specific events from the Windows Event Log would you as an investigator believe would be important to examine during a Windows CLI Investigation? Note: This will require research into the Windows Event Log and the types of events that are logged by the system.

11. Create an alternate data stream that will execute a program not only hide information.

ADDITIONAL RESOURCES

DHS. Homeland Security—critical infrastructure sectors. (n.d.). Official Website of the Department of Homeland Security, http://www.dhs.gov/critical-infrastructure-sectors. Accessed February 2016.

Microsoft TechNet. Command-line reference A-Z. (n.d.). https://technet.microsoft.com/en-us/library/bb490890.aspx. Accessed February 2016.

White House. Presidential Policy Directive—critical infrastructure security and resilience PDD-21. (n.d.). https://www.whitehouse.gov/the-press-office/2013/02/12/presidential-policy-directive-critical-infrastructure-security-and-resil. Accessed February 2016.

Operating the Proactive Incident Response Command Shell

4

Investigate: Word Origin
Early 16th century – from the Latin investīgātus, to search out or follow
a trail.

CHAPTER OUTLINE

INTRODUCTION

Now that we have a good starting point for conducting Windows Command Line Interface (CLI) investigations, we will introduce the Proactive Incident Response Command Shell (PIRCS) that will provide extended capabilities for collecting, encapsulating, and securing evidence collected during live investigative scenarios. The PIRCS technology provides an interface similar to that of a Windows CLI and is combined with a Secure Evidence Repository (SER). PIRCS provides a framework for maintaining evidence integrity, validation of evidence collection methods, preserving the investigative process, and providing nonrepudiation of actions taken by investigators.

PIRCS consists of three core components combined into a usable CLI overlay/ shell: (1) Secure real-time activity logging; (2) Evidentiary collection and encapsulation; and (3) SER. See Fig. 4.1(A).

A primary feature of PIRCS is the secure real-time activity logging of all command line actions performed (eg, commands executed and files collected). This includes full "service" level logging that generates time-stamped entries that are

Executing Windows Command Line Investigations. http://dx.doi.org/10.1016/B978-0-12-809268-2.00004-3

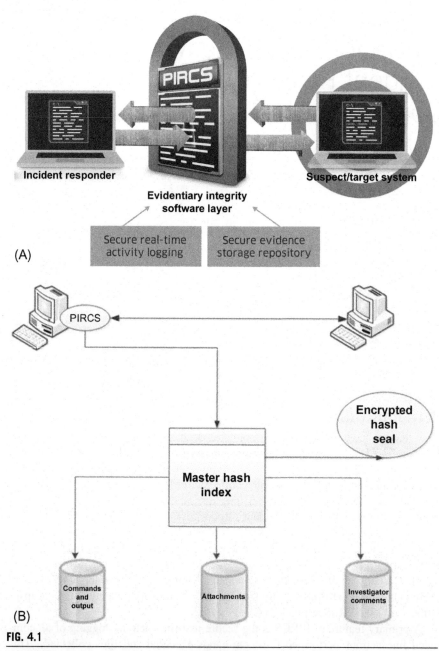

Incident responder

Suspect/target system

Evidentiary integrity
software layer

Secure real-time
activity logging

Secure evidence
storage repository

(A)

PIRCS

Encrypted
hash
seal

Master hash
index

Commands
and
output

Attachments

Investigator
comments

(B)

FIG. 4.1

(A) PIRCS evidence integrity model. (B) PIRCS SER.

stored in Greenwich Mean Time (GMT) and displayed in Local Time. All logs are populated in real-time with a verifiable hash value generated, recorded, and permanently stored for the purposes of maintaining and validating data integrity.

PIRCS also securely captures the bidirectional command line actions of the responder during an investigation by providing a live file collection and encapsulation process. This process provides automated and persistent encoding of metadata about the circumstances and individuals involved in an investigation directly within the SER. This metadata will be based on a series of definable fields, with a mix of automatically and manually populated entries. Examples of such fields include the name of the investigator (or other means of identification), case identifier, validated date/time of the data collection, suspect/target system details, and host system details.

PIRCS includes a SER that encapsulates data for secure evidence storage and logging. The SER securely authenticates incident response analysts, securely stores all evidentiary artifacts collected, and documents incident responder's interactions with stored evidence. Evidence is stored utilizing the Evidence Locker Format (ELF). This format was uniquely designed to facilitate the real-time, bit-stream encapsulation of individual evidentiary artifacts in a live incident response environment.

The PIRCS collection mechanism (Fig. 4.1B) stores all commands and their output in a "command database" which is continuously hashed. Downloaded attachments and evidence files are similarly stored in an attachment database, while investigator comments are stored in a comments database.

All three datasets are hashed and linked in the Master Hash Index. To provide security and nonrepudiation, the Master Hash Index is itself hashed and encrypted in the Hash Seal Locker. The combination of the Master Hash and the Hash seal is used by PIRCS to verify the integrity of the commands, attachments, and comments. The use of 128 bit Advanced Encryption Standard (AES) level encryption to protect the Hash Seal Locker provides nonrepudiation and accountability required for court room viability.

The PIRCS User's Manual is a great source of information for installing, operating, and accessing the advanced features of PIRCS, and we will not duplicate that documentation here. Instead, this chapter will focus on only two key issues; first, special considerations for utilizing PIRCS during live investigations; second, providing a detailed walk through of utilizing PIRCS, and the Windows Command Line. Specific use case examples will be covered in Chapter 5.

PIRCS OPERATIONAL CONSIDERATIONS

Fundamentally, there are three common methods of utilizing PIRCS; (1) install PIRCS on the system you intend to investigate; (2) install PIRCS on portable media such as a Universal Serial Bus (USB) device, or (3) install PIRCS within a corporate enterprise environment to remotely access targeted systems.

At first glance it may seem unusual to consider installing (copying) PIRCS to a system that you wish to investigate. However, for mission critical Microsoft Windows Server environments, preinstalling PIRCS on those servers can provide great value when the need arises for investigations. This application suite is small enough where savvy Chief Information Security Officers may choose to preinstall PIRCS on every server, desktop, and laptop device within the enterprise, only accessible by those with proper privileges.

On March 1, 2012, Robert Mueller, then Director of the FBI, addressed the audience at the annual RSA Cyber Security Conference in San Francisco, CA. He stated: "I am convinced that there are only two types of companies: those that have been hacked and those that will be. And even they are converging into one category: companies that have been hacked and will be hacked again."

James Comey said (2014): "There are those who've been hacked by the Chinese and those who don't know they've been hacked by the Chinese." (http://www.businessinsider.com/fbi-director-china-has-hacked-every-big-us-company-2014-10).

John Chambers, Cisco CIO, said: "There are two types of companies: those who have been hacked, and those who don't yet know they have been hacked." (http://www.weforum.org/agenda/2015/01/companies-fighting-cyber-crime/).

The second method would be to create a set of portable media devices that have PIRCS preinstalled and ready for use. The issue here is to determine: what type, how many, what size, what format, and how to ensure that the devices represent a metaphoric sanitized Petri dish. Let's examine the consideration for each of these.

What type? This of course depends upon the type of investigations that you perform. For example, USB devices (Fig. 4.2A) are the most popular, but have different capabilities.

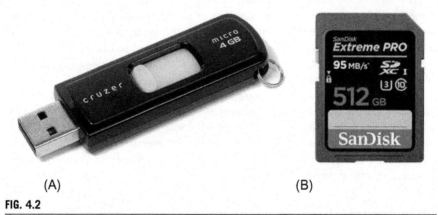

(A)   (B)

FIG. 4.2

(A) USB storage devices. (B) Secure digital memory—SD card.

For example, some devices have built-in encryption capabilities that will protect evidence if the devices were to be lost or stolen.

Some systems (most commonly, laptops) have secure digital memory (SD) cards (Fig. 4.2B) that may be more practical in certain situations.

How many? It would make sense to configure enough devices to satisfy the average number of investigations that you would typically perform per month. Then every month, revise your estimate based on experience and configure new devices.

What size? The size of the device will be based on the type of investigation. For example, if you plan to collect basic system and configuration information, collecting photographs, and documents, a 4 GB device would be sufficient. On the other hand, if you plan on extracting large amounts of data, such as e-mails, databases, memory captures, complete file systems, or large amounts of network data, you may need 500 GB–1 TB. Thus the best action would be to configure several different sizes and then choose the size based on the investigation at hand.

What format? Most smaller devices (4 GB or less today) come preconfigured with the simple File Allocation Table (FAT32) file system. It is important to note that older systems that you may be investigating may only support FAT32 devices so you should have some of these available. On the other hand, if you plan to be investigating more modern platforms where you may encounter larger file systems and large individual files, the New Technology File System (NTFS) would be preferred. Note that if you expect that you may need to copy files that are larger than 4 GB, then NTFS is a must as the FAT32 file system has an upper limit of 4 GB for individual file size (to be precise 4 GB-1 byte). Note that large video can easily exceed this size limit.

Petri dish considerations: Assuming that you have a USB or SD card that you wish to dedicate as a PIRCS device, we must prepare the device for use. This involves the following basic steps.

(1) Wipe the device of all data (note, even brand new devices can contain data and preinstalled software on the device, therefore brand new does NOT mean CLEAN)
(2) Format the device as FAT32 or NTFS depending on the type of investigation you are performing
(3) Label the device
(4) Install PIRCS on the device

PREPARING PIRCS FOR PORTABLE MEDIA

Next, we wish to prepare PIRCS for use from a portable media device, such as a USB device. In keeping with the command line nature of this book, we will undergo the process of creating a PIRCS mobile device utilizing the Windows Command Line and built-in capabilities.

Step one: wipe the device

Speaking with investigators around the world, they all seem to have their favorite method of cleaning or wiping drives, and the methods range from simple to complex. A couple of things to remember—we are discussing the wiping of solid-state memory based devices, either USB or SD cards. Thus, special consideration regarding residual data left on magnetic media is less of a concern. For this example, we are going to use the Windows Command Line and the built-in commands provided by Microsoft, namely *DISKPART*. It should be strongly noted that this is **DANGEROUS** and also requires the following disclaimer:

Disclaimer: Syngress and the Authors of this book are NOT responsible for lost user data. Be sure to back up any important data before performing this operation.

In order to utilize *DISKPART*, we must launch the Windows Command Prompt with Administrator privilege as shown in Fig. 4.3 and then enter the *DISKPART* command.

FIG. 4.3

Launching the Windows command line and DISKPART.

Next we will use *DISKPART* to list the available disks. The result shows Disk 0 is the main hard drive (931 GB), and Disk 1 is the smaller USB drive (30 GB) that was just inserted.

DISKPART> **LIST DISK**

Disk ###	Status	Size	Free	Dyn	Gpt
Disk 0	Online	931 GB	0 B		*
Disk 1	**Online**	**30 GB**	**0 B**		

To be sure, it makes sense to also list the volumes for all disks.

DISKPART> **LIST VOLUME**

Volume ###	Ltr	Label	Fs	Type	Size	Status	Info
Volume 0	C	OS	NTFS	Partition	920 GB	Healthy	Boot
Volume 1		ESP	FAT32	Partition	500 MB	Healthy	System
Volume 2		WINRETOOLS	NTFS	Partition	750 MB	Healthy	Hidden
Volume 3		PBR Image	NTFS	Partition	10 GB	Healthy	Hidden
Volume 4	D	Cruzer	FAT32	Removable	30 GB	Healthy	

As you can see, Drive C is the system disk containing four volumes labeled 0-3. Also, you see that volume 4 is a **removable** partition which is 30 GB in size, with the label Cruzer which matches the drive that will be cleaned.

Thus Disk 1 is selected as the disk to clean.

```
DISKPART> SELECT DISK 1

Disk 1 is now the selected disk.

DISKPART> CLEAN ALL

DiskPart succeeded in cleaning the disk.
```

Step two: format the device

Now that the disk has been cleaned, a partition needs to be created. In this case, it is a primary partition that will encompass the complete disk. The partition will then be formatted. I use the *CREATE PARTITION PRIMARY* command to accomplish the first part.

```
DISKPART> CREATE PARTITION PRIMARY

DiskPart succeeded in creating the specified partition.
```

Next, format the partition. The format command has many options as you can see by issuing the *HELP FORMAT* command.

```
DISKPART> HELP FORMAT

    Formats the specified volume for use with Windows.

Syntax:  FORMAT  [[FS=<FS>]  [REVISION=<X.XX>]  |  RECOMMENDED]
                  [LABEL=<"label">]
                  [UNIT=<N>]  [QUICK]  [COMPRESS]  [OVERRIDE]
                  [DUPLICATE]  [NOWAIT]
                  [NOERR]

    FS=<FS>      Specifies the type of file system. If no file system is given,
                 the default file system displayed by the FILESYSTEMS com-
                 mand is used.

    REVISION=<X.XX>

                 Specifies the file system revision (if applicable).

    RECOMMENDED  If specified, use the recommended file system and
                 revision instead of the default if a recommendation
```

exists. The recommended file system (if one exists) is displayed by the FILESYSTEMS command.

LABEL=<"label">

     Specifies the volume label.

UNIT=<N>   *Overrides the default allocation unit size. Default settings are strongly recommended for general use. The default allocation unit size for a particular file system is displayed by the FILESYSTEMS command.*

     NTFS compression is not supported for allocation unit sizes above 4096.

QUICK   *Performs a quick format.*

COMPRESS   *NTFS only: Files created on the new volume will be compressed by default.*

OVERRIDE   *Forces the file system to dismount first if necessary. All opened handles to the volume would no longer be valid.*

DUPLICATE   *UDF Only: This flag applies to UDF format, version 2.5 or higher. This flag instructs the format operation to duplicate the file system meta-data to a second set of sectors on the disk. The duplicate meta-data is used by applications, for example repair or recovery applications. If the primary meta-data sectors are found to be corrupted, the file system meta-data will be read from the duplicate sectors.*

NOWAIT   *Forces the command to return immediately while the format process is still in progress. If NOWAIT is not specified, DiskPart will display format progress in percentage.*

NOERR   *For scripting only. When an error is encountered, DiskPart continues to process commands as if the error did not occur. Without the NOERR parameter, an error causes DiskPart to exit with an error code.*

A volume must be selected for this operation to succeed.

Examples:

FORMAT FS=NTFS LABEL="New Volume" QUICK COMPRESS

FORMAT RECOMMENDED OVERRIDE

For this example we will format the partition as FAT32 and provide label PIRCS-FAT32.

```
DISKPART> FORMAT FS=FAT32 LABEL="PIRCS-FAT32" QUICK

    100 percent completed

DiskPart successfully formatted the volume.
```

Once *DISKPART* is finished, a cleaned, newly formatted, and labeled disk is created. In order to exit *DISKPART* and subsequently the privileged Windows Command Line, use the *EXIT* command as shown here.

```
DISKPART> EXIT
Leaving DiskPart...
C:\Windows\system32>exit
```

Step three: install PIRCS

Now that we have a clean PIRCS FAT32 formatted drive, we can copy the PIRCS files retrieved as defined in the PIRCS User's Manual and copy the files to the USB device. Download and unzip the PIRCS files to a folder on the desktop named PIRCS. Therefore, to copy the files to the PIRCS USB device, use the *xcopy* command shown here. Notice that it used the */E* and */V* options.

/E copies all directories and files including empty directories.

/V verifies that the copy was successful.

If you are interested in learning more about the *xcopy command*, you can always type *help xcopy*.

```
C:\Users\Chester>xcopy C:\Users\Chester\Desktop\PIRCS D:\PIRCS\ /E /V
C:\Users\Chester\Desktop\PIRCS\PIRCS User Manual.pdf
C:\Users\Chester\Desktop\PIRCS\PIRCS.exe
C:\Users\Chester\Desktop\PIRCS\PIRCSHookx64.dll
C:\Users\Chester\Desktop\PIRCS\PIRCSHookx86.dll
C:\Users\Chester\Desktop\PIRCS\PIRCSWoW.exe
C:\Users\Chester\Desktop\PIRCS\PIRCSx64.bin
C:\Users\Chester\Desktop\PIRCS\PIRCSx86.bin
C:\Users\Chester\Desktop\PIRCS\Cases\Test\master.elf
C:\Users\Chester\Desktop\PIRCS\Cases\Test\seal.slf
C:\Users\Chester\Desktop\PIRCS\Cases\Test\T256\T256-1.ef
C:\Users\Chester\Desktop\PIRCS\Cases\Test\T262\T262-1.ef
C:\Users\Chester\Desktop\PIRCS\Cases\Test\T262\T262-2.ef
C:\Users\Chester\Desktop\PIRCS\Cases\Test\T262\T262-3.ef
C:\Users\Chester\Desktop\PIRCS\Cases\Test\T262\T262-4.ef
C:\Users\Chester\Desktop\PIRCS\Cases\Test\T262\T262-5.ef
C:\Users\Chester\Desktop\PIRCS\Cases\Test\T262\T262-6.ef
```

```
C:\Users\Chester\Desktop\PIRCS\Cases\TestPS\master.elf
C:\Users\Chester\Desktop\PIRCS\Cases\TestPS\seal.slf
C:\Users\Chester\Desktop\PIRCS\Cases\TestPS\T256\T256-1.ef
C:\Users\Chester\Desktop\PIRCS\Cases\TestPS\T262\T262-1.ef
C:\Users\Chester\Desktop\PIRCS\Cases\TestPS\T262\T262-2.ef
C:\Users\Chester\Desktop\PIRCS\Macros\sample.cl
C:\Users\Chester\Desktop\PIRCS\Tools\ReadMe.txt
23 File(s) copied
```

To launch PIRCS you simply need to navigate to the newly created disk, directory, and execute the PIRCS command as shown here. Fig. 4.4 depicts the resulting PIRCS startup.

```
C:\Users\Chester>d:

D:\>cd PIRCS

D:\PIRCS>dir
  Volume in drive D is PIRCS-FAT32
  Volume Serial Number is F269-C309

  Directory of D:\PIRCS

01/16/2016  01:46 PM  <DIR>          .
01/16/2016  01:46 PM  <DIR>          ..
04/10/2014  10:39 AM      1,696,401 PIRCS User Manual.pdf
12/03/2015  12:24 PM      1,633,280 PIRCS.exe
12/03/2015  12:25 PM         73,216 PIRCSHookx64.dll
12/03/2015  12:24 PM         61,952 PIRCSHookx86.dll
12/03/2015  12:24 PM         84,992 PIRCSWoW.exe
12/03/2015  12:25 PM      4,772,864 PIRCSx64.bin
12/03/2015  12:24 PM      3,847,168 PIRCSx86.bin
01/16/2016  01:34 PM  <DIR>          Cases
01/16/2016  01:34 PM  <DIR>          Macros
01/16/2016  01:34 PM  <DIR>          Tools
               7 File(s)  12,169,873  bytes
               5 Dir(s) 33,189,380,096 bytes free

D:\PIRCS>PIRCS
```

Please note: The first time this command is executed, the user will be required to accept the end user license agreement.

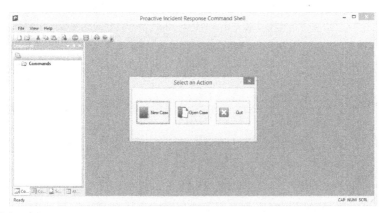

FIG. 4.4

PIRCS default start display executed from removable media.

PIRCS BASICS

As previously mentioned, the PIRCS User's Manual provides even more details, and Chapter 5 will walk through multiple investigative examples using PIRCS. However, a quick tour of the basics is in order. As was illustrated in Fig. 4.4, the initial startup display of PIRCS provides three options. New Case, Open Case, or Quit. Since this is our first use we will select New Case and fill in the basics of the case as shown in Fig. 4.5. A couple of important notes here:

(1) The information here is included when the console is exported for potential use in court. Therefore, make sure the information is complete.
(2) Select a strong password to ensure access control is maintained.
(3) The current date and time shown below is extracted from the system. Investigators may wish to specify a more accurate time that will then be synced with their investigative actions.

Once the information is filled in, select OK and PIRCS is ready to execute investigative commands as shown in Fig. 4.6.

To get things started, execute the *systeminfo* command as shown in Fig. 4.7. The screenshot is annotated with the numbers 1 and 2.

(1) Depicts the *systeminfo* results of the command entered in the PIRCS Console Windows.
(2) After entering several additional commands, the command list now displays the list of user executed commands in sequence. This is considered the

FIG. 4.5

PIRCS new case dialog entry.

FIG. 4.6

PIRCS ready for investigative commands.

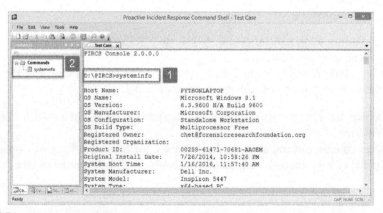

FIG. 4.7

PIRCS initial command entry.

FIG. 4.8

PIRCS command window sequence.

Command Window, as more commands are entered, this window will continue to expand and list the sequence of commands entered. See Fig. 4.8.

As shown in Fig. 4.9 any previously entered command can be selected from the Command Window and the PIRCS Console Windows will move back to that command for review. The commands panel depicts the sequence of commands entered, thus you can review the commands in the order they were executed.

In addition, if you wish to make a note or comment regarding the results of the command, highlight the information and right-click as shown in Fig. 4.10, revealing the option to add a comment associated with this command. Fig. 4.11 depicts the entry of the comment associated with the selected command.

By selecting the Comment Window tab at the bottom of the left panel shown in Fig. 4.12 (#1), you can display the Comment pane. By selecting the desired comment (#2), the comment will be displayed as a callout (#3). The PIRCS Console Window automatically moves to the command associated with the selected comment (#4).

Another important feature of PIRCS is the ability to take a screen capture. In many cases investigators wish to capture the screen of the computer under investigation. This can be accomplished by selecting Screen Capture from the Tools menu shown in Fig. 4.13.

This action will launch the Screen Capture Dialog Box and allow you to associate a comment with the screenshot as shown in Fig. 4.14.

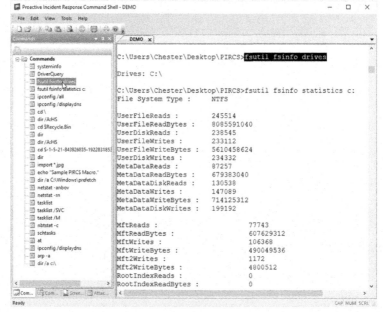

FIG. 4.9

Select and display a previously entered command.

FIG. 4.10

Right-click and select the add comment option.

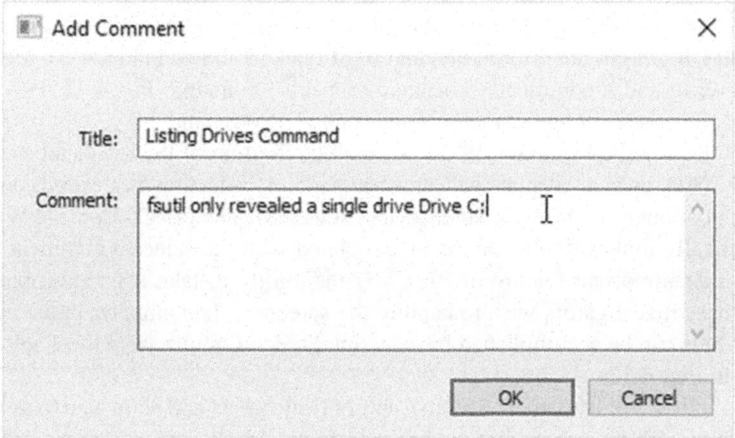

FIG. 4.11

Enter the comment associated with the command.

FIG. 4.12

Review previously stored case comments.

FIG. 4.13

Select screen capture from the PIRCS Tools menu.

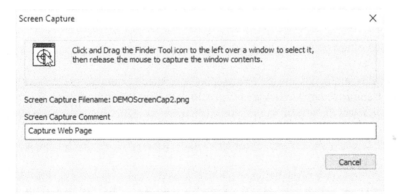

FIG. 4.14

Screen capture dialog box.

The investigator can then drag the screen capture icon to any window and capture that Window. For this illustration an open web page was captured that depicts the CCCleaner Web page as shown in Fig. 4.15.

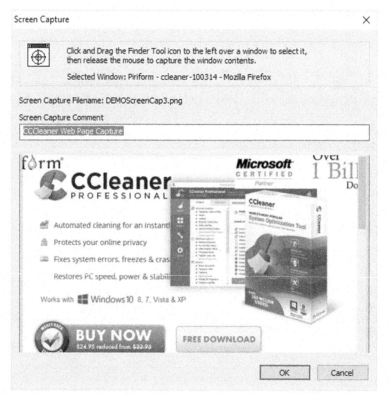

FIG. 4.15

Completed screen capture.

As with Commands and the Comments Pane, screen captures are listed within the Screen Capture Pane. As shown in Fig. 4.16, you first select the Screen Capture tab (#1), then select the screen capture you wish to review (#2). This, in turn, displays the callout (#3).

Once selected, the full screen capture will be displayed for investigative review as shown in Fig. 4.17.

Once you have completed your investigative session, you can exit PIRCS using the File Menu Option shown in Fig. 4.18 or simply press the "X" located at the top right corner of the PIRCS application.

If you wish to continue the investigation or review the results, you can simply launch PIRCS again and select the master.elf file of the specific case in question as shown in Figs. 4.19 and 4.20.

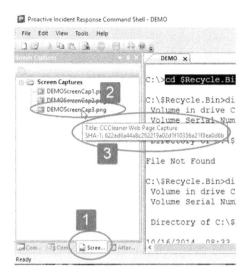

FIG. 4.16

Screen captures review process.

FIG. 4.17

Screen capture retrieval and display.

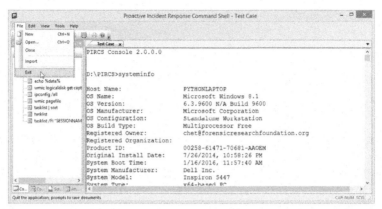

FIG. 4.18

Exiting PIRCS.

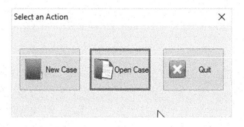

FIG. 4.19

PIRCS select and open an existing case.

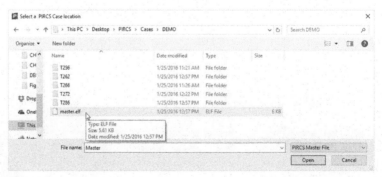

FIG. 4.20

Select the master.elf case file.

At this point PIRCS will give you the option to open the case to either *Review* or *Investigate* as shown in Fig. 4.21. You must enter the password associated with the case (#1) and then select either *Review Mode* or *Investigative Mode* (#2). If you select *Review Mode*, you will only be able to examine the case data versus *Investigative Mode* where you can enter new commands and continue to collect additional evidence.

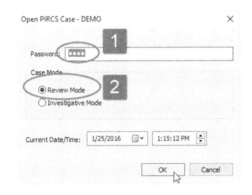

FIG. 4.21

Login and select review or investigator mode.

PIRCS ADVANCED CAPABILITIES

There are several advanced PIRCS features that provide extended value to investigators, that are covered in this section.

Exporting the console: First, is the ability to export the PIRCS console to a normal text file. This can be useful for both investigative review and for inclusion within court documents. You can export the console from the Tools menu by selecting the Export Console Action as shown in Fig. 4.22.

FIG. 4.22

Select export console from Tools menu.

The export console feature provides detailed information regarding the investigative process (Fig. 4.23). This includes case information (Item 1), PIRCS Console Information (Item 2) and then input and output of each command including the time stamp when the command was executed (Item 3). The output is in chronological order providing details of each step of the investigative process.

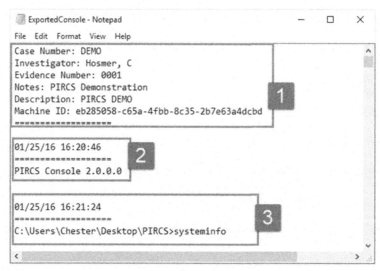

FIG. 4.23

Sample exported PIRCS console.

Including file acquisitions: Investigators performing live investigations in many cases will navigate the file system and acquire specific files of interest. PIRCS supports this capability using the *import* command, which allows the investigator to import specific files into the PIRCS case. In order to demonstrate this, a series of commands are executed in order to examine and then extract recently deleted files contained in the Windows Recycle Bin (Fig. 4.24).

FIG. 4.24

Command sequence.

Having basic knowledge of the Windows environment allows you to move to the C:\ directory where the Recycle Bin is typically located. After navigating to the C:\ directory using the *cd * command, the *dir /A:HS* command was performed revealing the Hidden and System Files in the current directory. The directory was then changed to the $Recycle.bin directory using the *C:\>cd $Recycle.Bin* command. Next, the contents of the directory were examined in order to identify the current day recycle bin using *dir /A:HS* again. The results are shown in Fig. 4.25.

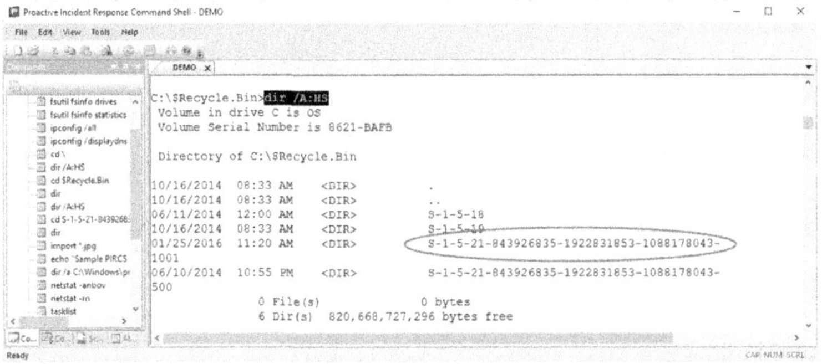

FIG. 4.25

Content list of the recycle bin.

Next we move into that directory once again using the change directory command *cd S-1-5-21-843926835-1922831853-1088178043-1001*. The directory is then listed using the *dir* command to get a sense of the contents and recently deleted files. Fig. 4.26 provides a partial listing of the file contents. Note: when executing commands like this; once you have typed the first few letters of a filename, pressing the Tab key will auto fill matching options.

FIG. 4.26

Contents of today's recycle.

Files with .jpg extensions were then collected and included in the case using the import command depicted in Fig. 4.27.

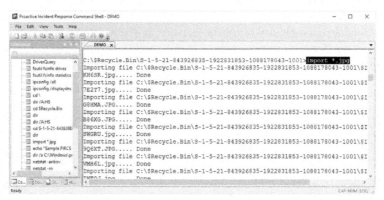

FIG. 4.27

Execution of the import command.

To review the results of any file imports we refer to the Attachment Pane as shown in Fig. 4.28. This figure depicts the two sections of this display, the Attachment Pane selection at the bottom right along with the list of attachments that have been imported into the case.

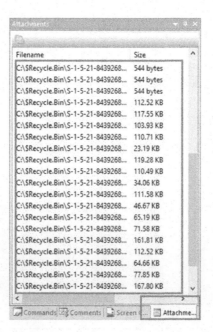

FIG. 4.28

Attachments included in the case.

Macros: Macros are predefined sets of commands that can be executed as a group in a specific sequence. Fig. 4.29 provides an example Macro File; Macro Files use a .cl extension and can be manually created with a simple text editor such as Notepad as shown here.

FIG. 4.29

Creation of the macro file.

To execute a Macro File you can select Run Macro from the Tools Menu as shown in Fig. 4.30, you then select the desired Macro from the File browser and the commands will execute in the order they were specified in the Macro File.

FIG. 4.30

Macro file execution.

If you include an *echo* command as the first command in the Macro File, it will be easy to identify the sequence of commands processed as part of the Macro. Adding an echo at the end of the Macro sequence will assist in identifying commands that were processed as a Macro versus those that were typed by a user. PIRCS also adds an entry at the end of a Macro that states a Macro was run and how long it took to execute. I have highlighted the commands that were executed using the Macro in Fig. 4.31.

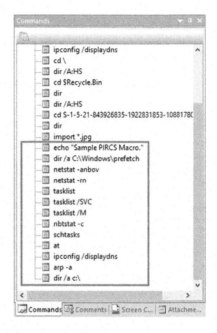

FIG. 4.31

Macro commands listed in the command pane.

CHAPTER 4 REVIEW

This chapter provided a quick tour of PIRCS along with the examination of some operational considerations. In addition, we examined how to create a clean removable device and then install PIRCS on that device for portable investigations. The best way to learn and become comfortable with PIRCS is to experiment with the tool in mock investigative scenarios. We also recommend that you reference the latest PIRCS User's Manual for up-to-date information and features.

CHAPTER 4 SUMMARY QUESTIONS

1. Install PIRCS on both a Desktop and USB Device.
   a. Create a new case
   b. Experiment with commands, screenshots, and comments
   c. Exit and then open the case in reviewer mode and examine the previous commands, screenshots, and comments
   d. Develop a list of pro's and con's for using PIRCS for live investigation scenarios both from a preinstalled and from a portable media point of view
2. Define additional capabilities that you see would be beneficial to investigators that are using PIRCS.

ADDITIONAL RESOURCES

Harris. (n.d.). *Proactive Incident Response Command Shell (PIRCS)© installation user maintenance instructions*. Version 2.0 or later.

Mueller, R., III (2012). Combating threats in the cyber world outsmarting terrorists and hackers. In *RSA conference, San Francisco, CA, March 1, 2012*. https://www.fbi.gov/news/speeches/combating-threats-in-the-cyber-world-outsmarting-terrorists-hackers-and-spies.

Use cases

5

Digital Evidence:
Any information or data of value to an investigation that is stored on,
received, or transmitted by an electronic device. This evidence is acquired
when data or electronic devices are seized and secured for examination.

CHAPTER OUTLINE

INTRODUCTION

The identification and collection of digital evidence is one of the, if not the, most crucial element of any cyber investigation, whether you work for law enforcement, corporate security, or as an independent consultant. Collection of digital evidence is similar to the

Executing Windows Command Line Investigations. http://dx.doi.org/10.1016/B978-0-12-809268-2.00005-5

collection of physical evidence. There is an established process for surveying the applicable crime scene, identifying potential artifacts that are relevant to the case at hand, handling, and storing the evidence such that there is a high level of assured integrity that can withstand verifiable scrutiny. Understanding and following this process is particularly important since the mere act of locating and collecting digital evidence has the potential to corrupt, destroy, or otherwise alter it. As such, it is imperative that proper preparation, awareness, documentation, and processes are established and tested prior to actual use "in-the-field." As seen in Chapter 3, there are a multitude of built-in Windows Command Line Interface (CLI) commands and functions that can be leveraged for an investigation, however they may not always be the best choice or provide the examiner with the level of evidentiary detail or assurance that is needed or warranted.

There is a myriad of third-party utilities available that can expand existing capabilities, provide new functionalities, or assist with validating digital evidence specifically when built-in Windows functions return evidence that, in some cases, cannot and should not be trusted at face value. There are many pieces of malware in the wild that intentionally hide, alter, obfuscate, or otherwise modify what the Windows operating system (OS) (and its built-in tools) can see and interact with. Additionally, the user of the suspect system could have maliciously altered commands, functions, or implemented a logic bomb that when reacted too could impede an investigation. In these instances it is imperative that alternative methods of safeguarding, identifying, and collecting evidence have been documented, tested, and readily available for implementation.

Logic Bomb

A Logic Bomb is a piece of software code or a set of instructions, that are embedded into a system or application that are executed if and when a particular set of conditions are met (such as running a Windows CLI command), usually with harmful or malicious intent.

One of the more recent variants of the RawPOS Point of Sale malware includes functionality that has been labeled as being a logic bomb. In this instance, the malware authors utilize this code in an effort to further protect and hide the presence of infection and compromise. Specifically, the binary file used by the malware for capturing memory is timed so it will not execute if approximately more than 1 months' time has passed from when it was compiled. This condition would limit malicious activity on a compromised system if the attacker could not regain access to it, and deter most dynamic sandbox analysis of the file.

A full technical report for this malware can be found on TrendMicro's website at: http://sjc1-te-ftp.trendmicro.com/images/tex/pdf/RawPOS%20Technical%20Brief.pdf.

It is often impossible, at the beginning of a computer investigation, to know the scope, impact, or actors involved. However, by leveraging standardized methods for evidence collection, handling, and storage you ensure that minimal evidence alteration has occurred, verifiable processes can be replicated as needed, and that the utilized methods will satisfy potential legal or regulatory requirements and other potential forms of evidence contestation.

As an example of evidentiary mandates and considerations, consider how the United States Federal Rules of Evidence "Best Evidence Rule" [Rule 1001(3)] was modified to provide for the inclusion of computer based evidence by adding the clause, "[if] data are stored in a computer or similar device, any printout or other output readable by sight, shown to reflect the data accurately, is an 'original'." Based on the definition and general interpretation of this rule, each copy of a piece of digital evidence can constitute an original copy of the evidence. If an examiner is working with contraband evidence, such as child pornography or other sensitive or regulated data, knowing the location of all copies of the data, as well as the documentation of actions taken to collect and analyze that data could be called into question in a court of law. This could have multiple implications to an organization if they are not able to identify, track, or validate evidence integrity, collection, handling, and storage.

Incidents will share some similarities to their predecessors, but each maintains its own unique elements. Therefore no "standard" set of step-by-step instructions can be compiled that encompasses all potentialities, but it is essential that initial baseline procedures and tools are documented, standardized, and vetted to allow for as much standardization and evidentiary assurance as possible.

GENERAL EVIDENCE COLLECTION GUIDELINES

It is important to note that not every incident will require a live forensic analysis and some may only require a portion of the investigation to implement live evidence collection methods. The criteria which would determine this is often based on the type of investigation that is being processed, the nature of the incident, and the defined processes and procedures of your respective industry and organization.

A standard issue with live response situations is that it is relatively impossible to fully and adequately document and delineate specific procedures that should be utilized for every case, due to the potentially endless variations that can be encountered during an investigation. Generally, while the overall process can be defined, specific step-by-step instructions for an examiner are decided in real-time and are based on a range of factors including:

- The technologies involved and the potential evidence available
- How the incident was identified or detected
- Previous experience with similar incidents
- Examiner experience and knowledge
- The scope and severity of the incident
- Systems, staff, or data affected
- The probability of eventual civil or criminal, legal action
- The potential for public exposure of the incident

Nonetheless, by understanding core principles, how to minimize evidence interaction and the overall volatility of data within the various Windows OSs, generalized processes and guidelines can be formulated. These processes and guidelines can best reflect the actions or scope of actions that can and should be taken in any given situation.

LOCARD'S PRINCIPLE

Locard's Exchange Principle, often called simply "Locard's Principle," was developed by Dr. Edmond Locard in the early 20th century and states that whenever an individual makes contact with another person, place, or thing; that contact results in some level of exchange of physical materials or trace evidence. While originally focused on the traditional physical forensic sciences, Locard's Principle also directly applies to digital forensics, since any interaction with a computer system generates various amounts and types of trace evidence. This is a guiding principle for performing live analysis of a computer system, as all actions performed either by an adversary or by an examiner will have a direct impact on a computer system and the evidence it contains. When an examiner interacts with a live system, every action affects the state of that system and has the potential of altering, corrupting, or destroying potential evidence.

When a computer system is running, background actions are occurring constantly, often times without user awareness or knowledge. Some of these activities can include, log files being written too, data moving around for efficiency, scheduled programming instructions and commands being read into and removed from memory space, or volatile memory being written to disk.

Therefore, certain actions need to be taken in sequence and in specific order, which will be discussed throughout this chapter. This will ensure that any changes to a computer system will only come after necessary and potentially affected evidence is collected and the potential scope and impact of those changes are defined, acknowledged, and documented. Since it is not known at the initial point of analysis and evidence collection, the full scope and scale of an investigation or incident, it is crucial for information about the current state of the affected system(s) to be collected first and that such actions are executed in a consistent and documented manner. This ensures that the collected evidence is appropriately prioritized and executed without risking evidence alteration.

ORDER OF VOLATILITY

One of the most important aspects to consider when obtaining evidence from a live system is the order of volatility of potential evidence and subsequent prioritization for collection. The volatility of digital evidence refers to the overall availability and stability of different types of data based on its usage and location. All data is volatile, however the reliability and accuracy of the data generally decreases over time. A computer system has highly volatile data that can range from the contents of active memory that could be unavailable in a matter of seconds, to a file that is stored on the hard drive that will be available for a much longer period of time. With this concept in mind, the order in which data is collected is important. Evidence that may have a higher level of volatility (such as the contents of memory) should have a higher priority than that of more persistent data (such as the contents of a file).

While not a comprehensive or complete set of all evidence that might be collected, the list below highlights the high level types of data available on a Windows-based system that might have evidentiary value in a live analysis situation. The data are listed in order of most volatile to least volatile.

• Random Access Memory (RAM) contents
• Network state and connectivity information
• Active and running process information
• Temporary files and memory swap space
• Windows Event Log contents
• Windows Registry contents
• Stored data on the system's hard drive or other media

TOOL SELECTION AND USAGE

Prior to any actual activity, triage, or evidence collection, one of the facets that examiners need to ensure is that they have a comprehensive and validated repository of tools that they can leverage.

As any interaction with a live system will have a direct impact on the system and the evidence obtained, the examiner must be selective in what tools are used and they need to understand, articulate, and be comfortable with any changes the tool may make to a system in the normal course of its operation. To understand these changes, it is essential that the examiner fully test all tools prior to actual use on a production system or an actual case. It is important that any tools employed, leave as much of a limited footprint on the system as possible.

Since command line tools do not have a Graphical User Interface (GUI), it is often believed that they leave less of a footprint on a system than that of tools with a GUI. In most respects this is a valid position, since the mere act of loading a GUI tool requires greater interactivity with the host OS. This activity includes increased memory space, system calls, and system resource allocations for presenting itself to the user, which in turn leaves a larger footprint on the system. Conversely, command line tools require an examiner to type in specific commands and requests, there is greater chance for typos and wrong commands to be entered due to human error. GUI based tools do provide point and click interfaces, which are often easier to use than typing in lengthy and cumbersome commands.

However, this is not a hard and fast rule either, as there are times where a GUI based tool will be needed or that CLI tools may not be able to execute. That is why it is important for an examiner to have a diverse and validated repository of tools at their disposal. An examiner should never assume or take someone else's word as to a tool's capabilities or the types of artifacts that it may leave behind. Outside of potential artifacts and trace evidence that is left behind, there are times where different tools may show different information, even if they are collecting the same information. This could be due to the way the technology queries the host OS, what system calls or components it queries, or some malicious behavior that may be affecting the output of one tool but not the other. The only true method of determining the actual footprint or usefulness of any particular tool is through thorough testing and validation.

It may seem like an onerous task to test and validate tools but it is a task that in the long run will save you a multitude of headaches and issues later on during an investigation and perhaps during any type of court proceedings. The overall process of performing these tests also provides you with a much better understanding as to how the tools function as well as greater insight into that particular area of potential evidence and its value.

FUNDAMENTAL DIGITAL EVIDENCE CATEGORIES

According to the National Institute of Standards and Technology's Guide to Integrating Forensic Techniques into Incident Response, "before the analyst begins to collect any data, a decision should be made by the analyst or management (in accordance with the organization's policies and legal advisors) on the need to collect and preserve evidence in a way that supports its use in future legal or internal disciplinary proceedings. In such situations, a clearly defined chain of custody should be followed to avoid allegations of mishandling or tampering of evidence. Throughout the process, a detailed log should be kept of every step that was taken to collect the data, including information about each tool used in the process. The documentation allows other analysts to repeat the process later if needed and if the evidence may not be needed for legal proceedings for an extended time, proper documentation enables an analyst to remember exactly what was done to collect data and can be used to refute claims of mishandling."

When performing live response and evidentiary triage, the actual order of operations and processes you use can and will vary greatly. This variation is due to the dynamic range of factors and situations that are unique to each investigation. In light of that, it is often times better to have a general understanding and awareness of the overall workflow, possible pitfalls, and potential evidence so that you are able to adjust and adapt to each situation as needed, versus being solely dependent on the usage or capabilities of a single piece of technology or methodology.

The type and priority of evidence that is deemed most useful is often times dependent on the specific situation the examiner is faced with. While Locard's Principle and Order of Volatility need to be considered, there are times when an investigation uncovers circumstances where evidence that may generally have a lower volatility needs immediate collection (i.e., Windows Event Logs are in risk of being destroyed or otherwise altered and, as such, their collection may supersede something with a higher volatility).

You will find as you process investigations that a lot of the evidence collection procedures will be redundant and overlap between the various tools and the data that may be of interest. The difference is more about when you should collect certain pieces of evidence, what pieces of evidence you need or should attempt to identify, and what to do if and when you run into problems or unknowns.

The sections below, which are in a relative order of volatility and with consideration to Locard's Principle, provide a number of examples of various methods, techniques, and considerations for the collection of common categories of evidence. Within each section, when possible, we review multiple ways in which the same, or similar, evidence can be collected and gathered. While the sections below are not all inclusive with every potential type of available evidence or associated tools and techniques that may be available, they do highlight several fundamental categories and methodologies that generally yield a high amount of actionable intelligence and evidence for incident response and related activities. As several of the commands that will be reviewed can generate a large volume of results, some of the output in our examples may be truncated.

The goal here is to focus on maintaining the integrity of the evidence and system under investigation, as well as to provide a broad level of insight and awareness of the multitude of possible methodologies, positive and negative impacts, and considerations that need to be weighed and validated. Moreover, this awareness is also meant to stress the importance and need of thoroughly testing, validating, documenting, and prioritizing processes and tools that are suitable for your needs and the organization.

As you will see in the below examples, there often are multiple ways to extract the same piece of information, each with their own pros and cons. Ideally you will want to utilize the methods that have the smallest footprint and results that are immediately usable and recognizable. However, knowing alternate methods of collecting potential evidence for use during times when some functions or commands will not work, for whatever reason, is just as important.

Several of the examples in the following sections make use of third-party CLI tools. At no time should an examiner ever install software onto a system that is being investigated. It is strongly recommended that Proactive Incident Response Command Shell (PIRCS) be installed on external media, as outlined in Chapter 4, and that any and all third-party tools be downloaded and added to the PIRCS Tools directory prior to any testing or field use. By copying these utilities within the PIRCS Tools directory, they will be available for usage directly off the portable media and nothing will be installed on the system that evidence is being collected from.

It is important to note that several of the tools referenced, when downloaded and extracted to your PIRCS Tools folder will be created within sub-folders. To utilize these tools you will need to navigate to the appropriate folder to execute them from within the PIRCS environment. As an example, extracting the Microsoft SysInternals PSTools suite to the PIRCS Tools folder, will create and extract the tools to a sub-folder called PSTools, that is, \PIRCS\Tools\PSTools\. To execute these utilities, you will need to navigate to this folder first. You can also specify the full path to the PIRCS Tools Folder and sub-folder to execute the program, for example: \PIRCS\Tools\PSTools\autorunsc. exe. Alternatively, you could move the files from the sub-folder directly into the PIRCS Tools folder to execute the program from any folder.

A complete listing of web links to referenced tools, as well as many others, can be found within Appendix A.

Give me six hours to chop down a tree and I will spend the first four sharpening the axe.

Abraham Lincoln

FULL MEMORY CAPTURE

Within the Window OS environment, there is no built-in mechanism for capturing and saving the contents of a system's RAM. A number of commercial forensic suites, such as Guidance Software's Encase Forensic and AccessData's FTK/FTK Imager, have utilities for imaging memory. Additionally, there are a number of free alternatives that are available as well, often made available by security organizations such as Mandiant (now FireEye), Magnet Forensics, HBGary, etc. However, not all of them maintain the same level of functionality, operability, and compatibility with newer Windows OS versions and both 32-bit and 64-bit architectures.

Capturing full RAM contents with Mandiant Memoryze

Mandiant's Memoryze software is well utilized and respected within the incident response community, and is also widely utilized by Mandiant/FireEye for their professional service engagements. This application has a high level of versatility and flexibility, and is compatible with all known Windows OS versions since Windows 2000. It is also able to function on both 32-bit and 64-bit platforms. This software can be obtained from https://www.fireeye.com/services/freeware/memoryze.html.

Initially, Memoryze is not immediately usable in a command line or portable manner. Refer to the Memoryze User's Guide on how to install it to portable media versus attempting to install it on a system under investigation. After installation onto your portable media, Memoryze creates two folders labeled x86 and x64. These folders contain the Memoryze executable(s) as well as several prebuilt batch files and eXtensible Markup Language (XML) templates that can be utilized to perform various types of memory acquisition from both 32-bit and 64-bit versions of Windows, respectively.

NOTE: As computers have advanced over time, memory sizes have and will continue to increase. It is very common to see desktop and laptops systems with at least 4, 8, 12, or even 16 GB of RAM. Make sure that prior to any attempted memory acquisitions that you are utilizing portable media of sufficient size.

- Based on the Initial Host Detail collection information, confirm if the Windows OS is 32-bit (x86) or 64-bit (x64), and navigate to the respective directory.

    D:\PIRCS\tools > cd x64

- The directory you navigated to in the command above contains multiple files, whose purposes and usages are fully explained within the Memoryze User's Guide. However, as we are looking to perform a full RAM capture, which is the purpose of the MemoryDD batch file. Executing the command below will spawn a separate process and window.

    D:\PIRCS\tools\x64 > MemoryDD.bat -output d:

When executed, Memoryze saves its output to the desired location and creates a series of nested directories with the following structure: \Audits\[System Name]\[Date & Time of Acquisition]. This hierarchy provides a method of categorizing the evidence collected in instances where multiple collections are performed on one or more systems. The output from this program contains details of the settings that were used for the memory collection, any errors or issues that were encountered (there will always be some), and a RAM dump file. As the RAM dump file is in RAW format, it can be analyzed by most memory analysis tools, including: Mandiant Redline, Volatility, Encase, etc.

INITIAL HOST DETAIL

When an investigation is initiated, there are essential components of the suspect computer system that should be immediately captured and documented. This provides the examiner with an understanding of the initial computing environment they are faced with, which in turn will often dictate how to proceed. Facets such as the system's name, Window OS version, system time, and network configuration information, all aid the examiner in confirming they are investigating the correct system, provide a means of attribution for gathered evidence, provide insight as to what tools should be used, and the potential evidence that may be available. As with traditional forensics, evidentiary attribution and reliability are central components of incident response and being able to document, recall, and identify the source of collected evidence is a crucial factor.

When to collect host information is a matter of debate and consideration amongst incident response professionals, as well as those within law enforcement. On any live system, as discussed previously in this chapter, any action taken have a direct impact to the state of evidence within that system. Any commands or utilities that are executed immediately and unavoidably change the contents of active RAM memory, in addition to the potential modification of numerous system files, registry entries, and date and time stamps. As such, there are experts that recommend the immediate capture of active RAM memory prior to the collection of any host details, as well as experts that recommend capturing initial host details first to provide primary system validation and evidence attribution, even if a memory capture is going to be performed.

In a law enforcement organization, the first responder may not have knowledge of a computer system beforehand. If he/she arrives at a scene and there is one or more live computer system that they have the authority to seize and process, they may not be as concerned with capturing system identification details prior to executing a full memory capture, so they can obtain this evidence with minimal contamination as possible. Whereas in a corporate setting, an examiner generally knows and is looking for a very specific computer system (usually by host name, IP address, or username, etc.), and by obtaining this level of host identification immediately they have the ability of validating that they are indeed investigating the correct system. Too many incident responders fall into the trap of immediately capturing memory, both when performing local or remote incident response, only to find out afterwards that they inadvertently connected to the wrong machine (ie, due to IP address changes, incorrect user, DNS resolution errors, etc.). In this environment, the minimal memory contamination caused by obtaining this information is outweighed by the validation that time is not being wasted and the correct system is being investigated. In all instances, it is critical to only capture the minimal amount of information needed to validate the system details as every unnecessary command has the potential of impacting the contents of active memory and valuable evidence can be lost or destroyed.

The relative implementation of process around the concepts of Order of Volatility and Locard's Principle is a risk/reward trade-off and needs to be defined based on your organization's risk threshold and prioritization levels, as defined by your corporate HR and legal teams, and may differ than what is outlined below.

Host name

- **Host name via Windows OS HOSTNAME command**. This method utilizes the built-in Windows OS command and quickly provides the host name of the system. This method does not use the environment variables to obtain this information and may provide a higher level of confidence in its results, as environment variables can be easily modified by a user or malware.

  *D:\PIRCS > **hostname***
  DemoWindowsdMachineName

- **Host name via third-party tool HOSTNAME**. There are several third-party tools that do provide the ability of displaying a system's host name. There may be instances where using third-party tools, rather than built-in functions, may be desirable or wanted, such as in cases of malware infections or highly compromised machines, as the built-in tools may provide inaccurate or deliberately altered information. In this example we are using the HOSTNAME. EXE program, which is a part of the GNU Win32 CoreUtil suite and can be obtained from http://gnuwin32.sourceforge.net/packages/coreutils.htm.

GNU Win32 CoreUtil Installation

This suite has multiple utilities that can benefit an examiner performing evidence collection and triage. However, there are a few steps that need to be taken to get these applications to run off portable media. Specifically you want to download both the BINARIES and DEPENDENCIES archive files using the above link. Each of these files will need to be extracted onto your portable media. For PIRCS usage, they should be extracted to the TOOLS directory within the PIRCS folder. When the Binary archive is extracted it will create a directory called BIN within the TOOLS folder. It is important to also extract the Dependencies archive into the BIN folder as well. The Binaries archive contains all of the actual utilities themselves, whereas the Dependencies archive contains two resource files that are required for these utilities to execute.

---

  *D:\PIRCS\Tools\bin > **hostname.exe***
  DemoWindowsdMachineName

Windows OS version

- **Windows OS version via built-in command**. This method utilizes the built-in Windows OS command and quickly provides the system version. However, the information listed may not be immediately identifiable for some, as it utilizes the relative version number of the Windows OS, not its common name.

*D:\PIRCS>**ver***
Microsoft Windows [Version 6.3.9600]

- **Windows OS version via a direct Windows Registry query**. This method initiates a query directly to the Windows Registry. As this function does access the registry, the information may have a higher level of assurance then other methods. However, it also maintains a higher footprint and directly accesses a repository of additional evidence. This method is generally not recommended, unless no other options are working or exist.

    *D:\PIRCS>**reg query "HKLM\Software\Microsoft\Windows NT\ CurrentVersion" /v "ProductName"***

    HKEY_LOCAL_MACHINE\Software\Microsoft\Windows NT\ CurrentVersion

    ProductName   REG_SZ   Windows 8.1 Pro

System time

Capturing the system time is imperative in any investigation. Not only does this information document and delineate when the evidence collection began, it also provides a baseline understanding for the chronological analysis of the collected evidence. The details around the active time on the system, such as time zone and daylight savings time, will provide the baseline for time based analysis and correlation throughout the investigation. When collecting the system time, an effort should be made to document the current time and time on the system, as well as an external source of time validation, such as from the examiner's cellular telephone—as cellular telephones are automatically updated and synchronized and considered an accurate time source. Any unexplained differences between the system's time and the validated time, outside of time zone or daylight savings time differences, may indicate intentional time manipulation or malware on the system.

One of the first actions you want to take when investigating a system is to capture the local system time. This provides the current time zone and any differences in time that you will need to be aware of as you collect and work to correlate different pieces of information and evidence.

As discussed in Chapter 3, the Windows OS has multiple built-in ways to collect the current system time, each with small differences that need to be considered prior to determining what is the best to utilize within your given situation.

- **Date and time via Windows Management Instrumentation Command-line (WMIC)**. This method utilizes the WMI API function within Windows and provides the date and time in a single string. Reading it from left to right you have; year, month, day, hour (24 hour clock), minute, second, millisecond—Time zone offset, in minutes. While it does provide a bit more detail (ie, Time Zone), this command does generate much more activity in the background as it is executing a direct Application Program Interface (API) call to the Windows OS.

D:\PIRCS>wmic OS get localdatetime

LocalDateTime

20160118154941.765000-300

- **Time zone via Window's TZUTIL utility**. This method executes a utility that is a part of every Windows OS version since Windows Vista. It provides the information quickly, but it only provides the name of the time zone, not the default offset value. While this is an application execution, the application is relatively small and has minimal footprint and impact to the system when executed.

D:\PIRCS>tzutil /g

Eastern Standard Time

- **Time zone via WMIC**. This method utilizes the Windows Management Instrumentation (WMI) API function within Windows. The results from this command are the GMT offset in minutes for the time zone the computer is set to, however it does not display the time zone name. This command does generate much more activity in the background as it is executing a direct API call to the Windows OS.

D:\PIRCS>wmic OS get currenttimezone

CurrentTimeZone

-300

- **Time zone via PowerShell**. This method utilizes the Windows PowerShell interface within Windows. In the background, this command actually loads the PowerShell interface, executes the included command, performs the API query, returns the results, and then closes the PowerShell interface. While the results include both the GMT offset, in minutes, as well as the time zone name, this method has the largest footprint and background activity of all of the methods listed here.

D:\PIRCS>powershell Get-CimInstance Win32_TimeZone

Bias	*SettingID*	*Caption*
- - - - -	- - - - - - - - -	- - - - - - -
-300		*(UTC-05:00) Eastern Time (US & Canada)*

PIRCS Architecture

The purpose of PIRCS is to deliver a command shell interface type of environment that provides an examiner with validated documentation and action attribution while maintaining the integrity of a suspect system to the extent that is possible. A key point of this architecture is that it effectively protects an examiner from leveraging certain commands that may cause inadvertent and undue alteration or leaves a larger and unwanted footprint to a system that is being investigated. Based on this design concept, as you utilize PIRCS you will notice that certain commands or actions may not work as they would from within the traditional Windows Command Shell. Some of these commands include the internal Windows CLI commands such as: DEL, MKDIR, RMDIR, DATE, TIME, and SET. Additionally, certain scripting functions are also restricted since they often load more data than anticipated into a systems memory, such as using the | (PIPE) command to chain multiple commands together.

However, in realizing and understanding that an examiner may have the need to utilize some of these commands and methods at some point during their investigation, you can invoke (ie, execute) either the systems CMD.EXE command processor or a trusted command processor that you have previously tested and copied onto your PIRCS USB device. When you execute CMD.EXE from within PIRCS, it will effectively load and present you with the full Windows Command Shell, which in turn will enable you to execute and run the aforementioned types of commands and methods. It is important to note that if you execute the current systems CMD.EXE and in cases of malware infection, it is possible that actions taken and data collected could be inaccurate and/or altered as the integrity of the interface cannot be validated. In either instance, PIRCS will still continue to perform full logging and recording of your activities, actions, and findings. To exit using the CMD.EXE process you can either type EXIT or utilize the STOP button on the PIRCS menu bar.

The methods and examples discussed below are all done under the premise of utilizing the PIRCS shell interface. Therefore, you may notice that certain commands that were discussed in Chapter 3 might not be utilized within the use cases described below.

So far, all of these examples utilize built-in Windows OS functions and utilities. Even with the multitude of ways to pull this information, you still have to execute multiple commands to get the data that is being sought after, namely the current system time and time zone. Another alternative is to locate and test third-party software and utilities that may do just as good, if not better job, for what you are looking for. To that end, and in continuing with the system time example, let us look at the DATE. EXE program, which is a part of the previously referenced GNU Win32 CoreUtil suite.

- **Date, time, and time zone via third-party tool DATE.** Even though this is a third-party tool, it maintains a relatively small footprint, provides its results very quickly, and its default output provides both sets of desired information together at one time. Additionally, while by default the output does not show sub-second details, it does maintain additional capabilities, through various command line options to customize its output and the level of detail to that needed. This utility is a part of the previously referenced GNU Win32 CoreUtils suite.

  D:\PIRCS\Tools\bin > date.exe

  Wed Jan 20 16:40:05 Eastern Standard Time 2016

Current network configuration

- **Current network configuration and connection state via built-in IPCONFIG command**. This method utilizes the same built-in Windows OS command as above, however it provides a greater level of depth and detail about various network settings that may be of value to an examiner, such as when the IP address was assigned to the host, network adapter Media Access Control (MAC) addresses, etc. It should be noted, that this method also provides another avenue of collecting and validating the host name of the system in question, as seen in the below example.

> *D:\PIRCS>**ipconfig /all***
>
> *Windows IP Configuration*
>   *Host Name . . . . : WindowsMachineName*
>   *Primary Dns Suffix . . . . :*
>   *Node Type . . . . : Hybrid*
>   *IP Routing Enabled. . . . . : No*
>   *WINS Proxy Enabled. . . . . : No*
>   *DNS Suffix Search List. . . . . . : twcny.rr.com*
>
> *Ethernet adapter Ethernet 2:*
>   *Media State . . . . : Media disconnected*
>   *Connection-specific DNS Suffix . :*
>   *Description . . . . : ASIX AX88179 USB 3.0 to Gigabit*
>   *Ethernet Adapter*
>   *Physical Address. . . . . : 00-0A-CD-28-37-40*
>   *DHCP Enabled. . . . . : Yes*
>   *Autoconfiguration Enabled . . . . : Yes*
>
> *Wireless LAN adapter Wi-Fi:*
>   *Connection-specific DNS Suffix . : twcny.rr.com*
>   *Description . . . . : Marvell AVASTAR Wireless-AC Network*
>   *Controller*
>   *Physical Address. . . . . : C0-33-5E-10-F8-25*
>   *DHCP Enabled. . . . . : Yes*
>   *Autoconfiguration Enabled . . . . : Yes*
>   *IPv4 Address. . . . . : 192.168.1.113(Preferred)*
>   *Subnet Mask . . . . : 255.255.255.0*
>   *Lease Obtained. . . . . : Saturday, January 23, 2016*
>   *2:32:02 PM*
>   *Lease Expires . . . . : Sunday, January 24, 2016 2:32:01 PM*
>   *Default Gateway . . . . : 192.168.1.1*
>   *DHCP Server . . . . : 192.168.1.1*
>   *DNS Servers . . . . : 192.168.1.1*
>   *NetBIOS over Tcpip. . . . . : Enabled*

Currently logged on user

- **Active user session via built-in WHOAMI command**. This method utilizes a built-in Windows OS command and quickly provides the user account name that is currently in use by the examiner. In instances where the examiner utilizes an active user session on a suspect system to perform evidence collection and triage, it is important to identify exactly what user account is being utilized. If the user account in question is a Windows Domain account, such as in a corporate network, the output of this command will prepend the domain name to the username, such as *domain\username*.

      D:\PIRCS> **whoami**

      jbartolomie

- **Currently logged on users via built-in QUSER utility**. This method utilizes a built-in Windows OS command and quickly provides a listing of all users that are currently logged into or have an active session on the suspect computer system. This method may not show users that may be remotely using shared resources of the system in question, such as accessing a shared folder or remotely opening a file.

      D:\PIRCS> **quser**

      USERNAME SESSIONNAME ID STATE IDLE TIME LOGON   TIME

      jbartolomie   console   2 Active   21:41 n   1/23/2016 1:37 PM

- **Currently logged on users via third-party tool PsLoggedOn**. There are multiple third-party tools that are available to provide more insight and details into currently logged on users, active user sessions, etc. One of the more popular is PsLoggedOn, which is available via the Microsoft SysInternals website. Even though this is a third-party tool, it maintains a relatively small footprint and is designed to provide details on currently logged on users as well as users that are logged on via shared resources. The SysInternals PsLoggedOn application can be obtained from https://technet.microsoft.com/en-us/sysinternals/bb897545.aspx.

      D:\PIRCS\Tools\PSTools> **psloggedon -accepteula**

      PsLoggedon v1.34 - See who's logged on
      Copyright (C) 2000-2010 Mark Russinovich
      Sysinternals - www.sysinternals.com

      Users logged on locally:
      *   1/23/2016 1:37:18 PM   workgroup\jbartolomie*

      No one is logged on via resource shares.

Initial host detail collection recommendation

Based on the above examples, and taking into consideration the following aspects including: information needed, impact to the system, standardized usage, and general applicability across multiple types of investigations, the left window within Fig. 5.1 highlights an initially recommended listing and sequence of commands.

FIG. 5.1

PIRCS initial host details sample screenshot.

NETWORK CONNECTIONS

It is important to identify and capture details surrounding current network connections and related activity. This information can reveal indicators of an attacker actively connected to a machine, malware that is attempting communication or waiting for instructions, or network resources that may be in use. In addition to this information's usefulness for identifying and correlating additional local system evidence, this detail is indispensable if you have access to or have been provided evidence from external sources, such as network or firewall traffic logs.

Active connections

- **Active connections via built-in NETSTAT utility**. This method utilizes a built-in Windows utility and can provide a very quick listing of established network connections as well as network connections that may be available on the host computer. This utility has a wide range of command line arguments that each can provide different levels of detail. The command listed below is a common one used within incident response as it not only lists active connections and their current state, but also correlates the process identifier (PID) that initiated the connection request itself.

Often times, malware has specific code and embedded instructions to either call out to specific location(s) on the Internet, such as a set of domain names or IP addresses, or to listen for specific incoming connections. There have been documented cases of malware that have been able to hide or otherwise obfuscate their active network connection in such a way that normal Windows OS utilities and commands would not report it. It is generally recommended in cases where malware might be present to utilize both built-in and third-party tools to identify active network connections, as any differences between the results could act as evidence in and of itself.

```
D:\PIRCS\>netstat -ano
Active Connections
   Proto Local Address      Foreign Address      State        PID
   TCP   0.0.0.0:5631        0.0.0.0:0           LISTENING    1748
   TCP   0.0.0.0:8083        0.0.0.0:0           LISTENING    2696
   TCP   192.168.1.113:37267 216.58.216.228:443  ESTABLISHED  5304
   TCP   192.168.1.113:37296 216.58.216.228:80   ESTABLISHED  5792
```

- **Active connections via third-party utility TCPVCON.** There are several third-party tools that are available to provide more insight and details into active network connections. One of the more widely maintained and utilized ones is the GUI based TCPView from Microsoft SysInternals. This utility comes bundled with a command-line version, TCPVCON, which can be utilized via the Windows CLI. This utility has a relatively small footprint and is designed to provide a listing of all active network connections, as well as map each to its parent process by name and PID. However, it should be noted that while this utility does display if the network connection is Transmission Control Protocol (TCP) or User Datagram Protocol (UDP) based, it does not provide applicable network port numbers that are in use for each connection. The SysInternals TCPVCON application can be obtained from https://technet.microsoft.com/en-us/sysinternals/tcpview.aspx.

```
D:\PIRCS\Tools\tcpview>tcpvcon -a -n -accepteula
TCPView v3.01 - TCP/UDP endpoint viewer
Copyright (C) 1998-2010 Mark Russinovich and Bryce Cogswell
Sysinternals - www.sysinternals.com

[TCP] iexplore.exe
    PID: 5304
    State: ESTABLISHED
    Local: 192.168.1.113
    Remote: 216.58.216.228
```

> *[TCP] iexplore.exe*
> *PID: 5792*
> *State: ESTABLISHED*
> *Local: 192.168.1.113*
> *Remote: 216.58.216.228*

- **Active connections via third-party utility CurrPorts.** Another more widely maintained and utilized network connection reporting utility is CurrPorts, by NirSoft. As with most NirSoft utilities, while it is primarily a GUI based utility, it can be executed directly via the command-line and have its output stored in a separate text file. This utility has a relatively small footprint and is designed to provide a listing of all active network connections, as well as additional information regarding each connection. Not only does this utility map network connections to their parent processes, it also includes details about the process itself, including when the process started and which user account executed the process. This software can be obtained from http://www.nirsoft.net/utils/cports.html.

> *D:\PIRCS\Tools\cport-x64 >* **cports /stext output.txt**

Sample of output from output.txt

```
===================================
Process Name    : IEXPLORE.EXE
Process ID      : 5304
Protocol        : TCP
Local Port      : 37267
Local Port Name :
Local Address   : 192.168.1.113
Remote Port     : 443
Remote Port Name : https
Remote Address  : 216.58.216.228
Remote Host Name :
State           : Established
Process Path    : C:\Program Files (x86)\Internet Explorer\
                      IEXPLORE.EXE
Product Name    : Internet Explorer
File Description : Internet Explorer
File Version    : 11.00.9600.16384 (winblue_rtm.130821-1623)
Company         : Microsoft Corporation
Process Created On: 1/26/2016 1:01:55 PM
User Name       : WORKGROUP\jbartolomie
Process Services :
Process Attributes: A
Added On        : 1/26/2016 1:26:45 PM
Module Filename :
```

Remote IP Country :
Window Title   :
=================================

=================================
Process Name   : IEXPLORE.EXE
Process ID   : 5792
Protocol   : TCP
Local Port   : 37296
Local Port Name :
Local Address   : 192.168.1.113
Remote Port   : 80
Remote Port Name : http
Remote Address   : 216.58.216.228
Remote Host Name :
State   : Established
Process Path   : C:\Program Files (x86)\Internet Explorer\
                  IEXPLORE.EXE
Product Name   : Internet Explorer
File Description : Internet Explorer
File Version   : 11.00.9600.16384 (winblue_rtm.130821-1623)
Company   : Microsoft Corporation
Process Created On: 1/26/2016 1:01:55 PM
User Name   : WORKGROUP\jbartolomie
Process Services :
Process Attributes: A
Added On   : 1/26/2016 1:26:45 PM
Module Filename :
Remote IP Country :
Window Title   :
=================================

- **Local system DNS history via built-in IPCONFIG command**. The Windows
  OS has a built-in command that enables a user to display the active cache of
  mapped DNS queries and their associated results. This method utilizes the
  IPCONFIG utility and can provide a very quick listing of recent queries and active
  DNS mappings, and maintains a small footprint on the system when executed.

  *D:\PIRCS>**ipconfig /displaydns***

  Windows IP Configuration

  www.google.com

```
----------------------------------------
Record Name . . . . . : www.google.com
Record Type . . . . . : 1
Time To Live . . . . : 16
Data Length . . . . . : 4
Section . . . . . . . : Answer
A (Host) Record . . . : 173.194.68.147

Record Name . . . . . : www.google.com
Record Type . . . . . : 1
Time To Live . . . . : 16
Data Length . . . . . : 4
Section . . . . . . . : Answer
A (Host) Record . . . : 173.194.68.99

Record Name . . . . . : www.google.com
Record Type . . . . . : 1
Time To Live . . . . : 16
Data Length . . . . . : 4
Section . . . . . . . : Answer
A (Host) Record . . . : 173.194.68.106

Record Name . . . . . : www.google.com
Record Type . . . . . : 1
Time To Live . . . . : 16
Data Length . . . . . : 4
Section . . . . . . . : Answer
A (Host) Record . . . : 173.194.68.103
```

- **Local system Address Resolution Protocol (ARP) cache via built-in ARP utility**. The Windows OS has a built-in command that enables a user to display the active ARP cache of the system, which can be used to identify other systems that have recently, or currently are, connected to the suspect system. The ARP cache provides a mapping of the connecting systems MAC addresses, otherwise known as hardware addresses, to their associated IP addresses. This command maintains a small footprint when executed.

```
D:\PIRCS>arp -a

Interface: 192.168.1.113 --- 0x4
  Internet Address      Physical Address      Type
  192.168.1.1           48-f8-b3-b3-c4-dc     dynamic
  192.168.1.255         ff-ff-ff-ff-ff-ff     static
```

224.0.0.22   01-00-5e-00-00-16 static
224.0.0.251   01-00-5e-00-00-fb static
224.0.0.252   01-00-5e-00-00-fc static
239.255.255.250 01-00-5e-7f-ff-fa static
255.255.255.255 ff-ff-ff-ff-ff-ff   static

- **Routing table via built-in ROUTE utility.** The Windows OS has a built-in command that enables a user to display active network routing information on the system. This information provides detail as to how requests to different IP ranges will be handled and directed. This command maintains a small footprint when executed.

*D:\PIRCS>**route PRINT***
```
=====================================
```
Interface List
7...c2 33 5e 10 f9 24 ......Microsoft Wi-Fi Direct Virtual Adapter
6...c0 33 5e 10 f8 26 ...... Bluetooth Device (Personal Area Network)
4...c0 33 5e 10 f8 25 ......Marvell AVASTAR Wireless-AC Network
Controller
1..........................Software Loopback Interface 1
8...00 00 00 00 00 00 00 e0 Microsoft ISATAP Adapter
9...00 00 00 00 00 00 00 e0 Teredo Tunneling Pseudo-Interface
```
=====================================
```

IPv4 Route Table
```
=====================================
```
Active Routes:

Network Destination	Netmask	Gateway	Interface	Metric
0.0.0.0	*0.0.0.0*	*192.168.1.1*	*192.168.1.113*	*25*
127.0.0.0	*255.0.0.0*	*On-link*	*127.0.0.1*	*306*
127.0.0.1	*255.255.255.255*	*On-link*	*127.0.0.1*	*306*
127.255.255.255	*255.255.255.255*	*On-link*	*127.0.0.1*	*306*
192.168.1.0	*255.255.255.0*	*On-link*	*192.168.1.113*	*281*
192.168.1.113	*255.255.255.255*	*On-link*	*192.168.1.113*	*281*
192.168.1.255	*255.255.255.255*	*On-link*	*192.168.1.113*	*281*
224.0.0.0	*240.0.0.0*	*On-link*	*127.0.0.1*	*306*
224.0.0.0 ·	*240.0.0.0*	*On-link*	*192.168.1.113*	*281*
255.255.255.255	*255.255.255.255*	*On-link*	*127.0.0.1*	*306*
255.255.255.255	*255.255.255.255*	*On-link*	*192.168.1.113*	*281*

```
=====================================
```
Persistent Routes:
None

Network connection collection recommendation

Based on the above examples, and taking into consideration certain aspects such as the information needed, impact to the system, standardized usage, and general applicability across multiple types of investigations, the left window in Fig. 5.2 highlights an initially recommended listing and sequence of commands.

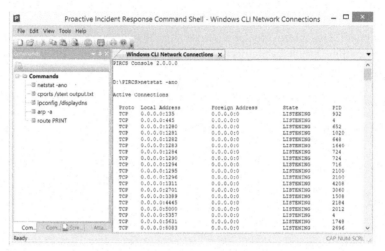

FIG. 5.2

PIRCS network connection collection sample screenshot.

ACTIVE PROCESS, SERVICES, AND SCHEDULED TASKS DETAILS

Knowing what processes, services, and scheduled tasks are actively running on a suspect system is a key component within incident response. Being able to identify current running applications, services, and tasks provides potential insight into how the system in question is being used and what it is being used for. Collecting information relating to running processes can be a full-time study in and of itself. There are multiple layers of depth, detail, and artifacts that can be collected, analyzed, and correlated to provide any layer of context and perspective needed. This includes utilizing methods and tools to perform partial memory captures, specific to individual processes of interest.

As with previous evidence categories, the following sections will review the high level areas of interest and methodologies that can be employed by an examiner to gain initial actionable intelligence in a manner that best maintains the overall integrity of the evidence and the system as a whole.

- **Basic process information via built-in TASKLIST utility**. This method utilizes a built-in Windows utility and provides a very quick listing of active processes and includes details such as the process name, the PIDs, the context under which it was started (such as a service or via a user session), and its overall memory usage. This utility has a wide range of command line arguments that each can provide different levels of detail. For this example we are going to use the basic command and take a look at its output.

D:\PIRCS>**tasklist**

Image Name	PID	Session Name	Session#	Mem Usage
System Idle Process	0	Services	0	4 K
System	4	Services	0	3,008 K
smss.exe	384	Services	0	548 K
csrss.exe	584	Services	0	2,608 K
wininit.exe	652	Services	0	2,148 K
services.exe	716	Services	0	8,828 K
lsass.exe	724	Services	0	21,816 K
svchost.exe	868	Services	0	13,288 K
svchost.exe	932	Services	0	10,164 K
svchost.exe	1020	Services	0	25,844 K
svchost.exe	420	Services	0	45,128 K

- **Process and loaded DLL information via built-in TASKLIST utility**. This method utilizes a built-in Windows utility and provides a very quick listing of active processes and includes details such as the process name, the PIDs, the context under which it was started (such as a service or via a user session), and its overall memory usage. This utility has a wide range of command line arguments that each can provide different levels of detail. For this example we are going to use a command-line argument to display all loaded system modules for each running process.

D:\PIRCS >**tasklist /m**

Image Name	PID	Modules
System Idle Process	0	N/A
System	4	N/A
smss.exe	384	N/A
csrss.exe	584	N/A
wininit.exe	652	ntdll.dll, KERNEL32.DLL, KERNELBASE.dll, msvcrt.dll, RPCRT4.dll, sechost.dll, profapi.dll, PGHook.dll, ADVAPI32.dll, CRYPTSP.dll, rsaenh.dll, bcrypt.dll, CRYPTBASE.dll, bcryptPrimitives.dll, PSAPI.DLL, wininitext.dll, USER32.dll, GDI32.dll, WS2_32.dll, NSI.dll, mswsock.dll, sspicli.dll, wtsapi32.dll, WINSTA.dll

- **Process and service information via built-in TASKLIST utility**. This method utilizes a built-in Windows utility and provides a very quick listing of active processes and includes details such as the process name, the PIDs, the context under which it was started (such as a service or via a user session), and its overall memory usage. This utility has a wide range of command line arguments that each can provide different levels of detail. For this example we are going to use a command-line argument to display any Windows services that may be associated with each running process.

*D:\PIRCS > **tasklist /svc***

Image Name	PID	Services
System Idle Process	0	N/A
System	4	N/A
smss.exe	384	N/A
csrss.exe	584	N/A
wininit.exe	652	N/A
services.exe	716	N/A
lsass.exe	724	KeyIso, Netlogon, SamSs, VaultSvc
svchost.exe	868	BrokerInfrastructure, DcomLaunch, LSM, PlugPlay, Power, SystemEventsBroker
svchost.exe	932	RpcEptMapper, RpcSs
svchost.exe	1020	Audiosrv, Dhcp, EventLog, lmhosts, Wcmsvc, wscsvc

- **Service information via built-in SC utility**. This method utilizes a built-in Windows utility and provides a listing of services that are currently installed and includes details such as the service name, the type of service, execution state, and PID.

*D:\PIRCS > **sc queryex***

```
SERVICE_NAME: AdobeARMservice
DISPLAY_NAME: Adobe Acrobat Update Service
        TYPE        : 10 WIN32_OWN_PROCESS
        STATE       : 4 RUNNING
                      (STOPPABLE, NOT_PAUSABLE,
                      IGNORES_SHUTDOWN)
        WIN32_EXIT_CODE   : 0 (0x0)
        SERVICE_EXIT_CODE : 0 (0x0)
        CHECKPOINT      : 0x0
        WAIT_HINT       : 0x0
        PID         : 1964
        FLAGS       :
```

SERVICE_NAME: Bonjour Service
DISPLAY_NAME: Bonjour Service
 TYPE : 10 WIN32_OWN_PROCESS
 STATE : 4 RUNNING
    (STOPPABLE, NOT_PAUSABLE,
    ACCEPTS_SHUTDOWN)
 WIN32_EXIT_CODE : 0 (0x0)
 SERVICE_EXIT_CODE : 0 (0x0)
 CHECKPOINT : 0x0
 WAIT_HINT : 0x0
 PID : 876
 FLAGS :

- **Process and user-mapping information via built-in TASKLIST utility**. This method utilizes a built-in Windows utility and provides a very quick listing of active processes and includes details such as the process name, the PIDs, the context under which it was started (such as a service or via a user session), and its overall memory usage. This utility has a wide range of command line arguments that each can provide different levels of detail. For this example we are going to a command-line argument to display the user account that was used to initiate each process.

 *D:\PIRCS\Tools > **tasklist /V /FO LIST***

 Image Name: System Idle Process
 PID: 0
 Session Name: Services
 Session#: 0
 Mem Usage: 4 K
 Status: Unknown
 User Name: NT AUTHORITY\SYSTEM
 CPU Time: 313:15:06
 Window Title: N/A

 Image Name: smss.exe
 PID: 384
 Session Name: Services
 Session#: 0
 Mem Usage: 548 K
 Status: Unknown
 User Name: NT AUTHORITY\SYSTEM
 CPU Time: 0:00:00
 Window Title: N/A

 Image Name: csrss.exe
 PID: 584

> Session Name: Services
> Session#:   0
> Mem Usage: 2,608 K
> Status: Unknown
> User Name: NT AUTHORITY\SYSTEM
> CPU Time: 0:00:11
> Window Title: N/A
>
> Image Name: wininit.exe
> PID: 652
> Session Name: Services
> Session#:   0
> Mem Usage: 2,148 K
> Status: Unknown
> User Name: NT AUTHORITY\SYSTEM
> CPU Time: 0:00:00
> Window Title: N/A

- **Process information via third-party tool PsList**. This method utilizes a third-party utility from Microsoft SysInternals called PsList. It provides a quick listing of running processes and can provide you with the amount of time each process has been running. PsList is a part of the Sysinternals PSTools suite and can be obtained from https://technet.microsoft.com/en-us/sysinternals/pslist.aspx.

> D:\PIRCS\Tools\PSTools>**pslist -accepteula**
> pslist v1.3 - Sysinternals PsList
> Copyright (C) 2000-2012 Mark Russinovich
> Sysinternals - www.sysinternals.com
>
> Process information for WindowsMachineName:

Name	Pid	Pri	Thd	Hnd	Priv	CPU Time	Elapsed Time
Idle	0	0	4	0	0	313:29:48.078	101:26:23.431
System	4	8	157	1747	3752	1:18:24.968	101:26:23.431
smss	384	11	2	44	284	0:00:00.406	101:26:23.416
csrss	584	13	10	577	2148	0:00:11.437	101:26:18.562
wininit	652	13	1	94	1640	0:00:00.187	101:26:18.202
services	716	9	4	320	6508	0:22:43.140	101:26:17.984
lsass	724	9	9	1967	14384	0:02:13.468	101:26:17.968
svchost	868	8	9	518	8632	0:00:32.328	101:26:12.695

- **Scheduled task information via built-in SCHTASKS utility**. This method utilizes a built-in Windows utility and provides a listing of all scheduled tasks and their associated details such as the task name, the next run time, and status. The output listed below has been formatted as a list.

```
D:\PIRCS>schtasks /Query
Folder: \
TaskName                    Next Run Time      Status
================================================
Adobe Acrobat Update Task        N/A              Ready
Adobe Flash Player Updater       1/26/2016 6:03:00 PM Ready
Microsoft_Hardware_Launch_ipoint_exe   N/A         Ready
Microsoft_Hardware_Launch_itype_exe    N/A         Ready
Microsoft_Hardware_Launch_mousekeyboardc N/A       Ready
Microsoft_MKC_Logon_Task_ipoint.exe    N/A         Ready
Microsoft_MKC_Logon_Task_itype.exe     N/A         Ready
User_Feed_Synchronization        1/26/2016 7:19:01 PM Ready

Folder: \Microsoft
TaskName                    Next Run Time      Status
================================================
INFO: There are no scheduled tasks presently available at your
      access level.

Folder: \Microsoft\Configuration Manager
TaskName                    Next Run Time      Status
================================================
Configuration Manager Health Evaluation N/A        Ready
Configuration Manager Idle Detection   N/A         Ready
Configuration Manager Maintenance      N/A         Ready
```

WINDOWS PREFETCH FILES

In an effort to provide process execution optimization, the Windows OS has the capability, if enabled, to create and utilize a prefetch file. These files contain details about the application in question, and are used as a method of providing execution details that will enable the application to launch quicker on subsequent uses. As such, if an application is executed on a Windows OS, it may generate a prefetch file. These files create a wealth of information about the application they were created for, including aspects such as the date when the program was first executed, the date of its most recent execution, the number of times it has been executed, and the path and related files that are accessed when the application is started. This information has the potential to provide insight into recent applications that have been executed, how often they are used, and could identify user or malicious activity.

- **Windows prefetch collection via third-party utility WinPrefetchView**. The Windows OS does not have a built-in prefetch collection or parsing utility. There are several utilities that can be used to collect and parse these files, and of the more commonly utilized ones is WinPrefetchView by NirSoft. As with most NirSoft utilities, while it is primarily a GUI based utility, it can be executed directly via the command-line and have its output stored in a separate text file. This utility has a relatively small footprint and is designed to automatically locate the default Windows OS prefetch storage path and parse all available prefetch files on the system in question. This software can be obtained from http://www. nirsoft.net/utils/win_prefetch_view.html.

*D:\PIRCS\Tools\winprefetchview-x64>**winprefetchview /stext output.txt***

Sample of output from output.txt

```
=====================================
Filename        : IEXPLORE.EXE-7A9337F2.pf
Created Time    : 12/21/2015 4:14:45 PM
Modified Time   : 1/26/2016 2:09:34 PM
File Size       : 115,066
Process EXE     : IEXPLORE.EXE
Process Path    : C:\PROGRAM FILES\INTERNET EXPLORER\
                    iexplore.exe
Run Counter     : 46
Last Run Time   : 1/26/2016 2:09:24 PM, 1/26/2016 12:37:58 PM,
                    1/26/2016 12:28:57 PM, 1/26/2016 12:16:35 PM,
                    1/26/2016 12:13:13 PM, 1/25/2016 5:17:46 PM,
                    1/25/2016 4:51:16 PM, 1/25/2016 3:43:59 PM
Missing Process : No
=====================================
=====================================
Filename        : PIRCSX64.BIN-1AE20AF6.pf
Created Time    : 1/4/2016 2:48:22 PM
Modified Time   : 1/25/2016 2:27:50 PM
File Size       : 59,420
Process EXE     : PIRCSX64.BIN
Process Path    : D:\PIRCS\PIRCSx64.bin
Run Counter     : 31
Last Run Time   : 1/25/2016 2:27:40 PM, 1/25/2016 2:14:23 PM,
                    1/25/2016 2:12:22 PM, 1/22/2016 12:53:14 PM,
                    1/20/2016 11:35:25 AM, 1/19/2016 5:39:43 PM,
                    1/19/2016 12:53:47 PM, 1/18/2016 8:58:48 PM
Missing Process : No
=====================================
=====================================
Filename        : PUTTY.EXE-D43C026F.pf
Created Time    : 1/5/2016 3:00:55 PM
```

```
Modified Time    : 1/22/2016 1:52:03 PM
File Size        : 39,512
Process EXE      : PUTTY.EXE
Process Path     : C:\PROGRAM FILES (X86)\PuTTY\putty.exe
Run Counter      : 8
Last Run Time    : 1/22/2016 1:52:02 PM, 1/21/2016 5:19:58 PM,
                   1/21/2016 12:27:31 PM, 1/20/2016 12:16:33 PM,
                   1/20/2016 11:14:20 AM, 1/18/2016 11:28:00 AM,
                   1/8/2016 1:29:52 PM, 1/5/2016 3:00:45 PM
Missing Process  : No
=====================================
=====================================
Filename         : REDLINE.EXE-55EEA7F1.pf
Created Time     : 1/22/2016 3:43:56 PM
Modified Time    : 1/22/2016 4:21:24 PM
File Size        : 353,986
Process EXE      : REDLINE.EXE
Process Path     : C:\PROGRAM FILES (X86)\Redline\Redline.exe
Run Counter      : 3
Last Run Time    : 1/22/2016 4:21:14 PM, 1/22/2016 3:49:13 PM,
                   1/22/2016 3:43:46 PM
Missing Process  : No
=====================================
```

WEB BROWSER HISTORY

There is a wide variety of web browsers available, including: Internet Explorer, Chrome, Firefox, and Safari. Each of these browsers, as well as different versions of these browsers, create and store different types and amounts of information, history, and cached data relating to a user's web browsing activity in locations and ways that are specific to themselves. Generally speaking, there are five distinct facets of data that an examiner could have interest with regard to a system's web browsing activity: website history, cookie history, file download history, cache files, and form history. This in turn, makes it more difficult for an incident responder to adequately collect web browsing history and artifacts from a suspect machine, as they often do not have foreknowledge of what browsers are, or were, in use on the system prior to their investigation.

There are a variety of tools that are available to help an examiner collect, parse, and analyze web browsing history. While software developers, such as NirSoft, provide full suites of useful software that are browser specific, there are very few free or low cost utilities that will look for artifacts from multiple web browsers at one time.

One of the utilities that will search for and parse objects for the most common web browsers is Mandiant's/FireEye's Redline software. This software package has a wide range of capabilities and functionalities, one of which is the ability to allow an examiner to create "Portable Collectors," which are user customized scripts. Once created, and copied onto appropriate portable media, these collectors can be utilized by executing within the Windows CLI by using the provided batch file. As with the full memory capture process previously discussed, the output from these collectors are stored within a folder hierarchy to help categorize them by individual systems and runtimes. However, unlike the memory capture process, the output of most of the collectors is in a specific and custom XML format. The good news here is that XML files are essentially text files and can be opened in any text editor and even within Microsoft Excel. Additionally, the output can be imported and analyzed within the Redline GUI, as seen in Fig. 5.3.

FIG. 5.3

Mandiant redline web browser history sample screenshot.

As a method of obtaining evidence with a high degree of integrity, unless the potentially used browsers are known beforehand, and raw browser history files are required by you or your organization, it is highly recommended to make use of this, or similar, technology. Refer to Redlines documentation as to the overall process used to create a portable collector.

WINDOWS REGISTRY DATA COLLECTION

The Windows OS registry is a hierarchical database that stores a wealth of configuration data settings for the overall OS as well as how applications make use of it. There is a profusion of viable evidence available within the registry, and as such there are many considerations that an examiner needs to weigh prior to interacting with it on a suspect system. As with other components within the Windows OS, interacting with and querying the registry can inject inadvertent and unrealized changes or alterations to it that may affect later analysis and findings. At its basic, the Windows Registry is composed of hives, keys, subkeys, and values. A hive is a logical grouping or collection of keys, subkeys, and values. At the storage level, each hive is made up of a set of supporting system files.

As the registry is a substantial repository of evidence, it is often a good idea to obtain a copy of their associated system files in their entirety prior to initiating various queries and searches against it. This way, the original state of the suspect system's registry is preserved as much as possible prior to any subsequent queries that need to be made against the running system's registry. Additionally, more robust and exhaustive registry based utilities can also be leveraged against the backed-up copies off of the suspect system.

The examples below will highlight where and how to backup the registry hives, as well as a few small utilities that can be executed on the suspect system to obtain quick details that could provide actionable intelligence for your investigation.

- **Backup of raw registry files via third-party utility HoboCopy**. Since the registry hive files are system files that are in a constant state of use, you cannot just simply copy them using normal utilities. There are several commercial third-party utilities that will enable you to copy locked or in-use files. As a free alternative, there is a tool called HoboCopy that works just as well. While the software is a little older, you can obtain versions for both 32-bit and 64-bit Windows OS's. HoboCopy has been tested to work on systems as new as Windows 8.1. Both versions of this software can be obtained from http://candera. github.io/hobocopy/.

> *D:\PIRCS\Tools\hobocopy >* **hobocopy c:\windows\system32\config**
>   **D:\RegistryBackup**
>
> *HoboCopy (c) 2006 Wangdera Corporation. hobocopy@wangdera.com*
>
> *Starting a full copy from c:\windows\system32\config\ to*
> *D:\registrybackup*
> *Copied directory*
> *Backup successfully completed.*
> *Backup started at 2016-01-26 21:03:15, completed at 2016-01-26*
>   *21:03:54.*
> *65 files (253.44 MB, 1 directories) copied, 0 files skipped*

- **USB history (registry query) via third-party utility USBDeview.** The Windows OS does not have a built-in utility to list the history of USB devices that have been connected to a system. There are several utilities that can be used to collect and parse these files. One of the more commonly utilized utilities is called USBDeview by NirSoft. As with most NirSoft utilities, while it is primarily a GUI based utility, it can be executed directly via the command-line and have its output stored in a separate text file. This utility has a relatively small footprint and is designed to automatically query the Windows registry to obtain and parse available history on USB devices that have been connected to the machine in question. This software can be obtained from http://www.nirsoft.net/utils/usb_ devices_view.html.

*D:\PIRCS\Tools\usbdeview-x64 >**usbdeview /stext output.txt***

Sample of output from output.txt

```
=====================================
Device Name     : Port_#0001.Hub_#0001
Description     : Apple iPhone
Device Type     : Still Imaging
Connected       : No
Safe To Unplug  : Yes
Disabled        : No
USB Hub         : No
Drive Letter    :
Serial Number   : 0
Created Date    : 1/15/2016 12:05:40 PM
Last Plug/Unplug Date: 1/7/2016 11:40:08 AM
VendorID        : 05ac
ProductID       : 12a8
Firmware Revision : 6.01
USB Class       : 06
USB SubClass    : 01
USB Protocol    : 01
Hub / Port      :
Computer Name   :
Vendor Name     :
Product Name    :
ParentId Prefix :
Service Name    : WUDFWpdMtp
Service Description:
Driver Filename : WUDFRd.sys
Device Class    : _X
Device Mfg      : Apple Inc.
Power           :
USB Version     :
Driver Description: Apple iPhone
Driver Version  : 6.3.9600.17415
Driver InfSection : MTP
Driver InfPath  : wpdmtp.inf
Instance ID     : USB\VID_05AC&PID_12A8&MI_00\0
Capabilities    : Removable, UniqueID, SurpriseRemovalOK
=====================================


=====================================
Device Name     : Port_#0003.Hub_#0002
Description     : WD My Passport 0740 USB Device
Device Type     : Mass Storage
```

```
Connected        : No
Safe To Unplug   : Yes
Disabled         : No
USB Hub          : No
Drive Letter     :
Serial Number    : WXH1C12F5688
Created Date      : 2/6/2015 2:01:08 PM
Last Plug/Unplug Date: 2/6/2015 2:01:08 PM
VendorID         : 1058
ProductID        : 0740
Firmware Revision : 10.19
USB Class        : 08
USB SubClass     : 06
USB Protocol     : 50
Hub / Port       :
Computer Name    :
Vendor Name      :
Product Name     :
ParentId Prefix  :
Service Name     : USBSTOR
Service Description: @usbstor.inf,%USBSTOR.SvcDesc%;USB
                    Mass Storage Driver
Driver Filename  : USBSTOR.SYS
Device Class     : _X
Device Mfg       : Compatible USB storage device
Power            :
USB Version      :
Driver Description: USB Mass Storage Device
Driver Version   : 6.3.9600.17331
Driver InfSection : USBSTOR_BULK.NT
Driver InfPath   : usbstor.inf
Instance ID      : USB\VID_1058&PID_0740\
                    575848314331324635363838
Capabilities     : Removable, UniqueID, SurpriseRemovalOK
=======================================
```

- **Auto-start on boot or logon applications via third-party utility AUTORUNSC.** There are several third-party tools that are available to provide more insight and details into active network connections. One of the more widely maintained and utilized utilities is the GUI based Autoruns from Microsoft SysInternals. This utility comes bundled with a command-line version, AUTORUNSC, which can be utilized via the Windows CLI. This utility has a relatively small footprint and is designed to query the various locations available for auto-start configurations. This software can be obtained from https://technet. microsoft.com/en-us/sysinternals/bb963902.aspx.

*D:\PIRCS\Tools\Autoruns > **autorunsc –a bl -accepteula***

Sysinternals Autoruns v13.51 - Autostart program viewer
Copyright (C) 2002-2015 Mark Russinovich
Sysinternals - www.sysinternals.com

HKLM\SOFTWARE\Microsoft\Windows\CurrentVersion\Run
  iTunesHelper
   "C:\Program Files\iTunes\iTunesHelper.exe"
   iTunesHelper
   Apple Inc.
   12.3.1.23
   c:\program files\itunes\ituneshelper.exe
   10/16/2015 4:19 AM

HKLM\SOFTWARE\Wow6432Node\Microsoft\Windows
  CurrentVersion\Run
  SunJavaUpdateSched
   "C:\Program Files (x86)\Common Files\Java\Java Update
     jusched.exe"
   Java Update Scheduler
   Oracle Corporation
   2.8.51.16
   c:\program files (x86)\common files\java\java update\jusched.exe
   6/8/2015 9:06 PM

WINDOWS EVENT LOGS

Depending on the version of Windows that is being investigated, a wide variation of
log files may be available. Windows event logs are a considerable repository of evidence, and if possible it is recommended to obtain a copy of them in their entirety and
perform parsing and/or viewing actions on a machine other than the one under analysis. However, it is important to note that depending on the version of Windows you
are investigating, the type, quantity, and location of the Windows Event Logs could
vary. Additionally, more robust and exhaustive registry based utilities can also be
leveraged against the backed-up copies, off of the suspect system.

- **Backup of raw Windows 8.1 event logs via third-party utility HoboCopy**. As
  the Windows event log files are system files that are in a constant state of use, you
  cannot just simply copy them using normal utilities. There are several
  commercial third-party utilities that will enable you to copy locked or in-use files,
  however there is a free alternative called HoboCopy that works just as well.
  While the software is a little older, you can obtain versions for both 32-bit and
  64-bit Windows OS's, and it has been tested to work on systems as new as

Windows 8.1. Both versions of this software can be obtained here: http://candera. github.io/hobocopy/.

> *D:\PIRCS\Tools\hobocopy > **hobocopy c:\windows\system32\winevt\ logs\ D:\LogBackup***

> *HoboCopy (c) 2006 Wangdera Corporation. hobocopy@wangdera.com*

> *Starting a full copy from c:\windows\system32\winevt\Logs\ to d:\ LogBackup*
> *Copied directory*
> *Backup successfully completed.*
> *Backup started at 2016-01-26 21:07:19, completed at 2016-01-26 21:08:06.*
> *192 files (245.14 MB, 1 directories) copied, 0 files skipped*

- **Windows event log parsing via third-party utility PsLogList**. There are several third-party tools that are available to parse and display the contents of the Windows event logs. Depending on your situation and circumstances, you may only be interested in a certain segment or duration of logs, have an immediate need to identify some details, or would otherwise rather parse the logs directly on the suspect system. This activity will have a variable footprint on the suspect system, depending on which event log is being parsed, the size of the event logs, and the scope of the parsing or export that is being executed. The example below is a query specifically looking for Windows 8.1 User Logon Events only.

There are a multitude of excellent online resources that provide insight and details into Windows Event Logs and associated Event IDs. Each version of the Windows OS tends to utilize different event types and event IDs. Additionally the types of events that are recorded within the Windows Event Logs can vary depending on OS version and various configurations and settings. A good resource for looking up specific Event IDs can be found at http://www.eventid.net/

> *D:\PIRCS\Tools\PSTools > **psloglist -i 4624 security -accepteula***

> *PsLoglist v2.71 - local and remote event log viewer*
> *Copyright (C) 2000-2009 Mark Russinovich*
> *Sysinternals - www.sysinternals.com*

> *Security log on \\WindowsMachineName:*
> *[119653] Microsoft-Windows-Security-Auditing*
> *Type: SUCCESS AUDIT*
> *Computer: WINDOWSMACHINENAME*
> *Time: 1/27/2016 2:12:01 PM ID: 4624*

An account was successfully logged on.
  Subject:
     Security ID: *S-1-5-18*
     Account Name: *JBARTOLOMIE*
     Account Domain: *WORKGROUP*
  Logon ID: *0x6e89984*
     Logon GUID: *{00000000-0000-0000-0000-000000000000}*
  Process Information:
     Process ID: *0xf58*
     Process Name: *C:\Windows\System32\winlogon.exe*
  Network Information:
     Workstation Name: *WINDOWSMACHINENAME*
     Source Network Address: 127.0.0.1
     Source Port: *0*
  Detailed Authentication Information:
     Logon Process: *User32*
     Authentication Package: Negotiate
     Transited Services: *-*
     Package Name (NTLM only):   *-*
     Key Length: *0*

FILE LISTINGS

Depending on the circumstances surrounding the investigation, as an examiner you may want to obtain at least a basic listing of files that are either within a specific location or on the system as a whole. While this can be done as needed with standard Windows CLI commands, doing so across the whole system or haphazardly can inject change onto the files themselves, such as by potentially altering their last access dates/times. As such, it is often times better to obtain a full listing of files and capture details such as their date and time stamp, as well as any additional information that may be of value, depending upon your need. The purpose, need, and impact of these actions are unique to each situation and as such, the impact from this activity is dependent on how the listing is obtained, the scope of the listing, and what details are being looked for.

One of the utilities that can be preconfigured to enumerate and generate a listing of files on a system is Mandiant's/FireEye's Redline software. This software package has a wide range of capabilities and functionalities, one of which is the ability to allow an examiner to create "Portable Collectors," which are user customized scripts. Once created and copied onto appropriate portable media, these collectors can utilized by executing within the Windows CLI by using the provided batch file. As with the full memory capture and web browsing history processes previously discussed, the output from these collectors are stored within a folder hierarchy to help categorize them by individual systems and runtimes. However, unlike the memory capture process, the output of most of the collectors is in a specific and custom XML format.

The good news here is that XML files are essentially text files and can be opened in any text editor and even within Microsoft Excel. Additionally, the output can be imported and analyzed within the Redline GUI.

As a method of obtaining evidence with a high degree of integrity, if you have the need to obtain a listing of all files on a suspect system, or need to obtain a deeper amount of information about all the files at the same time as obtaining a listing of them, it is highly recommended to make use of this, or similar, technology. Redline has a wide range of capabilities that can be enabled when enumerating a listing of files on a system, to include performing digital signature validation, performing hashing of the files, or even searching and reporting back only files that meet user defined criteria. Refer to Redlines documentation as to the overall process used to create a portable collector.

USE CASE EXAMPLES

The type and priority of potential evidence that is deemed most useful is generally dependent upon the specific situation and type of incident the examiner is faced with. Most investigations and evidence collection activities occur in an iterative fashion, meaning that data discovered is not simply documented and forgotten. Rather, data discovered from one source of information needs to be leveraged and correlated across other aspects of the investigation (network, host, and log). The iterative correlation of data should augment the scope of the investigation by enhancing the examiner's understanding of the situation at hand and identifying new potential evidence that should also be collected. Thus, the data that would be valuable to you and your investigation is contingent upon the type of case you are confronted with.

While Locard's Principle and Order of Volatility need to be considered, there are times when the investigation uncovers a situation where evidence, that may generally have a lower volatility, would need to be immediately collected (ie, Windows Event Logs are in risk of being destroyed or otherwise altered and as such their collection may supersede something with a higher volatility).

Take, for example, the following situations:

- You are faced with a situation that appears to be the result of a phishing attack on a corporate system. Generally, in these instances, evidence that may be of most value to you would consist of the suspicious email itself, temporary files, active processes, network connections and activity, process-to-network mapping details, and any recent system or service changes.
- You are confronted with an employee that is suspected of stealing or sending proprietary corporate information outside of the company. In this case, you may be interested in recently accessed files and network shares, a listing of all files on the user's computer, network connections and activity, web browsing history, etc.
- A critical corporate server is part of a known active corporate intrusion with customized or otherwise unknown malware. As this is a critical system with

an unknown threat on it, the best course of action may be to immediately initiate a full active memory capture to obtain the best possible level of evidence from this highly volatile source.

- A historical activity recreation investigation that is not focused on current system activities or running processes. The focus on this would be to collect evidence to construct a chronological string of events and activity for a corporate internal or external audit, then evidence of lower volatility, such as Windows Event Logs, may be collected prior to the collection of evidence with a higher volatility. In cases such as this, evidence of higher volatility may not even be needed as they have no bearing on the investigation.

As we discussed evidence categorization and a breakdown of methodologies within the previous section, this section is going to review a mix of different use cases and situational scenarios that may be encountered. These will provide a high level overview of potential evidence of value, acquisition prioritization, order of operations, impact considerations, and several best practices.

The purpose of the Use Case examples listed below is not to document a step-by-step set of procedures on specific tools or commands but to provide you with a starting point and understanding of potential key pieces of evidence, collection methods, and a high level walkthrough of potential evidence prioritization.

To standardize the context of each Use Case listed below, it is assumed that the examiner has physical access to the suspect system in question, that the system OS is Windows 7 or greater, it is unlocked, and that the analyst is utilizing a copy of PIRCS on a clean external USB thumb drive. As the PIRCS software provides an acceptable level of activity recording and integrity validation, steps that would normally be taken for aspects such as procedural and findings documentation will not be included within these Use Cases. In instances where PIRCS may not be in use, it is expected that you are leveraging the Windows CLI output redirection arguments (> and >>), as described in Chapter 3, to capture the output of your commands or tools where needed.

SPEAR PHISHING ATTACK SCENARIO

Spear phishing is a form of social engineering attack where a personalized email message is sent to a specific target with the intent of enticing them to either provide information, perform an action, or gain their trust.

To adequately tailor the email, the attacker often researches the targets recent activities, through available and public sources, such as social media. Alternatively, attackers have also been known to compromise the email accounts of individuals the target already knows and trusts, which in turn increases the likelihood of the target providing the requested information, or performing the requested or desired actions.

A senior executive in your organization received an email from what appeared to be from an outsourced financial consultant. The e-mail had a spreadsheet attached to it. The name of the spreadsheet made it appear to be related to the finances of a project in a different part of the organization on which the consultant was working. Upon trying to open the attachment in Microsoft Excel, the software crashed and since then, the executive's computer appeared to be running poorly. The executive reached out to the project manager and inquired as to why the email was sent, and it was discovered that the sender was not known to anyone and was not a part of the outsourced team.

You have been tasked with performing initial evidence collection and triage on the senior executive's computer system so that you can provide the evidence to the organization's incident response team for analysis.

When collecting evidence for analysis from a system that may involve malware, there needs to be a high level of focus and awareness of highly volatile data. Often times, a large amount of valuable information about a malware infection resides in the system's memory, is time sensitive, and can be easily and quickly lost. These types of cases are very dynamic, as the scope and depth of response is dictated by a multitude of factors including the organization's incident response or handling policy, the role and value of the system in question, and the scope of the investigation.

Handle all potential malware with caution

Malware authors develop their code so that it has the capability to self-replicate, morph in order to avoid detection by antivirus software, and impersonate other programs to bypass traditional cyber security defenses such as firewalls, intrusion prevention systems, and antivirus suites.

Cross contamination is always a concern and a risk whenever an examiner handles potential malware. Inadvertent execution or self-replication increases the chance of lateral infection to an examiner's portable media and/or systems. If the potential malware sample is an executable file, a common best practice is to rename the file extension, to something like .ex_, to prevent accidental execution. This small change will help prevent the unintentional execution of the potential malware by the examiner as well as anyone who may be unaware of the malicious nature of the file in question.

In a scenario such as this, while you are attempting to determine a malware infection or perform malware discovery, the basic outline below highlights a standard breakdown of evidence collection actions and priorities.

1. **Obtain system date and time details**
2. **Perform full memory capture**

  Note: As the system in question is known, the employee is known, and there is no question that you are at the correct machine, performing a full memory capture prior to anything else is a viable action in this case. In other instances of malware discovery, you may want to obtain details such as the system name and OS version first. In cases of malware, if you need to potentially obtain a copy of the malware for reverse engineering or other analysis, performing a full memory capture is always recommended. There are times when malware files themselves are encrypted and are only in a decrypted state when actively running on a computer system. Additionally there are times when only parts of the malware are stored as a file on the system or the malware is memory resident only. Being able to carve malware components and samples from memory can greatly aid in an investigation.

3. **Obtain system name and OS version**
4. **Identify network configuration details**
5. **Obtain currently logged on users**
6. **Identify all active network connections**

    Note: As this is a case where malware is potentially present, it is highly recommended, as mentioned in this Active Network Connections section above, that you utilize both the built-in Windows command as well as a tested third-party tool to collect and compare this information.

7. **Acquire the contents of DNS and ARP cache, and the systems routing table**
8. **Inspect running processes**

    Note: To obtain the best understanding of processes that are running, what files they may be using, when they were started, and who started them; there are several initial commands you may want to execute and capture the output from. An example of some of the commands/tools you may want to consider are provided below:

    a. tasklist /v
    b. tasklist /m
    c. tasklist /svc
    d. pslist

9. **Examine system services and scheduled tasks**
10. **Collect and parse Windows prefetch files**
11. **Copy or export Windows Registry hive**
12. **Copy or export Windows Event log files**
13. **Obtain a full listing of all files on the computer system**

    Note: In instances of malware, it is recommended to utilize a tool such as Redline, as it has the ability of providing deeper information about a file, such as verifying the digital signature of system files etc. Additionally, in some instances these utilities are able to identify and list files that may be intentionally and maliciously hidden from the OS itself.

As you can see in the above outline, we did not collect or capture any evidence relating to web browsing history. A majority of malware does not make use of web browsers or related technology to communicate externally. Since we already are aware of the most likely infection vector of the possible malware, an email attachment and not due to web browsing, there is no immediate need or value in collecting this information. In instances where a system has potential malware and the infection vector is unknown, we would have recommended performing a web browser history collection, as well as additional details from the registry such as recent USB devices as they are common infection vectors.

Human resources violation scenario

An anonymous employee reported to your local HR team that they saw a relatively new intern viewing pornographic material, multiple times, on their work computer. When an initial investigation was conducted and individuals around the suspected offender were questioned about this activity, several individuals hesitantly admitted that they may have seen similar activity, but couldn't be sure. They did mention, however, that whenever they went into this individual's cubicle, he immediately turned off his monitor or appeared to quickly close open applications and windows on his system. As this type of activity is a clear violation of Human Resource policies, management would like to determine whether this activity is, in fact, occurring. In an effort to validate this activity so they can take immediate remedial actions, and not falsely accuse the employee, the HR team has asked the corporate incident response team to investigate the suspect's computer for activities or files that may indicate he has been viewing or saving pornographic material.

You have been tasked with performing initial evidence collection and triage on the intern's computer system so that you can provide the evidence to the organization's incident response team for further analysis.

When collecting evidence for analysis from a system that may involve inappropriate material such as pornography, there are several considerations that need to be weighed. Experience shows that individuals that habitually browse pornography at their workplace often also save and store various amounts onto the local system. Since this type of employee activity could lead to their termination, care should be taken in regards to the scope, depth, and documentation of any actions taken on their computer system. It is critical to validate and attribute if the inappropriate materials are due to user activity versus instances of click fraud or other types of browser hijacking based malware. This level of consideration is warranted since it is possible for the employee to attempt legal action against the organization and as such any aspects of the investigation could be admitted as evidence in a court of law.

Click fraud is where an individual or automated software, usually malware, performs the actions of a legitimate user clicking of web based advertisements. Generally, individuals that own websites or are behind an advertisements posting, makes a certain amount of revenue based on the number of times advertisements that are displayed on their websites are clicked on. The goal of click fraud activity is to falsely inflate the number of clicks that the advertisements obtain, which in turn increases the amount of financial gain received.

In a scenario such as this, where you are attempting to determine initial web browsing history and local storage information, the basic outline below highlights a standard breakdown of evidence collection actions and priorities. This outline correlates to both the fundamental evidence categories discussed previously. Based on what we've discussed up to this point, the initial recommended evidence collection steps are:

1. **Obtain system date and time details**
2. **Obtain system name and OS version**
3. **Identify network configuration details**
4. **Obtain currently logged on users**
5. **Identify all active network connections**
6. **Acquire the contents of DNS and ARP cache, and the systems routing table**
7. **Obtain a basic listing of running processes**
8. **Extract and parse the Windows prefetch**
9. **Extract web browser history**

   Note: While this is a corporate system and as such should be utilizing a standard Internet browser, it is always possible for the usage of a separately installed browser to be in use. Due to that concern, it is recommended that you utilize a tool with similar functionality to Redline, as previously discussed, so that information from multiple browsers can be automatically collected. Performing a text search against the collected browser history for common pornographic keywords may quickly identify suspicious activity.

10. **Copy or export Windows Registry hive**

    Note: As previously noted, the Windows Registry provides a cornucopia of potential evidence. Based on these circumstances, additional details such as Most Recently Used files, recent documents, and even Windows media player history can all be collected through registry analysis.

11. **Obtain details of recent USB device connections**

    Note: Based on the potential of stored pornography in this scenario, it is useful to identify if the suspect may have used or connected any USB storage devices to the machine. This activity may indicate the potential transfer of material from the system to the portable media.

12. **Copy or export Windows Event log files**

    Note: Windows event logs provide a wealth of insight into actions taken on a system. In this instance, event log entries that could identify when the user logged on, when user logged off, and even when and what applications were started, all provide details and evidence that can be correlated together to create a timeline of events.

13. **Obtain a full listing of all files on the computer system**

    Note: Initially, a full file listing is recommended in order to quickly validate or review if any contraband may be stored on the system under investigation. Individuals that go through the steps to save pornographic material locally on their system, often save a lot of it. Performing a text search for common pornographic keywords, or even just reviewing the files within the user's profile, may quickly uncover a repository of prohibited material.

As you can see in the above outline, we only collected a basic listing of running processes and related prefetch history on this computer. Our interest here is not so much what the user is running on the system, but what type of web history and files they are storing. However, by obtaining this information, it could be possible to identify web browsing software that may be in use, or have been used, which in turn could aid in the investigation.

While attempting to locate inappropriate material as part of this investigation, locating it may not immediately implicate the suspect as performing the actions in question. A critical component of incident response and digital forensics as a whole, is attributing actions to a specific user, or validating to the highest degree possible that the user was the person at the keyboard when things happened. In this instance, all of the collected data should be correlated and used to create an overall timeline base. As an example, event log entries that identify when the user account logged on, when user logged off, and even when and what applications were started, can be correlated with the times that certain websites were accessed, when specific files were saved, or external data such as the user swiping their corporate badge to gain access to the building. This timeline can and will provide a much greater level of confidence placing the suspect at the keyboard when the activity occurred.

INSIDER DATA EXFILTRATION SCENARIO

Your organization recently bid on a major multiyear contract but, unfortunately, was not selected. It is later discovered that one of your competitors provided an almost identical response as your company but had a slightly lower bid and won the contract. Almost immediately after this, one of your employees, who had been a key contributor to this process, gave his notice and advised that he had accepted a senior position with the competing organization. The circumstances around the contract loss and job change have raised the concern and suspicions of management. They are concerned that the employee in question may have provided the competitor with confidential corporate intelligence and project details that may have allowed them to successfully undercut your organization's bid. In coordination with, and authorization from both corporate HR and legal teams, they want to have the employee's computer investigated prior to his last day of employment with the organization.

You have been tasked with performing initial evidence collection and triage on the employee's computer system to identify any evidence of potential communications, data transfer, unauthorized data collection, or other activities that may indicate the employee purposely shared confidential information for his own personal gain or any evidence of a quid pro quo.

An insider can be anyone who is a current or former employee, contractor, third-party trusted service provider, or any other business partner or trusted agent that has legitimate and authorized access to an organization's internal network, systems, or data.

There are two insider threat categories, namely, malicious and nonmalicious. A malicious insider is an individual that intentionally misuses or oversteps the authorized access in a manner that negatively impacts the organization. A nonmalicious insider is an individual that unintentionally causes a negative impact to the organization, through error, neglect, or unawareness to corporate policies.

There has been a number of cases over the years that highlight the short and long term impacts the insider threat can pose to an organization, such as the National Security Administration and the actions taken by Edward Snowden in 2013.

In a scenario such as this, where you are attempting to determine overall computer usage patterns, local storage details, and possible data movement. The basic outline below highlights a standard breakdown of evidence collection actions and priorities. This outline correlates to both the fundamental evidence categories discussed previously. Based on what we've discussed up to this point, the initial recommended evidence collection steps are:

1. **Obtain system date and time details**
2. **Obtain system name and OS version**
3. **Identify network configuration details**
4. **Obtain currently logged on users**
5. **Identify all active network connections**
6. **Acquire the contents of DNS and ARP cache, and the systems routing table**
7. **Obtain a basic listing of running processes**
8. **Extract and parse the Windows prefetch**
9. **Extract web browser history**

    Note: Due to the prevalence of web based email and file sharing services, being able to validate and review what websites the suspect has utilized can provide insight into potentially related activities.

10. **Copy or export Windows Registry hive**

    Note: Windows event logs provide a wealth of insight into actions taken on a system. In this instance, event log entries that could identify when the user logged on, when the user logged off, and even when and what applications were started, all provide details and evidence that can be correlated together to create a timeline of events.

11. **Obtain details of recent USB device connections**

    Note: Based on the potential of data transfer to external media, it is useful to identify if the suspect may have used or connected any USB storage devices to the machine.

12. **Copy or export Windows Event log files**
13. **Obtain a full listing of all files on the computer system**

    Note: Initially, a full file listing is recommended to be able to quickly validate or review the scope of potential proprietary data the user may have on their system, which may include data they should not be in possession of. Additionally, a lot of data exfiltration type cases make use of archive file formats, such as ZIP or RAR, as a means of storing a large number of files in a single compressed container. Locating a large amount of archive files, or archive files with a large size, may provide a cause for a deeper level of collection and analysis.

As you can see in the above outline, we only collected a basic listing of running processes and related prefetch history on this computer. Our interest here is not so much what the user is running on the system at this point in time, but to obtain an idea of the types of programs that may be normally run on this system, as well as identifying tools that can be used for file archive creation, file compression, or even antiforensic tools that may attempt to destroy evidence of system activities. Due to the nature of this case, a listing of suspicious files should be presented to the business leaders that requested the analysis, to determine whether or not the suspect should have had access to these files.

As with the previous scenario, locating files that violate corporate policy may not immediately implicate the suspect as performing the actions in question. A critical component of incident response and digital forensics as a whole, is attributing actions to a specific user, or validating to the highest degree possible that the user was the person at the keyboard when things happened. In this instance, all of the collected data should be correlated and used to create an overall timeline base. As an example, event logs entries that identify when the user account logged on, when the user logged off, and even when and what applications were started, can be correlated with the times that certain websites were accessed, when specific files were saved or created, or external data such as the user swiping their corporate badge to gain access to the building. This timeline can and will provide a much greater level of confidence placing the suspect at the keyboard when the activity occurred.

SUMMARY

Evidence collection is not just a simple matter of copying files or searching a suspect computer system. Every action taken on a system has the potential to add, modify, or destroy potential evidence. There are a multitude of methods and available tools that can be leveraged for the identification and gathering of evidence from a computer system, however not all of them are optimal or should be utilized for incident response activities. As such, there are multiple considerations that an examiner needs to be aware of beforehand so that they can obtain evidence in the best manner with minimal impact, as possible. Preparation is a crucial component of this activity and all methods and tools that are used should be fully tested, validated, and vetted by the organization and examiners.

CHAPTER 5 REVIEW

In this chapter we reviewed multiple facets of digital evidence to include its overall volatility, categorization, methods of acquisition, as well as other important aspects that need to be considered and weighed by an examiner. We examined several principals that have direct applicability to the overall integrity of digital evidence and discussed the need to perform thorough testing and validation of processes and technologies prior to any production usage.

We walked through a multitude of hands-on examples of methodologies, considerations, and tools that can be leveraged for digital evidence collection, for a series of fundamental evidence categories. Lastly we reviewed several scenarios and took a look at initial order of operations, the value of certain pieces of evidence, the dynamic nature of performing evidence collection, and various situations that an examiner may encounter.

CHAPTER 5 SUMMARY QUESTIONS

1. What is the importance of Locard's Principle and Order of Operations?
2. What is the United States Best Evidence Rule 1001(3) and how does it apply to digital evidence?
3. Is it, and if so why is it, important to thoroughly test technology and processes prior to real-world usage?
4. Why should you capture the host name of the system under investigation first?
5. Why is identifying and knowing the system time important to an investigation?
6. For what types of investigations should you capture live memory prior to any other actions?
7. Is it possible to correlate a logged in user with an active process and associated network connections? How?
8. What is the Windows registry and why is it of evidentiary value?
9. What factors can cause extracting web browsing history to be difficult?
10. Why would you want to acquire the registry hive and event log files for offline analysis versus parsing or searching them directly on the system under investigation?

ADDITIONAL RESOURCES

Barbara, J. (2010). *Triage a computer*. http://www.forensicmag.com/articles/2010/06/triage-computer.

Bay, J., & Zatyko, K. (2011). *The digital forensics cyber exchange principle*. http://www.forensicmag.com/articles/2011/12/digital-forensics-cyber-exchange-principle.

Brezinski, D., & Killalea, T. (2002). *Guidelines for evidence collection and archiving*. https://tools.ietf.org/html/rfc3227.

Carvey, H. (2014). *Windows forensic analysis toolkit*. Elsevier, ISBN: 978-0-12417-174-9.

Carvey, H. (2016). *Windows incident response blog*. http://windowsir.blogspot.com/.

Casey, E. (2011). *Digital evidence and computer crime* (3rd ed.). Elsevier, ISBN: 978-0-12374-268-1.

Cichonski, P., Grance, T., Millar, T., & Scarfone, K. (2012). *Computer security incident handling guide*. National Institute of Standards and Technology. http://nvlpubs.nist.gov/nistpubs/SpecialPublications/NIST.SP.800-61r2.pdf.

Cornell University Law School. Federal rules of evidence: Rule 1001 definitions. (n.d.). http://www.law.cornell.edu/rules/fre/rules.htm#Rule1001.

Federal Evidence Review. Federal rules of evidence: Rule 1001. (n.d.). http://federalevidence.com/rules-of-evidence#Rule1001.

Frieden, J., & Murray, L. (2011). The admissibility of electronic evidence under the federal rules of evidence. *Richmond Journal of Law and Technology*, *XVII*(2). http://jolt.richmond.edu/v17i2/article5.pdf.

Kent, K., Chevalier, S., Grance, T., & Dang, H. (August 2006). *Guide to integrating forensic techniques into incident response*. National Institute of Standards and Technology. http://csrc.nist.gov/publications/nistpubs/800-86/SP800-86.pdf.

Ligh, M., Adair, S., Hartstein, B., & Richard, M. (2010). *Malware analyst's cookbook.* Wiley, ISBN: 978-0-47061-303-0.

Malin, C., Casey, E., & Aquilina, J. (2012). *Malware forensics field guide for windows systems.* Elsevier, ISBN: 978-1-59749-472-4.

Mukasey, M. B., Sedgwick, J. L., & Hagy, D. W. (2008). *Electronic crime scene investigation: A guide for first responders* (2nd ed.). US Department of Justice. https://www.ncjrs.gov/pdffiles1/nij/219941.pdf.

SBE Council. Visa security alert: "Rawpos" malware targeting lodging merchants. (n.d.). http://www.sbecouncil.org/2015/03/30/visa-security-alert-rawpos-malware-targeting-lodging-merchants/.

Scarfone, K., & Souppaya, M. (2013). *Guide to malware incident prevention and handling for desktops and laptops.* National Institute of Standards and Technology. http://nvlpubs.nist.gov/nistpubs/SpecialPublications/NIST.SP.800-83r1.pdf.

Scientific Working Group on Digital Evidence (SWGDE) (2014). *SWGDE recommended guidelines for validation testing.* https://www.swgde.org/documents/Current%20Documents/2014-09-05%20SWGDE%20Recommended%20Guidelines%20for%20Validation%20Testing%20V2-0.

TrendLabs Security Intelligence Blog. RawPOS technical brief. (n.d.). http://sjc1-te-ftp.trendmicro.com/images/tex/pdf/RawPOS%20Technical%20Brief.pdf.

Wilding, S. (2012). *Locard's exchange principle.* Forensichandbook. http://www.forensichandbook.com/locards-exchange-principle/.

Future considerations

Future: Word Origin
(13c.), from Latin futurus "to grow or to become"

CHAPTER OUTLINE

INTRODUCTION

When you picked up this book, you might have thought, "Who uses the Windows Command Line for investigations and more importantly why?" Even more so, you might have thought, "Well if the Command Line is not dead now it will be dead very soon." There is no question that the advances in Graphical User Interface (GUI), mobile and laptop touch interfaces, holographic displays, augmented reality, and of course, the Speech Interpretation and Recognition Interface (better known as SIRI), provide a far better human experience. So why would one ever investigate or respond to an incident via the command line? Who could forget the famous scene in Star Trek IV The Voyage Home where Scotty picks up the mouse and tries to speak directly to the Apple Computer?

The answer is: Regardless of how many human interface layers of abstraction we place between us and the underlying processor and hardware, investigators still want to query the computer in very discrete and specific ways using the least abstracted method. Today that interface still needs to take place via the command line. There are many reasons for the propensity to want to probe systems from the command line:

- Reduce the levels of abstraction between User and the hardware.
- Extract evidence that is not easily provided from GUI tools.

- Sequence commands based on specific investigative needs or circumstances.
- Extract trace evidence using special low level commands and executable(s).
- Get as close to the hardware as possible to eliminate malware obfuscation.
- Locard's Principle considerations.
- Volatility of Data and the impact on the investigation.

WINDOWS 10.X

From a Microsoft Windows point of view, Windows 10 is now available and there are several esthetic changes to the Windows Command Line. A couple of these visual changes are depicted below in Fig. 6.1.

(1) Demonstrates the ability to control the level of transparency of the command window and allows investigators to see windows and the desktop through the command window.
(2) Allows investigators to modify the size and shape of the command window by using more traditional window control points.

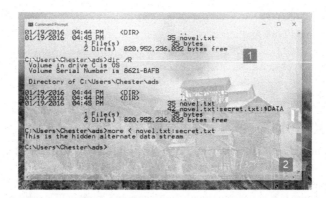

FIG. 6.1

Windows 10 command line processor application.

In addition, the new Command Window has incorporated a plethora of new keyboard sequences to automate previous manual functions. A description of all these new changes can be found at: *https://blogs.windows.com/buildingapps/2014/10/07/console-improvements-in-the-windows-10-technical-preview/*.

WINDOWS EMBEDDED

In addition to the Windows Desktop and Server operating systems, Windows also offers *Windows Embedded*. This allows developers to embed the Windows OS into devices such as the *Internet of Things*, or IoT. Windows Embedded has been around for quite some time, however, some investigators may not be aware of its presence in IoT devices, automobiles, appliances, multimedia devices, and robotics. Typically, when these devices are built they include a built-in command line, where most, if not all of the standard command line functions are available. You can learn more about Windows Embedded OS at: *https://www.microsoft.com/windowsembedded/en-us/ windows-embedded.aspx.*

ADVANCED AUTOMOTIVE TECHNOLOGY

In addition, as we move forward in time, we find that computers and networks that require investigation are everywhere. Here are just a few examples of computers and networks that contain valuable evidence that we need to investigate now and in the near future.

Fig. 6.2 shows the Tesla in the car infotainment system. This system provides the driver with access to information about the car's operation, navigation system, entertainment options, service requirements, and communication systems. Fig. 6.3 depicts

FIG. 6.2

Tesla cockpit infotainment interface.

FIG. 6.3

Tesla backend MCU.

the backend media control unit (MCU) that contains a 3.2 GHz Targa Quad Core Processor with a Solid State Drive and multiple digital and analog sensors. The live and postmortem information available from this system can provide evidence related to crash and/or criminal activities. The operating system running on the main CPU is Linux, not Windows, with drivers and interfaces for the specialized control and information systems proprietary to Tesla.

RASPBERRY Pi

Another popular device that arrived on the scene in Feb. 2012, and continues to be updated in its hardware, operating system, and software, is the Raspberry Pi, a fully self-contained, credit card sized computer (Fig. 6.4).

FIG. 6.4

Raspberry Pi.

The Raspberry Pi is not only being used as a standalone device, but is also being used in IoT environments due to its versatility. The Pi can support several operating systems, the most popular being Raspbian which at its core is based on the Linux Debian standard. Launching a terminal window on the Pi, you can enter many standard Linux commands. By way of example, several commands provide details of the Pi you are examining, such as *cat /proc/version* and *cat /proc/cpuinfo*, as shown below.

```
pi@raspberrypi ~ $ cat /proc/version
Linux version 3.18.7+ (dc4@dc4-XPS13-9333) (gcc version 4.8.3 20140303
  (prerelease) (crosstool-NG linaro-1.13.1+bzr2650 - Linaro GCC 2014.03))
  #755 PREEMPT Thu Feb 12 17:14:31 GMT 2015
pi@raspberrypi ~ $ cat /proc/cpuinfo
processor   : 0
model name      : ARMv6-compatible processor rev 7 (v6l)
BogoMIPS   : 2.00
Features  : half thumb fastmult vfp edsp java tls
```

```
CPU implementer    : 0x41
CPU architecture: 7
CPU variant    : 0x0
CPU part  : 0xb76
CPU revision  : 7

Hardware  : BCM2708
Revision  : 0010
Serial    : 0000000009088d46
```

You can checkout the attached USB devices attached to the Raspberry Pi by using the *lsusb* command shown here.

```
pi@raspberrypi ~ $ lsusb
Bus 001 Device 002: ID 0424:9514 Standard Microsystems Corp.
Bus 001 Device 001: ID 1d6b:0002 Linux Foundation 2.0 root hub
Bus 001 Device 003: ID 0424:ec00 Standard Microsystems Corp.
Bus 001 Device 004: ID 046d:c52b Logitech, Inc. Unifying Receiver
```

More standardized Linux commands such as *ifconfig* allows you to configure or view the network interface configurations, as shown here.

```
pi@raspberrypi ~ $ ifconfig
eth0      Link encap:Ethernet  HWaddr b8:27:eb:08:8d:46
          inet addr:192.168.0.138  Bcast:192.168.0.255
Mask:255.255.255.0
          UP BROADCAST RUNNING MULTICAST  MTU:1500  Metric:1
          RX packets:29 errors:0 dropped:0 overruns:0 frame:0
          TX packets:29 errors:0 dropped:0 overruns:0 carrier:0
          collisions:0 txqueuelen:1000
          RX bytes:2846 (2.7 KiB)   TX bytes:3366 (3.2 KiB)

lo        Link encap:Local Loopback
          inet addr:127.0.0.1  Mask:255.0.0.0
          UP LOOPBACK RUNNING  MTU:65536  Metric:1
          RX packets:8 errors:0 dropped:0 overruns:0 frame:0
          TX packets:8 errors:0 dropped:0 overruns:0 carrier:0
          collisions:0 txqueuelen:0
          RX bytes:1104 (1.0 KiB)   TX bytes:1104 (1.0 KiB)
```

Since Raspberry PI uses small Solid State Memory the *cat /proc/meminfo* command provides details about current system memory operations.

```
pi@raspberrypi ~ $ cat /proc/meminfo
MemTotal:       445740 kB
MemFree:        303040 kB
MemAvailable:   374680 kB
Buffers:         30220 kB
Cached:          60748 kB
```

```
SwapCached:          0 kB
Active:          87088 kB
Inactive:        36992 kB
Active(anon):    33252 kB
Inactive(anon):    836 kB
Active(file):    53836 kB
Inactive(file):  36156 kB
Unevictable:         0 kB
Mlocked:             0 kB
SwapTotal:      102396 kB
SwapFree:       102396 kB
Dirty:               0 kB
Writeback:           0 kB
AnonPages:       33124 kB
Mapped:          32500 kB
Shmem:             980 kB
Slab:             8372 kB
SReclaimable:     4256 kB
SUnreclaim:       4116 kB
KernelStack:      1328 kB
PageTables:       1496 kB
NFS_Unstable:        0 kB
Bounce:              0 kB
WritebackTmp:        0 kB
CommitLimit:    325264 kB
Committed_AS:   292168 kB
VmallocTotal:   565248 kB
VmallocUsed:      3088 kB
VmallocChunk:   321968 kB
```

WEARABLE TECHNOLOGY

Wearable technologies, such as Android and Apple Watch (Fig. 6.5), and fitness technologies such as FitBit and Garmin (Fig. 6.6), also utilize different operating systems under the hood that can be accessed via the command line. One example is the Smart Development Bridge (SDB), a command line technology used for discrete device management. SDB behaves as an intermediary between your wearable device and a traditional computer. The SDB can access files, perform specific device management capabilities and can access the sensors and other data elements of wearable devices via the command line.

NEW COMMAND LINE APPLICATIONS

Over the past several years investigators, undergraduate and graduate students, researchers, professors, and for-profit and nonprofit groups have begun to develop new command line tools for investigators and incident response applications.

FIG. 6.5

Apple and android watches.

FIG. 6.6

Garmin and fitbit wearable fitness devices.

Today, the language of choice is Python; based on its versatility, ease of use and development, out-of-the-box cross platform capabilities, open source fundamentals, extensive built-in standard library, and built-in data structures that are ideally suited for investigative solutions, along with a global user and support community. Fig. 6.7 depicts Python usage on the command line.

Philip Guo, an Assistant Professor of Computer Science at the University of Rochester, reported in the Mar. 2015 issue of the *Communications of the ACM*, "Python, an open source scripting language, has become the most popular introductory teaching language at top US universities ... At schools including the Massachusetts Institute of Technology (MIT), Carnegie Mellon University, and the University of California, Berkeley, Python emerged as the leading language to teach novices." These facts have created and continue to create a plethora of new computer science

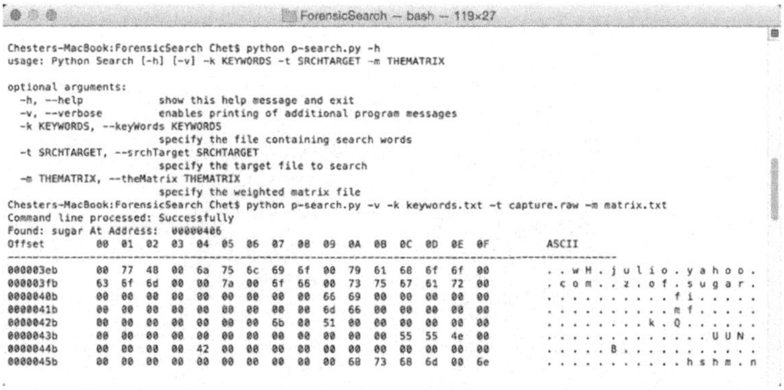

FIG. 6.7

Python command line execution.

students with core skills in Python looking for challenging problems to solve. http://cacm.acm.org/magazines/2015/3/183588-python-for-beginners/fulltext.

In addition to Python, the *Go* Programming Language, often referred to as *golang*, was developed at Google by programming language legends Ken Thompson, Rob Pike, and Robert Griesemer. The language was specifically developed for "systems programming" applications where forensics and incident response solutions squarely focus. This new language and environment is likely to deliver new innovations and investigative applications in the coming years.

IN CLOSING

New cyber innovations continue to expand the ability to investigate and respond to cyber crimes that accompany these new inventions and technologies. Because of this, the future response is likely to move more quickly from postmortem to live investigation. Whether the investigation focuses on traditional servers, desktops, laptops, phones or tablets, or we find ourselves attempting to extract evidence from wearable devices, IoT, automobiles, or embedded systems, we are likely to find ourselves behind the keyboard probing these technologies from the command line once again.

ADDITIONAL RESOURCES

Hosmer, C. (2014). *Python forensics: A workbench for inventing and sharing digital forensic technology*. Syngress. ISBN 978-0124186767.

Kernighan, B., & Donovan, A. (2015). *The Go programming language*. Addison-Wesley. ISBN 978-0134190440.

Shein, E. (2015). Python for beginners. *Communications of the ACM, 58*(3), 19–21. http://cacm.acm.org/magazines/2015/3/183588-python-for-beginners/fulltext.

Third-party Windows CLI tools

INTRODUCTION

The following tables contain information on commonly used third-party Windows Command Line Interface (CLI) tools that can be utilized to gather evidence during an investigation. These tools span genres including: host information collection; process utilities; file and disk utilities; security utilities; and networking utilities. These tools are free but consideration must be made to each of the tool's licensing terms and conditions to ensure compliance. Web site addresses to access and download each of the tools listed in this Appendix have been provided for your reference. Please note that the following list is not intended to be an exhaustive listing of all third-party tools that are available. It is simply a representative sampling of the types of tools that are available by third-party vendors.

Name: Autorunsc	**Developer:** Microsoft Sysinternals
Genre: Host information collection	**License:** Custom/Proprietary
Platform: Windows XP or higher	**Web site:** https://technet.microsoft.com/en-us/sysinternals/bb963902.aspx
Description taken from vendor's web site on Dec. 9, 2015: "Autorunsc is the command-line version of Autoruns. This utility, which has the most comprehensive knowledge of auto-starting locations of any startup monitor, shows you what programs are configured to run during system bootup or login, and when you start various built-in Windows applications like Internet Explorer, Explorer, and media players. These programs and drivers include the ones in your startup folder, Run, RunOnce, and other Registry keys. *Autoruns* reports Explorer shell extensions, toolbars, browser helper objects, Winlogon notifications, auto-start services, and much more. *Autoruns* goes way beyond other auto-start utilities"	

Name: ChromeCacheView v1.67	**Developer:** NirSoft
Genre: Internet history collection	**License:** Freeware
Platform: "Any version of Windows, starting from Windows 2000, and up to Windows 7/8/2008/10"	**Web site:** http://www.nirsoft.net/utils/chrome_cache_view.html
Description taken from vendor's web site on Dec. 29, 2015: "ChromeCacheView is a small utility that reads the cache folder of Google Chrome Web browser and displays the list of all files currently stored in the cache. For each cache file, the following information is displayed: URL, Content type, File size, Last accessed time, Expiration time, Server name, Server response, and more. You can easily select one or more items from the cache list, and then extract the files to another folder, or copy the URLs list to the clipboard"	

Name: Crowd Response

Genre: Host information collection

Platform: "32 bit and 64 bit versions of Windows from XP and above"

Developer: CrowdStrike

License: Custom/Proprietary

Web site: http://www.crowdstrike.com/community-tools/index.html

Description taken from vendor's web site on Dec. 30, 2015: "Crowd Response is a lightweight Windows console application designed to aid in the gathering of system information for incident response and security engagements. The application contains numerous modules, each of them invoked by providing specific command-line parameters to the main application. Modules are all built into the main application in C++ language utilizing the Win32 API to achieve their functionality"

Name: CurrPorts v2.20

Genre: Networking utilities

Platform: "Windows NT, Windows 2000, Windows XP, Windows Server 2003, Windows Server 2008, Windows Vista, Windows 7, Windows 8, and Windows 10. There is also a separated download of CurrPorts for x64 versions of Windows. If you want to use this utility on Windows NT, you should install psapi.dll in your system32 directory"

Developer: NirSoft

License: Freeware

Web site: http://www.nirsoft.net/utils/cports.html

Description taken from vendor's web site on Dec. 29, 2015: "CurrPorts is a network monitoring software that displays the list of all currently opened TCP/IP and UDP ports on your local computer. For each port in the list, information about the process that opened the port is also displayed, including the process name, full path of the process, version information of the process (product name, file description, and so on), the time that the process was created, and the user that created it"

Name: Encrypted Disk Detector v2

Genre: Host information collection

Platform: Windows XP, Vista, 7, 8, 10, 2003, 2008, 2012 (32 and 64 bit support)

Developer: Magnet Forensics Inc.

License: Custom/Proprietary

Web site: https://www.magnetforensics.com/free-tool-encrypted-disk-detector/

Description taken from vendor's web site on Dec. 30, 2015: "Encrypted Disk Detector (v2 released Apr. 22, 2013) is a command-line tool that can quickly and nonintrusively check for encrypted volumes on a computer system during incident response"

Name: ExifTool v10.08

Genre: Metadata extraction

Platform: "Requires Perl 5.004 or later. No other libraries or software required. For Windows users: A stand-alone Windows executable version of ExifTool is available which doesn't require Perl"

Developer: Phil Harvey

License: Custom/Proprietary

Web site: http://www.sno.phy.queensu.ca/~phil/exiftool/

Description taken from vendor's web site on Dec. 30, 2015: "A platform-independent Perl library plus a command-line application for reading, writing, and editing meta information in a wide variety of files"

Name: GNC Core Utilities v. 5.3.0

Genre: System utilities

Platform: "MS-Windows 95/98/ME/NT/ 2000/XP with msvcrt.dll"

Developer: Multiple (Free Software Foundation)

License: Custom/Proprietary

Web site: http://gnuwin32.sourceforge. net/packages/coreutils.htm

Description taken from vendor's web site on Jan. 25, 2016: "The GNU Core Utilities are the basic file, shell, and text manipulation utilities of the GNU operating system. These are the core utilities which are expected to exist on every operating system"

Name: Handle v4.0

Genre: Process utilities

Platform: Client: Windows XP and higher

Server: Windows Server 2003 and higher

Developer: Microsoft Sysinternals

License: Custom/Proprietary

Web site: https://technet.microsoft.com/en- us/sysinternals/handle

Description taken from vendor's web site on Dec. 9, 2015: "Handle is a utility that displays information about open handles for any process in the system. You can use it to see the programs that have a file open, or to see the object types and names of all the handles of a program"

Name: Hobocopy

Genre: Imaging/acquisition

Platform: Windows XP, Vista, 7, 8, 10, 2003, 2008, 2012 (32 and 64 bit support)

Developer: Craig Andera

License: Free/Open Source

Web site: http://candera. github.io/hobocopy/

Description taken from vendor's web site on Dec. 9, 2015: "Hobocopy is a free, open- source backup tool for Windows. It can copy files that are locked, so you can do things like back up your Outlook.pst files without closing Outlook"

Name: IECacheView v1.55

Genre: Internet history collection

Platform: "Windows, from Windows 98 to Windows 8, with Internet Explorer 6.0–11.0"

Developer: NirSoft

License: Freeware

Web site: http://www.nirsoft.net/ utils/ie_cache_viewer.html

Description taken from vendor's web site on Dec. 29, 2015: "IECacheView is a small utility that reads the cache folder of Internet Explorer, and displays the list of all files currently stored in the cache. For each cache file, the following information is displayed: Filename, Content Type, URL, Last Accessed Time, Last Modified Time, Expiration Time, Number Of Hits, File Size, Folder Name, and full path of the cache filename. You can easily save the cache information into text/html/xml file, or copy the cache table to the clipboard and then paste it to another application, like Excel or OpenOffice Spreadsheet"

Name: IECookiesView v1.77

Developer: NirSoft

Genre: Internet history collection

License: Freeware

Platform: "Windows 95/98/ME, Windows NT, Windows 2000, Windows XP, or Windows Vista" "Internet Explorer, Versions 4.0–9.0. There is only limited support for Internet Explorer 10.0, due to a change in the way that cookies index information is stored"

Web site: http://www.nirsoft. net/utils/iecookies.html

Description taken from vendor's web site on Dec. 29, 2015: "IECookiesView is a small utility that displays the details of all cookies that Internet Explorer stores on your computer"

Name: IEHistoryView v1.70

Developer: NirSoft

Genre: Internet history collection

License: Freeware

Platform: "Any version of Windows operating system with Internet Explorer version 4.00 or greater." "Currently, IEHistoryView doesn't support IE10 and IE11. In order to view the history of IE10/IE11, you can use BrowsingHistoryView utility"

Web site: http://www. nirsoft.net/utils/iehv.html

Description taken from vendor's web site on Dec. 29, 2015: "Each time that you type a URL in the address bar or click on a link in Internet Explorer browser, the URL address is automatically added to the history index file. When you type a sequence of characters in the address bar, Internet Explorer automatically suggests you all URLs that begin with character sequence that you typed (unless AutoComplete feature for Web addresses is turned off). However, Internet Explorer doesn't allow you to view and edit the entire URL list that it stores inside the history file"

"This utility reads all information from the history file on your computer, and displays the list of all URLs that you have visited in the last few days. It also allows you to select one or more URL addresses, and then remove them from the history file or save them into text, HTML, or XML file. In addition, you are allowed to view the visited URL list of other user profiles on your computer, and even access the visited URL list on a remote computer, as long as you have permission to access the history folder"

Name: IE PassView v1.32

Developer: NirSoft

Genre: Internet history collection

License: Freeware

Platform: "Supports all versions of Internet Explorer, from version 4.0 and up to 11.0"

Web site: http://www.nirsoft.net/ utils/internet_explorer_password.html

Description taken from vendor's web site on Dec. 29, 2015: "IE PassView is a small password management utility that reveals the passwords stored by Internet Explorer Web browser, and allows you to delete passwords that you don't need anymore." "For each password that is stored by Internet Explorer, the following information is displayed: Web address, Password Type (AutoComplete, Password-Protected Web Site, or FTP), Storage Location (Registry, Credentials File, or Protected Storage), and the user name/password pair. You can select one or more items from the passwords list and export them into text/ html/csv/xml file"

Name: InsideClipboard v1.12

Developer: NirSoft

Genre: Desktop utilities

License: Custom/Proprietary

Platform: Any version of Windows, from Windows 98 to Windows Vista

Web site: http://www.nirsoft.net/utils/inside_clipboard.html

Description taken from vendor's web site on Feb. 10, 2016: "Each time that you copy something into the clipboard for pasting it into another application, the copied data is saved into multiple formats. The main clipboard application of Windows only displays the basic clipboard formats, like text and bitmaps, but doesn't display the list of all formats that are stored in the clipboard

InsideClipboard is a small utility that displays the binary content of all formats that are currently stored in the clipboard, and allows you to save the content of specific format into a binary file"

Name: IOC Finder

Developer: Mandiant/FireEye

Genre: Host information collection

License: Custom/Proprietary

Platform: Windows XP, Windows Vista, Windows 7 (32-bit and 64-bit)

Web site: https://www.fireeye.com/services/freeware/ioc-finder.html

Description taken from vendor's web site on Dec. 9, 2015: "Mandiant's indicators of compromise (IOC) Finder is a free tool for collecting host system data and reporting the presence of IOCs. IOCs are open-standard XML documents that help incident responders capture diverse information about threats"

Name: ListDLLs v3.1

Developer: Microsoft Sysinternals

Genre: Process utilities

License: Custom/Proprietary

Platform: Client: Windows XP and higher

Server: Windows Server 2003 and higher

Web site: https://technet.microsoft.com/en-us/sysinternals/bb896656

Description taken from vendor's web site on Dec. 9, 2015: "ListDLLs is a utility that reports the DLLs loaded into processes. You can use it to list all DLLs loaded into all processes, into a specific process, or to list the processes that have a particular DLL loaded. ListDLLs can also display full version information for DLLs, including their digital signature, and can be used to scan processes for unsigned DLLs"

Name: LiveContactsView v1.26

Developer: NirSoft

Genre: Internet history collection

License: Freeware

Platform: "Works only with Windows Live Messenger"

Web site: http://www.nirsoft.net/utils/live_messenger_contacts.html

Description taken from vendor's web site on Dec. 29, 2015: "LiveContactsView is a small utility that allows you to view the details of all contacts in your Windows Live Messenger. For each contact, LiveContactsView displays the following fields: Email address, nickname, quick name, first name, last name, and more. You can easily select one or more contacts and then export them into text/xml/html/csv file, or copy them into the clipboard and then paste them into Excel or to other spreadsheet application"

Name: LogonSessions v1.3

Genre: Host information collection

Platform: Client: Windows XP (32-bit) and higher

Server: Windows Server 2003 and higher

Developer: Microsoft Sysinternals

License: Custom/Proprietary

Web site: https://technet.microsoft.com/en-us/sysinternals/logonsessions

Description taken from vendor's web site on Dec. 9, 2015: "LogonSessions lists the currently active logon sessions and, if you specify the -p option, the processes running in each session"

Name: Log Parser v2.2

Genre: File utilities

Platform: "Windows 2000, Windows Server 2003, Windows XP Professional Edition"

Developer: Microsoft©

License: Custom/Proprietary

Web site: https://www.microsoft.com/en-us/download/details.aspx?id=24659

Description taken from vendor's web site on Jan. 20, 2016: "Log parser is a powerful, versatile tool that provides universal query access to text-based data such as log files, XML files, and CSV files, as well as key data sources on the Windows® operating system such as the Event Log, the Registry, the file system, and Active Directory®"

Name: Magnet RAM Capture

Genre: Imaging/acquisition

Platform: "Windows XP, Vista, 7, 8, 10, 2003, 2008, 2012 (32 and 64 bit support)"

Developer: Magnet Forensics Inc.

License: Custom/Proprietary

Web site: https://www.magnetforensics.com/free-tool-magnet-ram-capture/

Description taken from vendor's web site on Dec. 30, 2015: "Magnet RAM Capture is a free imaging tool designed to capture the physical memory of a suspect's computer, allowing investigators to recover and analyze valuable artifacts that are often only found in memory"

Name: Memoryze

Genre: Imaging/acquisition

Platform: Windows 2000 Service Pack 4 (32-bit)
Windows XP Service Pack 2 and Service Pack 3 (32-bit)
Windows Vista Service Pack 1 and Service Pack 2 (32-bit)
Windows Vista Service Pack 2 (64-bit)
Windows 2003 Service Pack 2 (32-bit and 64-bit)
Windows 7 Service Pack 0 (32-bit and 64-bit)
Windows 2008 Service Pack 1 and Service Pack 2 (32-bit)
Windows 2008 R2 Service Pack 0 (64-bit)
Windows 8 Service Pack 0 (32-bit and 64-bit)

Developer: Mandiant/FireEye

License: Custom/Proprietary

Web site: https://www.fireeye.com/services/freeware/memoryze.html

Continued

Windows Server 2012 Service Pack 0
(64-bit)

Description taken from vendor's web site on Dec. 9, 2015: "Mandiant's Memoryze™ is
a free memory forensic software that helps incident responders find evil in live memory.
Memoryze can acquire and/or analyze memory images and on live systems can include the
paging file in its analysis"

Name: Microsoft File Checksum Integrity
Verifier

Developer: Microsoft

Genre: Hashing utility

License: Custom/Proprietary

Platform: "Windows 2000, Windows 2000
Advanced Server, Windows 2000 Server,
Windows 2000 Service Pack 2, Windows 2000
Service Pack 3, Windows 2000 Service Pack
4, Windows XP, Windows XP Home Edition,
Windows XP Professional Edition, Windows XP
Service Pack 1"

Web site: http://www.microsoft.com/
en-us/download/details.aspx?
id=11533

Description taken from vendor's web site on Dec. 9, 2015: "The Microsoft File
Checksum Integrity Verifier tool is an unsupported command-line utility that computes MD5
or SHA1 cryptographic hashes for files"

Name: MozillaCacheView v1.69

Developer: NirSoft

Genre: Internet history collection

License: Freeware

Platform: "Any version of Windows, From
Windows 98 to Windows 10"

Web site: http://www.nirsoft.net/utils/
mozilla_cache_viewer.html

Description taken from vendor's web site on Dec. 29, 2015: "MozillaCacheView is a
small utility that reads the cache folder of Firefox/Mozilla/Netscape Web browsers, and
displays the list of all files currently stored in the cache. For each cache file, the following
information is displayed: URL, Content type, File size, Last modified time, Last fetched
time, Expiration time, Fetch count, Server name, and more. You can easily select one or
more items from the cache list, and then extract the files to another folder, or copy the URLs
list to the clipboard"

Name: MozillaCookiesView v1.50

Developer: NirSoft

Genre: Internet history collection

License: Freeware

Platform: "All versions of Windows (Windows 9x/ME,
Windows NT, Windows 2000, and Windows XP) and it
can read the cookies file created by any version of
Netscape/Mozilla browser"

Web site: http://www.nirsoft.
net/utils/mzcv.html

Description taken from vendor's web site on Dec. 29, 2015: "MozillaCookiesView is an
alternative to the standard 'Cookie Manager' provided by Netscape and Mozilla
browsers. It displays the details of all cookies stored inside the cookies file (cookies.txt)
in one table, and allows you to save the cookies list into text, HTML, or XML file, delete
unwanted cookies, and backup/restore the cookies file"

Name: MozillaHistoryView v1.56

Genre: Internet history collection

Platform: "Any version of Windows, From Windows 98 to Windows Vista. For all Firefox/ Mozilla versions except Firefox 3, you can use this utility even if Firefox/Mozilla is not installed on your system, as long as you have the history file (history. dat or places.sqlite) that you want to inspect"

Developer: NirSoft

License: Freeware

Web site: http://www.nirsoft.net/ utils/mozilla_history_view.html

Description taken from vendor's web site on Dec. 29, 2015: "MozillaHistoryView is a small utility that reads the history data file (history.dat) of Firefox/Mozilla/Netscape Web browsers, and displays the list of all visited Web pages in the last days. For each visited Web page, the following information is displayed: URL, First visit date, Last visit date, Visit counter, Referrer, Title, and Host name. You can also easily export the history data to text/HTML/Xml file"

Name: MyLastSearch v1.64

Genre: Internet history collection

Platform: "Up to Windows 10"

Developer: NirSoft

License: Freeware

Web site: http://www.nirsoft.net/utils/my_last_search. html

Description taken from vendor's web site on Dec. 29, 2015: "MyLastSearch utility scans the cache and history files of your Web browser, and locates all search queries that you made with the most popular search engines (Google, Yahoo, and MSN) and with popular social networking sites (Twitter, Facebook, and MySpace). The search queries that you made are displayed in a table with the following columns: Search Text, Search Engine, Search Time, Search Type (General, Video, and Images), Web Browser, and the search URL. You can select one or more search queries and then copy them to the clipboard or save them into text/html/xml file"

Name: Network Users v1.22

Genre: User information collection

Platform: "Windows NT 4 or later"

Developer: Optimum X, Marty List

License: Freeware

Web site: http://www.optimumx.com/downloads. html#NetUsers

Description taken from vendor's web site on Jan. 25, 2016: "Displays a current or historical list of users logged on to a remote Windows system. Requires the Remote Registry service to be running, which is not set to Automatic start on Windows 7. Use "sc.exe\\ computername start remote registry" to start the service. Use "sc.exe\\computername config remote registry start=auto" to set the service to auto start. Use 'NetUsers/?' to view the syntax"

Name: OpenedFilesView v1.61

Genre: Host information collection

Platform: "Windows 2000, Windows XP, Windows 2003/2008, Windows Vista, Windows 7, Windows 8, Windows 10"

Developer: NirSoft

License: Freeware

Web site: http://www.nirsoft.net/utils/opened_files_view.html

Description taken from vendor's web site on Dec. 29, 2015: "OpenedFilesView displays the list of all opened files on your system. For each opened file, additional information is displayed: handle value, read/write/delete access, file position, the process that opened the file, and more ..."

Name: OperaCacheView v1.40

Genre: Internet history collection

Platform: "Any version of Windows, From Windows 98 to Windows 7. However, for Windows 98/ME, you have to download the non-Unicode version"

Developer: NirSoft

License: Freeware

Web site: http://www.nirsoft.net/utils/opera_cache_view.html

Description taken from vendor's web site on Dec. 29, 2015: "OperaCacheView is a small utility that reads the cache folder of Opera Web browser, and displays the list of all files currently stored in the cache. For each cache file, the following information is displayed: URL, Content type, File size, Last accessed time, and last modified time in the server. You can easily select one or more items from the cache list, and then extract the files to another folder, or copy the URLs list to the clipboard"

Name: OperaPassView v1.10

Genre: Internet history collection

Platform: "Any version of Windows, starting from Windows 2000 and up to Windows 7/2008"

Developer: NirSoft

License: Freeware

Web site: http://www.nirsoft.net/utils/opera_password_recovery.html

Description taken from vendor's web site on Dec. 29, 2015: "OperaPassView is a small password recovery tool that decrypts the content of the Opera Web browser password file (wand.dat) and displays the list of all Web site passwords stored in this file. You can easily select one or more passwords in the OperaPassView window, and then copy the passwords list to the clipboard and save it into text/html/csv/xml file"

Name: PasswordFox v1.56

Genre: Internet history collection

Platform: "Windows 2000, Windows XP, Windows Server 2003, Windows Vista, Windows 7, and Windows 8"

Developer: NirSoft

License: Freeware

Web site: http://www.nirsoft.net/utils/passwordfox.html

Description taken from vendor's web site on Dec. 29, 2015: "PasswordFox is a small password recovery tool that allows you to view the user names and passwords stored by Mozilla Firefox Web browser. By default, PasswordFox displays the passwords stored in your current profile, but you can easily select to watch the passwords of any other Firefox profile. For each password entry, the following information is displayed: Record Index, Web Site, User Name, Password, User Name Field, Password Field, and the Signons filename"

Name: Peframe

Genre: Security utilities

Platform: "Up to Windows 10"

Developer: Gianni Amato

License: Custom/Proprietary

Web site: https://github.com/guelfoweb/peframe

Description taken from vendor's web site on Dec. 30, 2015: "To perform static analysis on Portable Executable malware"

Name: Port Reporter

Genre: Networking utilities

Platform: "Windows 2000, Windows Server 2003, Windows XP"

Developer: Microsoft

License: Custom/Proprietary

Web site: http://www.microsoft.com/en-us/download/details.aspx?id=9964

Description taken from vendor's web site on Dec. 9, 2015: "Port Reporter logs TCP and UDP port activity on a local Windows system. Port Reporter is a small application that runs as a service on Windows 2000, Windows XP, and Windows Server 2003. On Windows XP and Windows Server 2003, this service is able to log which ports are used, which process is using the port, if the process is a service, which modules the process has loaded and which user account is running the process. On Windows 2000 systems, this service is limited to logging which ports are used and when. In both cases, the information that the service provides can be helpful for security purposes, troubleshooting scenarios, and profiling systems' port usage"

Name: Prefetch-Parser

Genre: Host information collection

Platform: "Up to Windows 10"

Developer: Red Wolf Computer Forensics

License: Custom/Proprietary

Web site: http://redwolfcomputerforensics.com/index.php?option=com_content&task=view&id=42&Itemid=55

Description taken from vendor's web site on Dec. 30, 2015: "Parse the prefetch files and display information"

Name: ProcDump v7.01

Genre: Process utilities

Platform: Client: Windows XP and higher

Server: Windows Server 2003 and higher

Developer: Microsoft Sysinternals

License: Custom/Proprietary

Web site: https://technet.microsoft.com/en-us/sysinternals/dd996900

Description taken from vendor's web site on Dec. 9, 2015: "ProcDump is a command-line utility whose primary purpose is monitoring an application for CPU spikes and generating crash dumps during a spike that an administrator or developer can use to determine the cause of the spike. ProcDump also includes hung window monitoring (using the same definition of a window hang that Windows and Task Manager use), unhandled exception monitoring and can generate dumps based on the values of system performance counters. It also can serve as a general process dump utility that you can embed in other scripts"

Name: PsExec v2.11
Genre: Remote connection utility
Platform: Client: Windows XP and
higher
Server: Windows Server
2003 and higher

Developer: Microsoft Sysinternals
License: Custom/Proprietary
Web site: https://technet.microsoft.com/en-us/sysinternals/psexec

Description taken from vendor's web site on Dec. 9, 2015: "PsExec is a lightweight telnet-replacement that lets you execute processes on other systems, complete with full interactivity for console applications, without having to manually install client software. PsExec's most powerful uses include launching interactive command-prompts on remote systems and remote-enabling tools like IpConfig that otherwise do not have the ability to show information about remote systems"

Name: PsFile v1.02
Genre: Host information collection
Platform: Client: Windows XP and
higher
Server: Windows Server
2003 and higher

Developer: Microsoft Sysinternals
License: Custom/Proprietary
Web site: https://technet.microsoft.com/en-us/sysinternals/psfile

Description taken from vendor's web site on Dec. 9, 2015: "PsFile is a command-line utility that shows a list of files on a system that are opened remotely, and it also allows you to close opened files either by name or by a file identifier"

Name: PsInfo v1.77
Genre: Host information collection
Platform: Client: Windows XP and
higher
Server: Windows Server
2003 and higher

Developer: Microsoft Sysinternals
License: Custom/Proprietary
Web site: https://technet.microsoft.com/en-us/sysinternals/psinfo

Description taken from vendor's web site on Dec. 9, 2015: "PsInfo is a command-line tool that gathers key information about the local or remote Windows NT/2000 system, including the type of installation, kernel build, registered organization and owner, number of processors and their type, amount of physical memory, the install date of the system, and if it's a trial version, the expiration date"

Name: PsKill v1.14
Genre: Process utilities
Platform: Client: Windows XP and
higher
Server: Windows Server
2003 and higher

Developer: Microsoft Sysinternals
License: Custom/Proprietary
Web site: https://technet.microsoft.com/en-us/sysinternals/pskill

Description taken from vendor's web site on Dec. 9, 2015: "PsKill is a kill utility that not only does what the Resource Kit's version does, but can also kill processes on remote systems. You don't even have to install a client on the target computer to use PsKill to terminate a remote process"

Name: PsList v1.3

Genre: Process Utilities

Platform: Client: Windows XP and higher

Server: Windows Server 2003 and higher

Developer: Microsoft Sysinternals

License: Custom/Proprietary

Web site: https://technet.microsoft.com/en-us/sysinternals/pslist

Description taken from vendor's website on 12/9/2015: "pslist exp would show statistics for all the processes that start with "exp", which would include Explorer.

–d Show thread detail.

–m Show memory detail.

–x Show processes, memory information and threads.

–t Show process tree.

–s [n] Run in task-manager mode, for optional seconds specified. Press Escape to abort.

–r n Task-manager mode refresh rate in seconds (default is 1).

||computer Instead of showing process information for the local system, PsList will show information for the NT/Win2K system specified. Include the –u switch with a username and password to login to the remote system if your security credentials do not permit you to obtain performance counter information from the remote system.

–u username If you want to kill a process on a remote system and the account you are executing in does not have administrative privileges on the remote system then you must login as an administrator using this command-line option. If you do not include the password with the -p option then PsList will prompt you for the password without echoing your input to the display.

–p password This option lets you specify the login password on the command line so that you can use PsList from batch files. If you specify an account name and omit the -p option PsList prompts you interactively for a password.

name Show information about processes that begin with the name specified.

–e Exact match the process name.

pid Instead of listing all the running processes in the system, this parameter narrows PsList's scan to tthe process that has the specified PID. Thus:

pslist 53 would dump statistics for the process with the PID 53."

Name: PsLoggedOn v1.34

Genre: Host information collection

Platform: Client: Windows XP and higher

Server: Windows Server 2003 and higher

Developer: Microsoft Sysinternals

License: Custom/Proprietary

Web site: https://technet.microsoft.com/en-us/sysinternals/psloggedon

Description taken from vendor's web site on Dec. 9, 2015: "PsLoggedOn is an applet that displays both the locally logged on users and users logged on via resources for either the local computer, or a remote one. If you specify a user name instead of a computer, PsLoggedOn searches the computers in the network neighborhood and tells you if the user is currently logged on"

Name: PsLogList v2.71

Genre: Host information collection

Platform: Client: Windows XP and higher

Server: Windows Server 2003 and higher

Developer: Microsoft Sysinternals

License: Custom/Proprietary

Web site: https://technet.microsoft.com/en-us/sysinternals/psloglist

Description taken from vendor's web site on Dec. 9, 2015: "The Resource Kit comes with a utility, elogdump, that lets you dump the contents of an Event Log on the local or a remote computer. PsLogList is a clone of elogdump except that PsLogList lets you login to remote systems in situations where your current set of security credentials would not permit access to the Event Log, and PsLogList retrieves message strings from the computer on which the event log you view resides"

Name: PsService v2.24

Genre: Host information collection

Platform: Client: Windows XP and higher

Server: Windows Server 2003 and higher

Developer: Microsoft Sysinternals

License: Custom/Proprietary

Web site: https://technet.microsoft.com/en-us/sysinternals/psservice

Description taken from vendor's web site on Dec. 9, 2015: "PsService is a service viewer and controller for Windows. Like the SC utility that's included in the Windows NT and Windows 2000 Resource Kits, PsService displays the status, configuration, and dependencies of a service, and allows you to start, stop, pause, resume, and restart them. Unlike the SC utility, PsService enables you to logon to a remote system using a different account, for cases when the account from which you run it doesn't have required permissions on the remote system. PsService includes a unique service-search capability, which identifies active instances of a service on your network. You would use the search feature if you wanted to locate systems running DHCP servers, for instance"

Name: RawCopy

Genre: File utilities

Platform: "Windows 2000, Windows XP, Windows 2003/2008, Windows Vista, Windows 7, Windows 8, Windows 10"

Developer: Joakim Schicht

License: Custom/Proprietary

Web site: https://github.com/jschicht/RawCopy

Description taken from vendor's web site on Dec. 30, 2015: "Console application that copy files off NTFS volumes by using low level disk reading method"

Name: RegRipper v2.8

Genre: Host information collection

Platform: Windows 2000, XP, 2003, and Vista

Developer: H. Carvey

License: Custom/Proprietary

Web site: https://github.com/keydet89/RegRipper2.8

Description taken from vendor's web site on Dec. 30, 2015: "Extracting, correlating, and displaying specific information from Registry hive files ..."

Name: Strings v2.52

Genre: File utilities

Platform: Win2K, Windows 95, Windows NT

Developer: Microsoft Sysinternals

License: Custom/Proprietary

Web site: https://technet.microsoft.com/en-us/sysinternals/bb897439.aspx

Description taken from vendor's web site on Jan. 20, 2016: "Working on NT and Win2K means that executables and object files will many times have embedded UNICODE strings that you cannot easily see with a standard ASCII strings or grep programs. So we decided to roll our own. Strings just scan the file you pass it for UNICODE (or ASCII) strings of a default length of 3 or more UNICODE (or ASCII) characters"

Name: Systeminfo

Genre: System utilities

Platform: All versions of Windows

Developer: Microsoft

License: Custom/Proprietary

Web site: https://technet.microsoft.com/en-us/library/bb491007.aspx

Description taken from vendor's web site on Feb. 10, 2016: "Displays detailed configuration information about a computer and its operating system, including operating system configuration, security information, product ID, and hardware properties, such as RAM, disk space, and network cards"

Name: TCPView and TCPVCon v3.05

Genre: Networking utilities

Platform: Client: Windows XP and higher
        Server: Windows Server 2003 and higher

Developer: Microsoft Sysinternals

License: Custom/Proprietary

Web site: https://technet.microsoft.com/en-us/sysinternals/tcpview

Description taken from vendor's web site on Dec. 9, 2015: "TCPView is a Windows program that will show you detailed listings of all TCP and UDP endpoints on your system, including the local and remote addresses and state of TCP connections. On Windows Server 2008, Vista, and XP, TCPView also reports the name of the process that owns the endpoint. TCPView provides a more informative and conveniently presented subset of the Netstat program that ships with Windows. The TCPView download includes Tcpvcon, a command-line version with the same functionality"

Name: USBDeview v2.51

Genre: Host information collection

Platform: "Windows 2000, Windows XP, Windows 2003, Windows Vista, Windows Server 2008, Windows 7, Windows 8, and Windows 10"

Developer: NirSoft

License: Freeware

Web site: http://www.nirsoft.net/utils/usb_devices_view.html

Description taken from vendor's web site on Dec. 29, 2015: "USBDeview is a small utility that lists all USB devices that are currently connected to your computer, as well as all USB devices that you previously used. For each USB device, extended information is displayed: Device name/description, device type, serial number (for mass storage devices), the date/time that device was added, VendorID, ProductID, and more .... USBDeview also allows you to uninstall USB devices that you previously used, disconnect USB devices that are currently connected to your computer, as well as to disable and enable USB devices. You can also use USBDeview on a remote computer, as long as you login to that computer with admin user"

Windows CLI reference synopsis

INTRODUCTION

This appendix provides an overview of *some* of the most common Windows Command Line commands used by investigators with specific examples, along with rationale for their use. In addition, web resources are provided that contain the most up-to-date information relating to the availability and syntax for all the Microsoft Windows built-in commands.

MICROSOFT TECHNET

Fig. B.1 shows the Microsoft TechNet web page "Command Reference A-Z," which was last updated Nov. 23, 2015. This specific reference covers the following Microsoft Operating System versions:

Windows Server 2012
Windows Server 2008 R2
Windows Server 2008
Windows Server 2003 R2
Windows Server 2003
Windows 8
Windows 7
Windows Vista
Windows XP

The web page provides quick access to all commands. Detailed descriptions of the selected command are illustrated. For example, in Fig. B.2, the *arp* command was selected. The first section of the page provides an overview of the command.

As shown in Fig. B.3, scrolling down the page shows details of each parameter associated with the command.

Thus, to test the provided information, we first specify the *arp /?* command to reveal the help information.

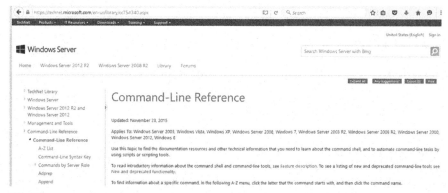

FIG. B.1

Microsoft TechNet A-Z command reference.

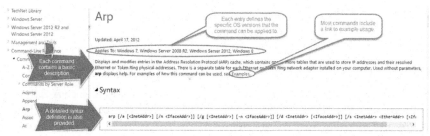

FIG. B.2

TechNet individual command details.

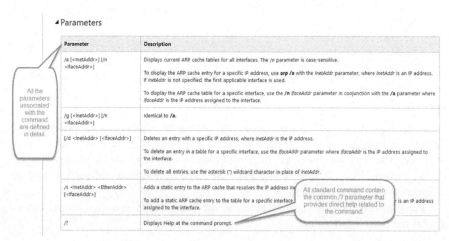

FIG. B.3

TechNet command parameters.

```
C:\Users\Chester>arp /?
```

Displays and modifies the IP-to-Physical address translation tables used
by address resolution protocol (ARP).

```
ARP -s inet_addr eth_addr [if_addr]
ARP -d inet_addr [if_addr]
ARP -a [inet_addr] [-N if_addr] [-v]
```

-a	Displays current ARP entries by interrogating the current protocol data. If inet_addr is specified, the IP and physical addresses for only the specified computer are displayed. If more than one network interface uses ARP, entries for each ARP table are displayed.
-g	Same as -a.
-v	Displays current ARP entries in verbose mode. All invalid entries and entries on the loop-back interface will be shown.
inet_addr	Specifies an internet address.
-N if_addr	Displays the ARP entries for the network interface specified by if_addr.
-d	Deletes the host specified by inet_addr. inet_addr may be wildcarded with * to delete all hosts.
-s	Adds the host and associates the Internet address inet_addr with the Physical address eth_addr. The Physical address is given as 6 hexadecimal bytes separated by hyphens. The entry is permanent.
eth_addr	Specifies a physical address.
if_addr	If present, this specifies the Internet address of the interface whose address translation table should be modified.

If not present, the first applicable interface will be used.
Example:
> arp -s 157.55.85.212 00-aa-00-62-c6-09 .... Adds a static entry.
> arp -a   .... Displays the arp table.

Making modifications to the arp table are not advisable during an investigation. Therefore, using the arp -a option will simply display the current arp entries as shown here.

```
C:\Users\Chester>arp -a
Interface: 192.168.21.1 --- 0x7
  Internet Address       Physical Address     Type
  192.168.21.254         00-50-56-ff-1d-29    dynamic
  192.168.21.255         ff-ff-ff-ff-ff-ff    static
  224.0.0.22             01-00-5e-00-00-16    static
  224.0.0.251            01-00-5e-00-00-fb    static
```

```
  224.0.0.252              01-00-5e-00-00-fc      static
  239.255.255.250          01-00-5e-7f-ff-fa      static
  255.255.255.255          ff-ff-ff-ff-ff-ff      static

Interface: 192.168.163.1 --- 0x8
  Internet Address         Physical Address       Type
  192.168.163.254          00-50-56-e3-29-fd      dynamic
  192.168.163.255          ff-ff-ff-ff-ff-ff      static
  224.0.0.22               01-00-5e-00-00-16      static
  224.0.0.251              01-00-5e-00-00-fb      static
  224.0.0.252              01-00-5e-00-00-fc      static
  239.255.255.250          01-00-5e-7f-ff-fa      static
  255.255.255.255          ff-ff-ff-ff-ff-ff      static
Interface: 192.168.0.128 --- 0x9
  Internet Address         Physical Address       Type
  192.168.0.1              00-00-ca-00-00-03      dynamic
  192.168.0.103            f4-81-39-7c-43-2a      dynamic
  192.168.0.112            00-0c-8a-97-9d-36      dynamic
  192.168.0.129            a8-66-7f-0a-87-4d      dynamic
  192.168.0.139            02-0f-b5-e8-3b-a9      dynamic
  192.168.0.255            ff-ff-ff-ff-ff-ff      static
  224.0.0.22               01-00-5e-00-00-16      static
  224.0.0.251              01-00-5e-00-00-fb      static
  224.0.0.252              01-00-5e-00-00-fc      static
  239.255.255.250          01-00-5e-7f-ff-fa      static
  255.255.255.255          ff-ff-ff-ff-ff-ff      static
Interface: 192.168.56.1 --- 0x1a
  Internet Address         Physical Address       Type
  192.168.56.255           ff-ff-ff-ff-ff-ff      static
  224.0.0.22               01-00-5e-00-00-16      static
  224.0.0.251              01-00-5e-00-00-fb      static
  224.0.0.252              01-00-5e-00-00-fc      static
  239.255.255.250          01-00-5e-7f-ff-fa      static
  255.255.255.255          ff-ff-ff-ff-ff-ff      static
Interface: 192.168.99.1 --- 0x23
  Internet Address         Physical Address       Type
  192.168.99.100           08-00-27-92-a5-c2      dynamic
  192.168.99.255           ff-ff-ff-ff-ff-ff      static
  224.0.0.22               01-00-5e-00-00-16      static
  224.0.0.251              01-00-5e-00-00-fb      static
  224.0.0.252              01-00-5e-00-00-fc      static
  239.255.255.250          01-00-5e-7f-ff-fa      static
  255.255.255.255          ff-ff-ff-ff-ff-ff      static
```

Now that you have an idea of how to identify and obtain usage information for Command Line commands, you should explore and practice them. The most difficult aspect for new Command Line users is how to specify the Command Line parameters. This takes some practice and patience, along with a careful study of each command and their associated options. In some cases, the parameter syntax will contain special characters that have important meaning.

<text inside angle brackets>	Indicates that a value must be supplied
[text inside square brackets]	Indicates that a value is optional
{text inside braces}	Indicates a set of possible items; you must choose one
Vertical Bar |	Indicates mutually exclusive items; choose only one
3 dots ...	Indicates items can be repeated

POPULAR COMMANDS FOR AN EXAMINATION

To limit the scope of this Appendix, the most widely used commands for information acquisition and examination have been chosen. The following table contains the commands, basic descriptions, forensic relevance, and Windows OS that support the command.

As stated earlier, this is a short list of useful commands for investigators. The sheer number of commands and variations of commands range in the thousands. Many web pages provide examples of command use, however always reference the Windows TechNet web site for the official reference. Also, make sure that you clearly understand the usage, parameters, potential risks of any command that you employ during an investigation. The best advice is to practice the commands in a safe environment before you attempt them in the field. Also, stick with display only and nondestructive commands and proceed carefully.

CMD	Description	Relevance	Example	Support OS
CD	Displays the name of the current directory or changes directory if one is specified	Used to navigate the file system under investigation	Display the current directory *CD* Change Directory to the root of the C Drive *CD C:*	ALL
DATE	Display or allow for the setting of a new system date	Record the current date of the system you are executing the command line	*DATE*	ALL
DIR	List the contents of a directory	One of the most well-known commands. The command lists the contents of a directory. Based on parameters to the command sub directories, system files, hidden files, and alternate data streams can be revealed	List content of current directory *DIR* List content of current directory and sub directories *DIR / S* List only files with the SYSTEM or HIDDEN attribute set in the current directory *DIR / A:HS* List only files in the current directory that include alternate data streams *DIR / R*	ALL

DISKPART	Utility for managing, configuring, or obtaining information regarding PC Disk Drives	Recording the state of the current disk drives is vital for investigation purposes	*DISKPART* **WARNING**: IMPROPER USE OF DISKPART CAN DESTROY DATA. THUS A DETAILED UNDERSTANDING OF EACH DISKPART COMMAND IS REQUIRED **NOTE**: ADMINISTRATIVE PRIVILEGE IS REQUIRED	Windows Vista, Windows Server 2008, Windows 7, Windows Server 2008 R2, Windows Server 2012 R2, Windows Server 2012, Windows 8
FC	File Compare Command to determine differences between similar files	In some cases, it is valuable to compare files to determine if they have been modified or altered	Compare two text files A and B *FC fileA fileb* Compare two binary files A and B *FC /B fileA fileB* Compare two text files A and B, case insensitive *FC /C fileA fileB*	Windows Vista, Windows Server 2008, Windows 7, Windows Server 2008 R2, Windows Server 2012, Windows 8
FIND	Searches for a text string in a file and displays lines that are found to match	Searching for names, places, email addresses can be useful in an investigation	Search for the string "EXIF" in the file image.jpg */I* ignore case */C* only displays the number of occurrence of the string *FIND /I /C "EXIF" image.jpg*	Windows Vista, Windows Server 2008, Windows Server 2012, Windows 8

Continued

CMD	Description	Relevance	Example	Support OS
FINDSTR	Not to be confused with FIND, FINDSTR searches for patterns of text	Useful for searching one or many files for specific patterns	Search for the string "gun" in the current directory and any subdirectories */s* include subdirectories */i* ignore case */m* print only the file name when a match is found `FINDSTR /s /i /m "\<gun\>"*.*`	Windows Vista, Windows Server 2008, Windows Server 2012, Windows 8

GETMAC	Display the Media Access Control (MAC) address for either the local or specified remote computer for all network interface cards found	Mapping known MAC addresses to specific computers may assist in identifying computers involved in malicious network activity	Displays MAC addresses found on the local computer
			`GETMAC`
			`GETMAC /S system-name`
				Windows Server 2008, Windows Server 2008 R2, Windows Server 2012, Windows 8

IPCONFIG	Displays all current TCP/IP network configuration values	Capturing current network configuration provide network context during live investigations	Displays the complete TCP/IP configuration for all adapters
			`IPCONFIG /ALL`
			Display the current DNS revolver cache showing recently cached DNS translations
			`IPCONFIG /DISPLAYDNS`
				Windows Vista, Windows Server 2008, Windows Server 2008 R2, Windows Server 2012, Windows 8

MORE	Used to display a single page of information at a time. For example, display the contents of a file, or paging the output of a command that contains many pages of output	Use to quickly examine the contents of a file or used in conjunction with long output commands such as IPCONFIG/ALL or DIR/S, etc.	`MORE filename` `DIR /S	MORE` `IPCONFIG /ALL	MORE`	Windows Vista, Windows Server 2008, Windows Server 2012, Windows 8

NETSH	Launches a command line scripting utility that can display or even modify the network configuration of a currently running computer	Useful to investigators that are needed to display or access more detailed network information	*NETSH*	Windows Server 2003, Windows Server 2008, Windows Server 2003 R2, Windows Server 2008 R2, Windows Server 2012, Windows 8
NETSTAT	Displays active network connections and ports on the current computer	Identifying connections to local and remote hosts can reveal unintended, unauthorized, or malicious connections	Display all active TCP and UDP Ports *NETSTAT -a* Display statistics for just TCP connections *NETSTAT -s -p TCP* Display Ethernet statistics such as packets sent, packets received, and errors *NETSTAT -e*	Windows Server 2008, Windows Server 2008 R2, Windows Server 2012, Windows 8
PING	Used to Verify that Internet Protocol Connectivity exists by sending Internet Control Message Protocol (ICMP) Echo Request Messages	Investigators can use this command to assess network connectivity	Verify connectivity to the Loopback Port *PING 127.0.0.1* Verifies connectivity from the local computer to a public Internet Address. This command also verifies that DNS is running and configured *PING google.com*	Windows Server 2003, Windows Vista, Windows XP, Windows Server 2008, Windows 7, Windows Server 2003 R2, Windows Server 2008 R2, Windows Server 2000, Windows Server 2012, Windows 8
POWERSHELL	Invoke the Windows PowerShell Environment	Investigators can launch PowerShell and then run specialized scripts to perform automated operations	**POWERSHELL**	Windows Vista, Windows XP, Windows Server 2008, Windows 7, Windows Server 2003 with SP2, Windows Server 2008 R2, Windows Server 2012, Windows 8

Continued

CMD	Description	Relevance	Example	Support OS
SC	Provides the ability to communicate with the service controller	Allows investigators to stop services that may be interfering or dangerous to an investigation	Sends a stop request to a specific service **SC STOP** Allows investigators to obtain information about a specific service or driver **SC QUERY**	Windows Server 2003, Windows Vista, Windows Server 2008, Windows 7, Windows Server 2003 with SP2, Windows Server 2003 R2, Windows Server 2008 R2, Windows Server 2012, Windows Server 2003 with SP1, Windows 8
SET	Displays, sets, or removes CMD.EXE environment variables	For investigative purposes using SET with no parameters will list the current cmd.exe environment variables	**SET**	Windows Server 2003, Windows Vista, Windows XP, Windows Server 2008, Windows 7, Windows Server 2003 R2, Windows Server 2008 R2, Windows Server 2000, Windows Server 2012, Windows 8
SFC	The SFC command performs a scan verifying the integrity of all protected system files	Verifying the environment before proceeding with command line investigation can reveal possible tampering of the underlying operating system	*SFC / VERIFYONLY* **WARNING**: It is important to use the/VERIFYONLY option in order to avoid unintentional modification of the system **NOTE**: Command requires administrator privilege	Windows Vista, Windows Server 2008, Windows Server 2008 R2, Windows Server 2012, Windows 8, Windows Server 2008 R2 with SP1

Command	Description	Usage	Supported versions
SORT	Typically used in conjunction with other commands to sort the output using a pipe	Allows investigators to SORT the output of commands for better organization	**TASKLIST | SORT** **TASKLIST /v /FO CSV | SORT**	Windows Server 2003, Windows Vista, Windows Server 2008, Windows Server 2003 with SP2, Windows Server 2003 R2, Windows Server 2008 R2, Windows Server 2000, Windows Server 2012, Windows Server 2003 with SP1, Windows 8
SYSTEMINFO	Provides detailed configuration computer information including: operating system, system configuration, security information, product identification, hardware characteristics (such as RAM, disk space, and network cards)	Creating a snapshot of the environment that you are investigating is a vital step in recording information regarding the system under test. This can be a local computer or a specific computer name or IP address	For local computer *SYSTEMINFO* To review remote computer configuration *SYSTEMINFO /S* *system-name*	Windows Server 2003, Windows Vista, Windows XP, Windows Server 2008, Windows 7, Windows Server 2003 R2, Windows Server 2008 R2, Windows Server 2000, Windows Server 2012, Windows 8
TASKLIST	Displays a list of currently running processes. The command can be applied to a local computer	Determining the current running tasks can provide investigators with information related to current activity and when used in conjunction with NETSTAT as discussed in Chapter 3 investigators can link tasks with open network ports	Provides a simple dump of the currently running tasks **TASKLIST** To provide a comma separated value output a useful command is **TASKLIST /v FO CSV**	Windows Server 2003, Windows XP, Windows Server 2008, Windows 7, Windows Server 2003 R2, Windows Server 2008 R2, Windows Server 2000, Windows Server 2012, Windows 8

Continued

CMD	Description	Relevance	Example	Support OS
TIME	Display or allow for the setting of a new system time	Record the current time of the system you are executing the command line	*TIME*	ALL
VER	Displays the currently operating system version	When documenting the system under investigation the VER command provides succinct details regarding the OS	**VER**	Windows Server 2003, Windows Vista, Windows XP, Windows Server 2008, Windows 7, Windows Server 2003 with SP2, Windows Server 2003 R2, Windows Server 2008 R2, Windows Server 2000, Windows Server 2012, Windows Server 2003 with SP1, Windows 8
XCOPY	Provides the ability to copy files, directories, and subdirectories	In some cases, investigators have the need to directly copy files or even whole file systems in a live setting	Consult the TechNet web site for specific examples of XCOPY. The XCOPY command contains over 30 optional parameters and many use cases	Windows Server 2003, Windows Vista, Windows Server 2008, Windows 7, Windows Server 2003 R2, Windows Server 2008 R2, Windows Server 2000, Windows Server 2012, Windows 8

ADDITIONAL RESOURCES

Microsoft TechNet. Command-line reference A-Z. (n.d.). https://technet.microsoft.com/en-us/library/cc772390.aspx.

Index

Note: Page numbers followed by *f* indicate figures, and *t* indicate tables.

Printed in the United States
By Bookmasters